An Introduction
to
Philosophy

An Introduction to Philosophy

*The Perennial Principles
of the Classical Realist Tradition*

By

Daniel J. Sullivan

TAN Books

Charlotte, North Carolina

Nihil Obstat:
John A. Schulien, S.T.D. Censor Librorum
Imprimatur:
Albert G. Meyer Archbishop of Milwaukee
January 26, 1957

TAN Books
Charlotte, North Carolina
1992

To the memory of

EMMANUEL C. CHAPMAN

CONTENTS

FOREWORD

Intended as a first introduction to philosophy, for the general reader as well as for the student, the primary purpose of this book has been to present the elements of philosophy with simplicity and clarity. To this end we have begun with the study of philosophy in its primitive historical setting, tracing the evolution of philosophical problems from their simplest origins. We have tried also to use as far as possible the vocabulary and forms of everyday speech, preferring to sacrifice some of the precision and refinement which a technical vocabulary makes possible for the literary and pedagogical advantages of a more familiar language.

Since the average reader usually comes to philosophy for the first time from a predominantly literary background, a second aim of this work has been to smooth the transition from the realm of literary imagery to the world of philosophical abstractions. This consideration has dictated the sequence of the parts following the historical introduction, which begin with the more immediate and concrete problems about man himself and extend to problems of a more remote and abstract nature—an order that parallels at least roughly the natural order of interest and discovery. Other sequences are possible. Some teachers might prefer, for example, to place the sections on the philosophy of nature and metaphysics before the sections on man and his destiny, as being a more logical order. The parts are sufficiently self-contained to allow a wide flexibility on this point.

Working in the great classical, realist tradition of Plato, Aristotle, Augustine, Aquinas, and their modern-day inheritors, we have tried to expose the perennially valid and vital principles of philosophy in a contemporary setting as well as in a contemporary idiom. By emphasizing its profound moral and social implications we have sought to demonstrate to the student that philosophy is a good deal more than a classroom exercise. Since, too, this work is intended for use by Catholic students, we have not hesitated, particularly in the field of ethics, where the purely philosophical answers would be incomplete, to point out how the conclusions of philosophy may be complemented by the truths of revelation. We feel, moreover, that this is consistent with the tradition of the perennial philosophy, which, while scrupulously guarding the distinction between natural and revealed wisdom, envisages their union in the whole man.

Since this book is an introduction it makes no claim to completeness. Neither, for many of the problems raised, has any attempt been made at anything like a final solution. We have thought it sufficient to arouse that sense of wonder which Aristotle says is the beginning of philosophy, for we are confident that once the beginner glimpses the fascination of "divine philosophy" he will not withhold the effort that its study calls for.

A work of this general nature inevitably owes a great deal to others, and the writer is only too conscious of his debt to his teachers, those who have taught him from books as well as in the classroom, and to his colleagues and students over the years. Particular thanks are due to the many publishers and authors who have so generously given permission to quote from their works. The writer is grateful also to Fordham University for the sabbatical year which made the completion of this work possible. Special thanks are due to Father Joseph Hassett, S.J., and to Dr. William Dunphy who read parts of the manuscript and whose criticisms were most valuable; to the editors of The Bruce Publishing Company for their most helpful suggestions; to Dr. Howard and Dorothy Lowensten for their unfailing and generous encouragement; and to my sister, Margaret Cullen, for her indispensable assistance in the preparation of the manuscript.

SCHOOL OF EDUCATION
FORDHAM UNIVERSITY
December 5, 1956

INTRODUCTION

CHAPTER 1

What Is Philosophy?

Wonder is the feeling of a philosopher, and philosophy begins in wonder.
PLATO, *THEAETETUS*, 155

It is owing to their wonder that men both now begin and at the first began to philosophize.
ARISTOTLE, *METAPHYSICS*, I, 2.

Until late in the history of our race the reason of man tended to be under the sway of his senses and imagination and the accounts given to explain the universe took for the most part the form of myth and legend. The Greeks alone among the peoples of antiquity succeeded in recognizing the difference between a purely rational explanation of things as distinct from mythical, poetical, or religious explanations. Those among them who displayed great gifts in the intelligent manipulation of the forces of nature and in tracing out the reasons for things were called wise men.

The earliest meaning of wisdom is very broad and refers to the cultivation of learning in general. "The word *sophia* covered all we mean by science and a good deal more besides, such as the art of making pontoons and guessing riddles."[1] With the passage of time, however, it became apparent that not all kinds of explanation were the same. The inquiry into what a thing is, for example, was seen to

---

1   J. Burnet, *Greek Philosophy from Thales to Plato* (London: Black, 1948), p. 11.

be different from the inquiry into how to do something. Particular fields of investigation, too, came to be separated out into special, self-contained branches of study such as geometry, physics, biology. The term wisdom ultimately was reserved for the study of things in their deepest and most general aspects: speculation about the fundamental reality of things, where things come from, why there is anything, and similar questions.

The Origin of the Term Philosopher

The word "philosopher" is traced back to Pythagoras, a famed sage who founded a community of scholars in southern Italy in the sixth century before Christ. Pythagoras is supposed to have disclaimed the title "sophist," or wise man, for the reason that "no man, but only God, is wise." Since the goal of perfect wisdom is beyond the attainment of mortal man, it is more fitting that one who searches after wisdom be called a philosopher, a lover of wisdom, rather than a wise man. Later men of learning also emphasized the disparity between true wisdom and human wisdom: "Only God is really wise," said Socrates at his trial. Not until the time of Aristotle, though, does the term philosophy take on a technical meaning, setting it off as a special branch of learning distinct from other kinds of investigation.

To understand what philosophy is in the strict, technical sense requires a knowledge of philosophy. It is impossible, therefore, to start with a definition of philosophy in the strict sense which will have much meaning for one who is just beginning his study of philosophy. For the present we will content ourselves with the most general description of what philosophy is, leaving the formulation of a precise definition to the end of our work after we have examined just what philosophy does.

The Meaning of Philosophy In the Wide Sense

The numerous schools of philosophy that have arisen have offered many different explanations of what philosophy is. Most of them agree, though, that it is concerned with the broad view of things.

Where the scientific specialist concerns himself with a single feature of reality—the astronomer, for example, with the study of the heavenly bodies—the philosopher seeks to view the whole of reality in a single comprehensive glance, to organize all aspects of reality into a unified world view. "All sciences tend to generalize, to reduce multitudes of particular facts to single general laws. Philosophy carries this process to the highest limit. It generalizes to the utmost. It seeks to view the entire universe in the light of the fewest possible principles, in the light, if possible, of a single ultimate principle."[2]

A second point on which nearly all philosophers are agreed is that philosophy must be distinguished from revealed religion, from supernatural wisdom, which also gives man a unified, comprehensive view of reality. Whereas religious beliefs are based on the truthfulness of a God who reveals, the principles of philosophy rest on a purely rational foundation.

Besides the disinterested inquiry into the nature of things, the use of philosophy in the wide sense usually covers also the order of practical wisdom—particularly the shrewd ordering of one's daily life. This is the sense of philosophy which persists in expressions such as "armchair philosopher" and "cracker-barrel sage."

In the light of these considerations we can give a tentative, descriptive definition of philosophy—philosophy taken in the wide, popular sense—as a superior kind of knowledge, "a sort of higher curiosity," whereby we endeavor to dig down to the very roots of things and through the exercise of reason try to find out why we hold our basic, most fundamental convictions about the nature of reality.

Philosophy is not, however, found embalmed in definitions. It is found in living men, and the best place to study it is in the philosophers themselves. For this reason we shall begin our study by retracing the footsteps of some of the first philosophers. In doing so we shall at the same time ourselves be learning to philosophize. First, however, let us inquire why we should philosophize at all.

---

2   W. T. A. Stace, *A Critical History of Greek Philosophy* (London: The Macmillan Company, 1920), p. 3.

Why Study Philosophy?

One of the earliest answers to this question can again be traced back to Pythagoras, who held that philosophy seeks knowledge simply for its own sake, apart from any question of gain or usefulness. He compared the community of man to the great crowds who used to come from all parts of Greece to celebrate the Olympic games. Some men come to compete and win prizes and honors.

These are like the politicians and soldiers who compete for honors from the community. Others come to buy and sell, setting up booths to provide for the needs of the crowd. These are like the merchants and tradesmen who spend their lives in the pursuit of gain. Still others, and they are the most favored of all, come simply as onlookers to see and enjoy the spectacle, seeking neither applause nor profit. This is the role of the philosopher in the community of men. "And as at games it is most befitting a free man to be a spectator seeking nothing for himself, so in life contemplation and understanding far surpass all other ambitions."[3]

Philosophy can be compared to the fine arts in that like them it has an intrinsic value and importance. We listen to music, read poetry, attend the theater, study paintings and statues because these things are enjoyable for their own sakes and not necessarily for the sake of anything else. Similarly, men philosophize not for purely practical ends but simply because it brings them pleasure. Anyone who has enjoyed working out a scientific experiment or solving a difficult problem in geometry has experienced the fact that knowledge brings pleasure. And this joy that knowledge brings is its own justification.

The arts and philosophy are of such great worth precisely because they are not to be used but to be loved and enjoyed just for themselves. For it is the exercise of his higher powers of knowing and loving that separates man from the lower animals. To the degree, then, that human beings devote themselves to the disinterested enjoyment of the arts and the pursuit of knowledge, to the degree

---

3 See Cicero, *Tusculan Disputations*, V, 3.

that they are not tied down to the useful, they and their culture ripen into what is most distinctively human.

All Men Philosophize

In the wide sense in which we have used the word philosophy, all men philosophize, whether they know it or not. Our most commonplace expressions of optimism or pessimism, selfishness or high-mindedness, idealism or cynicism, carry along with them unacknowledged assumptions about the nature of the universe as a whole and man's place in it. "The most practical and important thing about a man," says G. K. Chesterton, "is still his view of the universe. We think that for a landlady considering a lodger, it is important to know his income, but still more important to know his philosophy. We think that for a general about to fight an enemy, it is important to know the enemy's numbers, but still more important to know the enemy's philosophy. We think the question is not whether the theory of the cosmos affects matters, but whether in the long run anything else affects them."[4]

A philosophy none the less real because it is unrecognized is hidden in the words we speak and write, in our newspapers, in our motion pictures. A philosophy of one kind or another, some implied way of life, is embodied in works of art, in painting, music, dancing, in political institutions and social customs, in all sorts of unsuspected places.

The choice before us, then, is not between accepting or rejecting philosophy, since each of us—whether he knows it or not—already has one, but between holding it consciously or unconsciously. Unless we free our minds by becoming critically conscious of what we hold unconsciously and uncritically, we are liable to become victims of our own unconsciously held philosophy or of the philosophy of others, which may rule us all the more tyrannically because it is hidden and operates in the dark. What we hold implicitly, vaguely, confusedly, must be rendered explicit, definite, and clear in the light

---

4 G. K. Chesterton, *Heretics* (New York: Dodd, Mead and Company, 1905), p. 15.

7

of reason and the evidence of things. For in the words of Socrates, one of the greatest of all philosophers, "The unexamined life is not worth living."[5]

Summary

The beginnings of philosophy are traced back to the sages of early Greece who were the first men on record to appreciate the requirements of a purely rational explanation of reality. The term philosophy, the love of wisdom, came into use with the recognition that the wisdom open to man is at best partial and limited. Philosophy is used in both a broad, loose sense and a narrow, precise sense. The examination of the exact definition of philosophy is postponed until we have some acquaintance with what philosophy has meant in practice. In the broad sense we can say that it is the search for ultimates, conducted by reason alone, in order to satisfy man's curiosity about himself and the universe of which he is a part.

Note: A useful complement to the beginner's first studies in philosophy is the reading of some history of philosophy. A select list of these as well as a list of other *Introductions to Philosophy* will be found in the Reading List at the end of the volume.

---

5 Plato, *Apology*, 38. All quotations from Plato are taken from the translation of Benjamin Jowett as found in *The Dialogues of Plato* (Oxford: The Clarendon Press, 1920). The references to the works of Plato are based on an edition of the Greek text which appeared in Paris in 1578. Almost all modern editions keep the page numbers and marginal letters of this edition.

PART I:

THE HISTORICAL RISE OF PHILOSOPHY

CHAPTER 2

The First Beginnings of Philosophy

Let us call to our aid those who have attacked the investigation of being and philosophized about reality before us.
ARISTOTLE, METAPHYSICS, I, 3.

The Philosophers of Nature

The first philosopher on record is a man called Thales. Thales lived at the beginning of the sixth century B.C., at Miletus, a Greek colony on the coast of Asia Minor. He was one of the legendary Seven Wise Men of Ancient Greece and knew the famed lore of the Chaldeans. The Chaldeans had centuries-long records of the movements of the heavenly bodies, and they used this information to cast horoscopes. Thales and other early Greek philosophers, however, instead of trying to tell fortunes by the position of the planets, used this knowledge of the heavens to try to explain rationally the nature of the heavenly bodies themselves and their movements.

This at once marks off the early Greek philosophers from the other wise men of antiquity. The Greeks endeavored to find explanations for natural phenomena which did not bring in magic or the activity of the gods, not because they were necessarily atheists or had no use for religion, but because they recognized that magical, religious, allegorical, or mythical explanations differed from a rational, scientific explanation.

Beyond this universal concern of the first philosophers to explain the nature of the heavens by reason alone, they desired also to find out what everything comes from. Thales said everything comes from water. Another thinker, Anaximenes, said air is the source of everything. Still another, Heraclitus, said fire; and another, Empedocles, suggested the four elements—earth, air, fire, and water. These answers may appear naïve at first sight, but they are more profound than they seem. Thales and the other early philosophers were not unaware of the variety and multitude of things. What they were really trying to get at was the connection of things, the interrelations between them. Their question really is, "What do all things have in common?" for it seemed to them that, behind the vast multiplicity of things that make up the universe, there is some principle of unity, the very insight that is embodied in our word *universe*, which means "combined into one."

These early philosophers were called cosmogonists, because they tried to discover the matter of which the cosmos is made up. They are also called philosophers of nature because their interest was directed mainly to the external world. Still another name given to them is the term hylozoist, which comes from two Greek words meaning "living matter." They held that the stuff from which everything comes is alive. The world, in other words, is like a great animal, or a human being enormously magnified. "Just as our soul, being air, holds us together, so do breath and air surround the whole universe."[1]

A final label attached to these first philosophers is the term sensist. This means that they take into account only what falls under our senses. Only the things we can see and touch and otherwise sense are real. Unlike later sensists, these early philosophers did not deny the existence of intellect. They simply did not know about it.

---

1 This is the single complete sentence that has come down to us from Anaximenes, one of the Milesian School. It is also the first instance in the history of philosophy of the comparison between man and the world, the view that man is a microcosm, a world in miniature, or conversely that the macrocosm, the great world, is like man magnified.

However, Pythagoras, the next pioneer we are going to study, took for his field of investigation the mysterious realm of numbers. His speculations were to suggest that there is more to the reality of things than their surface appearance, and that the senses are not of themselves sufficient to account for everything we know.

Pythagoras and the Philosophy of Number

Pythagoras (572-497 B.C.)[2] was born at Samos, an island off the coast of Asia Minor, and came in contact there with the Milesian philosophers. To evade the rule of a political tyrant, Pythagoras emigrated from his homeland to Croton, in southern Italy, where he founded along religious lines a community of men dedicated to a life of scholarship and good works. They stressed philosophy as a way of life rather than a body of doctrine, a tradition continued later on by Socrates and Plato.

The greatest achievements of the Pythagoreans were in the realm of mathematics and they made important discoveries in the field of arithmetic and geometry. At this period the Greeks used the letters of the alphabet to designate numbers. Pythagoras used dots instead of letters, the dots being a kind of substitute for the pebbles with which the first counting was apparently done. This usage is not original with Pythagoras, for it had been anticipated by the gamblers of antiquity who used dots to mark the numbers on dice.

Pythagoras discovered that numbers could be fitted into regular patterns. The series of whole numbers, 1, 2, 3, 4, 5, etc., were made up of triangular numbers, thus:

1.   1.   1.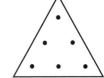
   2.
   2.
   3.

---

2 Most of the dates given for these early philosophers are approximate.

The series of odd numbers fitted into square patterns (we still speak of "square" roots):

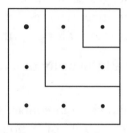

Even numbers make up oblong figures:

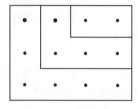

These numbers are called "figurate," from the Greek word *eidos* which means "pattern" or "figure." When today we say we are "figuring out" the answer, or when we refer to a column of "figures," we are reflecting the persistence through the long centuries of this ancient Pythagorean concept.

The Pythagoreans elaborated many of the theorems which were later gathered and systematized by Euclid. Among them is the important theorem which states that the square on the hypotenuse of a right-angled triangle is equal to the sum of the squares on the other two sides. This is still called the Pythagorean theorem, and Pythagoras is said to have sacrificed an ox to celebrate his great discovery.

Out of the Pythagorean interest in mathematics and music grew the conviction that reality itself consists of numbers. Everything we can see and touch is made up of numbers. Number therefore is more basic than water or fire or any other of the physical aspects of things. Numerical proportion and harmony account for the order and arrangement of things in their various forms.

The Pythagoreans[3] taught the doctrine of the transmigration of souls—the passage of the soul, that is, from one animal body to another. (An early poem makes fun of Pythagoras with the story that he stopped someone from beating a dog, saying that he recognized in the dog's anguished yelping the voice of a departed friend.) The only way the soul could be freed from its captivity within the body was by a process of self-discipline and purification. It was the task of the Pythagorean Brotherhood to bring about this liberation. Besides mathematics, they specialized in the study of music and medicine, and we are told that they purged the body by medicine and the soul with music.

A favorite comparison of the Pythagoreans was that which likened the body to a musical instrument, with the bodily contraries of hot and cold, wet and dry, corresponding to high and low pitch in music. The healthy body was one in which the various elements were properly blended just as the sounds given out by the strings of the lyre must be properly blended to produce music. And just as we speak of an instrument being in tune, so too we speak of body tone. The metaphor survives to this day when we say we need a spring tonic, that our system is out of tune, that we are under too much tension and need relaxation, or contrariwise, that we are all unstrung.

The Pythagorean strain, with its emphasis on the mysterious properties of numbers and the unsuspected harmonies within nature, was to be of the highest importance in the later development of Greek philosophy. The Brotherhood itself, however, came to an untimely end. They had in the course of time gained political control of Croton and other places in southern Italy. The inhabitants eventually rebelled against their rule because of an attempt,

---

3 None of the writings of Pythagoras have survived, and as in the case of so many of these men of very old times we are not sure of how much should be ascribed to the Master and how much to his disciples.

according to one tradition, to impose the dietary restrictions of the sect—including the prohibition of beans—on the population at large. The semi-monastic centers of the Brotherhood were destroyed and the few survivors scattered.

CHAPTER 3

The Problem of Change and Permanence

The One remains, the many change and pass.
SHELLEY, ADONAIS.

O ne of the most striking and mysterious of all the appearances in the world about us is that of change. The problem early arose as to how things can change and yet remain themselves, be infinitely diverse and yet stem from a single or a few basic elements. This is what is known as the problem of change and permanence, and it was destined to dominate Greek philosophy for a century and a half. The philosophers we are now going to study set the ultimate extremes for all time in the explaining of change and permanence.

Heraclitus and the Philosophy of Change

The first man on our stage is Heraclitus (535-475 B.C.), a native of Ephesus. He had the reputation of being a very bad-tempered man and we know at least that his was a sharp pen. He had a profound and outspoken contempt for just about everybody. According to him, Homer deserved to be whipped, and Pythagoras was an imposter. "Most men are bad," is one statement attributed to him.

As a reflection of his contempt for the run of mankind Heraclitus took little pains to make himself easily understood. He deliberately wrote in riddles, declaring that if you want gold you have to dig for it. He earned the title "the obscure" or "the dark" from the people of his day.

Heraclitus is still known as the philosopher of change. Change, for him, was the key to the universe. Nothing is so universal as the fact of change, from the movement of the heavenly bodies to the rhythm of growth and decline among terrestrial bodies. You plant an acorn, for example, and in a few years you have a towering oak tree. The question naturally arises, Is there any of the original acorn left in the oak tree? Humans change. The change is going on while this sentence is being read. We are some seconds older. We are not exactly the same person as when we arose this morning. Still less are we the person we were last year, and much less the person we were fifteen years ago. It is very difficult to see the eight pound infant in the two hundred pound adult with the double chin. Can we say there is any of the original infant left in the grown adult?

Even lifeless bodies are always changing. A thousand invisible hammers are tearing away at the objects around us—tables, chairs, books, buildings. What would happen if they were left to themselves for a thousand years, for five thousand years? The tombs of ancient kings who were buried with their furniture and their treasures long ages ago tell us that these things all crumble to dust. And a little reflection will remind us that this wasting away does not happen in one sudden moment, but that it is a continuous process that is going on even now. Even such solid-seeming things as gold and platinum, we know from modern physics, are centers of movement and pulsation, with the particles of the atom whirling around the central nucleus as the planets whirl around our sun.

"All things are in a state of flux," declared Heraclitus. Reality is a torrent of change and just as "you can never step into the same river twice," so too the world is never the same at successive instants. Heraclitus used the example of a burning candle to illustrate his point. The flame of the candle seems constant, yet we know that the solid body of the candle is slowly melting and being taken up into the flame of the candle where it is changed into smoke.

The world itself changes just like the flame of the candle. In fact, fire is the basic stuff out of which everything is made. Heraclitus chose fire as the ground of all things because it was the element that seemed most "alive." Things are always changing into and out of fire. Imagine the smoke from the burning candle turning back into wax and you are fairly close to Heraclitus' idea of the rhythm of change. The four elements are the various forms of fire: earth, the lowest and heaviest form of matter, melts into water; water changes into air, and air into fire. This is what Heraclitus called the upward path. The reverse changes of fire into air, water, and earth consti-tute the downward path.

The proportion of the elements varies in the course of end-less changes, the varying proportions of earth, water, air, and fire accounting for the changes of day and night, and the various sea-sons. The preponderance of moisture, for example, is the cause of winter, the encroachment of dryness the reason for summer.

What happens in the great world happens also in the little world of man. (Heraclitus too adopted the comparison of man and the world which is expressed by the notions of the microcosm and the mac-rocosm.) Man's body is mainly earth, but it is constantly changing into water, air, and fire, which is the soul; then, just as in the case of the great world itself, the fire changes back into air, moisture, earth. Sleep is due to the excessive proportion of moisture, as we can see in the case of drunkenness. Waking is caused by the restoration of the proper balance between the elements. If moisture, or any of the elements, gets the upper hand over the others, death follows.

As far as the appearances of things are concerned, then, it seemed to Heraclitus and his followers that we cannot name a single thing in the world around us which is not undergoing change. And, as Heraclitus furthermore stressed, if a thing is changing it is not the same from one moment to the next. In the very act of naming it, it is becoming something else. Things don't last long enough even to be named. They don't have even a relative permanence.

Parmenides and the Philosophy of Permanence

Shortly after Heraclitus had elaborated his doctrine of change, another philosopher called Parmenides (b. 510 B.C.), a native of Elea, in southern Italy, set up the opposite extreme to Heraclitus' position. Parmenides wrote a philosophic poem, fragments of which have come down to us. The poem is divided into two parts. The first part gives us Parmenides' doctrine, the second a summary of contemporary opinions which he dismisses as error. The two parts correspond to what Parmenides calls the two paths: the way of truth and the way of error, the way of reason and the way of the senses.

According to Parmenides the change of which Heraclitus made so much is an illusion and there is no such thing, really, as change. As philosophers, he said, we should try to get behind the appearances of things to their reality. Now the true reality of all things is not air, fire, or anything like that. The one thing we can say about all things in common is that they exist, that they are being. Being, not change or becoming, is the key to reality.

Everything which is is a being. If a thing is not a being it is a non-being, nothing. But change could come about only through a mixture of being with something else—with nothing, in other words. Change, therefore, is impossible.

Another important consequence follows from the fact that each thing is a being. If each thing is a being then each thing is what everything else is. A tree, for example, is a being and a horse is a being. They are, therefore, the same thing—being. There is no real difference between the tree and the horse—or as a matter of fact between any beings. All being, then, is one. Reality is just being, one single solitary unchanging being. Reality is the One.

All differences, including all changes, are just appearances. Naturally, things seem different, things seem to change, but reason proves that this appearance of change and diversity is simply the deception of the senses.

The Paradoxes of Zeno

A disciple of Parmenides, Zeno (b. 490 B.C.) by name, undertook to demonstrate the truth of his master's doctrine. He put forth a number of arguments which became known as the paradoxes of Zeno.

One of these paradoxes uses the ancient fable of the race between

Achilles and the Tortoise. The Tortoise is given a head start on Achilles. Before Achilles can catch the Tortoise he must cover the distance between himself and the point from which the Tortoise started. But when he reaches the point from which the Tortoise started, the Tortoise has in the meantime advanced part of the way toward the goal. Before Achilles can catch the Tortoise he must advance to that new point. But when he reaches the new point, the Tortoise will have again advanced toward the goal. Since the Tortoise is always moving toward the goal, Achilles is always faced with a prior task of crossing the distance between his starting point and the Tortoise's ever shifting starting point. Therefore, appearances to the contrary, the fleet-footed Achilles will never catch the Tortoise.

As a matter of fact, we can prove that Achilles never gets off his mark. Before Achilles can catch the Tortoise, he must cover half the distance between himself and the Tortoise. But before he can reach the halfway point of that distance, he has to cover half the first half. But half that distance has to be covered first, and so on and so on. It may be infinitesimally small, but there is always a first half of some distance to be covered before any of the further points can be reached. Achilles, then, cannot even get going, let alone catch the Tortoise.

Another paradox offered by Zeno was that of an arrow in flight. If anything seems to be in motion, it is an arrow flying swiftly through the air. But here again appearances are deceiving and reason tells us differently.

Consider the arrow in mid-flight. At the exact moment when we consider it, it is displacing the air to the extent of its own volume at one certain place and no other place. To displace its own volume of the atmosphere it has to be there, where the displacement is taking place—in that place and no other place. It is, therefore, in one precise geographical position, which could be accurately calculated— and while it is in one place it cannot be in any other place at the same time. For that exact moment, then, the arrow is here, and no place else. In other words, at that precise moment, while it is in that place and before it goes on to the place in front of it, it is not moving.

But this is true for any given moment of the arrow's flight. The arrow's flight, in other words, is made up of a series of motionless moments.

In a sense, the illustration is superfluous, for, as we have seen, the arrow could not have reached the halfway point in the first place.

Summary and Conclusion

Common sense is, naturally, shocked to hear from the disciples of Parmenides that all change and all differences are illusion, and that everything is an undifferentiated oneness—just as common sense is also shocked to hear from the disciples of Heraclitus that the things we call constant and stable are really in a state of endless flux and that stability, sameness, permanence, are all illusion.

Thus, at this very early age were set up in terms of their extreme limits certain classic problems in philosophy—what came to be called through the ages the problem of the One and the Many, of Sameness and Difference, of Change and Permanence, of Appearance and Reality.

Still another contrast divides the two philosophers. Heraclitus represents the climactic extreme of the sensist position—the doctrine that the only reality is what falls immediately under our senses. Parmenides, working in the tradition of Pythagoras, represents another extreme—the stress of reason to the point of excluding the testimony of our senses. (This will later be called rationalism.) The reconciliation of these extremes is destined to be henceforth one of the permanent problems of philosophy.

On the solution of all these problems Greek philosophers divided into two camps. Since each side seemed to have unanswerable arguments in favor of completely opposite positions, many men came to feel that the search for truth was a hopeless one: a despair of truth which was to lead quickly into an era of skepticism.

CHAPTER 4

The Age of the Sophists

His tongue
Dropt manna, and could make the worse appear
The better reason.
MILTON, PARADISE LOST, II, 112.

To understand the philosophers we are now about to study, a knowledge of the background against which they performed is necessary. The philosophers we have studied up to this point were found in the various Greek colonies and settlements scattered around the shores of the Mediterranean from the coast of Asia Minor to the island of Sicily. With the rise of the Sophists and later with Socrates, Plato, and Aristotle, the peninsula of Hellas, and particularly the city of Athens, becomes the center of our story.

The Golden Age of Greece

Twice at the beginning of the fifth century B.C.—once in the year 490 and again ten years later—the Greek city-states under the combined leadership of Sparta and Athens met and repulsed the great armed hordes of the mighty Empire of the Persians. Animated and invigorated by their wars for survival, these little communities were destined to reach a peak of blazing glory for which there is no parallel in all history.

"During the half century that followed this epoch," says Diodorus, writing on the effects of the Persian War,[1] "Hellas made vast strides

---

1   Diodorus, Bk. XII, Chaps. 1-2. From A. Toynbee, *Greek Historical Thought* (Boston: The

in prosperity. During this period the effects of the new affluence showed themselves in the progress of the arts, and artists as great as any recorded in history, including the sculptor Phidias, flourished at the time. There was an equally signal advance in the intellectual field, in which philosophy and public speaking were singled out for special honor throughout the Hellenic world and particularly at Athens. In philosophy there was the school of Socrates, Plato, and Aristotle; in public speaking there were such figures as Pericles, Isocrates, and Isocrates' pupils; and these were balanced by men of action with great military reputations, like Miltiades, Themistocles, Aristides, Cimon, Myronides and a long array of other names too numerous to mention. In the forefront of all, Athens achieved such triumphs of glory and prowess that her name won almost worldwide renown."

The Rise of Athens

After the defeat of the Persians, the Athenians rapidly assumed the maritime leadership of the eastern Mediterranean. With her rule firmly established over the neighboring islands, Athens became the center of a naval and commercial empire which was to bring her both wealth and power. "We have forced every sea and land to be the highway of our daring, and everywhere, whether for evil or for good, have left imperishable monuments behind us," was the just boast of Pericles.[2]

Politically, Athens was to lead the way also, realizing a degree of democratic self-government which was unique in the ancient world. Again in the words of Pericles, "Our constitution does not copy the laws of neighboring states; we are rather a pattern to others than imitators ourselves. Its administration favors the many instead of the few; this is why it is called a democracy. If we look to the laws, they afford equal justice to all in their private differences; if no social standing, advancement in public life falls to reputation for capacity, class considerations not being allowed to interfere with

Beacon Press, 1950), p. 161. 20

2 Thucydides, *History of the Peloponnesian War*, II, 41; Modern Library College Edition (New York: Random House, 1951), p. 126.

merit; nor again does poverty bar the way, if a man is able to serve the state, he is not hindered by the obscurity of his condition. The freedom which we enjoy in our government extends also to our ordinary life."[3]

So deep was the imprint left by this little city that the passage of centuries has hardly dimmed it. "We think and feel differently," says Edith Hamilton, "because of what a little Greek town did during a century or two, twenty-four hundred years ago. What was then produced of art and of thought has never been surpassed and very rarely equalled, and the stamp of it is upon all the art and all the thought of the Western World. . . . No sculpture comparable to theirs; no buildings ever more beautiful; no writings superior. Prose, always a late development, they had time only to touch upon, but they left masterpieces. History has yet to find a greater exponent than Thucydides; outside of the Bible there is no poetical prose that can touch Plato. In poetry they are all but supreme; no epic is to be mentioned with Homer; no odes to be set beside Pindar; of the four masters of the tragic stage three are Greek."[4]

The Sophists

With the sudden intensification of political and commercial activity among the Greeks after the Persian Wars there arose a demand for some kind of professional training to meet the needs and opportunities which were multiplied on all sides. This demand was met by a group of men called the Sophists,[5] that is, wise men, teachers who traveled from town to town offering courses not only in the familiar

---

3   *Ibid.*, II, 37; Modern Library College Edition, p. 123.

4   Edith Hamilton, *The Greek Way* (New York: W. W. Norton, 1940), pp. 15-17.

5   The term Sophists, originally applied to all men of unusual learning and great practical skill, takes on a specialized meaning at this period. The Sophist is now distinguished from the earlier philosophers whose interest was speculative rather than practical. The fact that they took money for imparting their wisdom also set them apart. A final characteristic that ties together this otherwise very diverse group is their common trend toward skepticism. At first a term of respect, the name Sophist quickly took on the unfavorable connotation which it still possesses today. (Compare the decay of the word politician in our own society.)

subjects of grammar, rhetoric, and literature, but also in such speci-
alities as statesmanship and generalship or whatever else promised
to offer worldly success.

Since the Sophists demanded pay for their services, they were
usually identified with the households of the well-to-do and the
powerful. Answering the special needs of their wealthy and influential clients, these teachers came very early to specialize in the arts
of eloquence and persuasion as a preparation for careers in the law
courts and on the public platform.

"Man is the Measure of All Things"

The first of the new professional teachers known to us is a man
called Protagoras. A native of Thrace, Protagoras was born about
the year 480 B.C. He came to Athens in middle age. He does not
share the bad reputation of the later Sophists, for we know that
he was entrusted by Pericles to draw up the constitution of a new
colony and he is portrayed sympathetically in two of the dialogues
of Plato. After the death of Pericles he was expelled from Athens,
and one tradition has it that he was drowned in the year 410 B.C.,
while crossing the sea to Sicily.

The philosophers who had come before Protagoras claimed
each to have the truth about the nature of things. Unfortunately,
though, they all seemed to have conflicting ideas about the nature
of truth. In the light of these oppositions and contradictions Protagoras apparently despaired of the possibility of reaching truth
and declared that it is the private concern of each individual person. "Man is the measure of all things, of things that are that they
are, and of things that are not that they are not," is a saying of Protagoras that has come down to us. The subject of much argument,
the sentence seems to mean that no one really knows what is outside of himself. For each one the appearance of things is different.
To a man with jaundice, for example, all things seem yellow. For
him that is true, although at the same time it is not true for another
person who is in a normal state of health. Whatever appears to be
the case for you is true even though to me it is false. Thus everyone

is always right; no one can ever be wrong.

For Protagoras, then, and for the Sophists in general, there are no answers to our questions about reality. There is no truth apart from our private feelings about things, or if there is it cannot be discovered.

The Sophist Attack on Morals

In the realm of morals the denial of the possibility of knowing truth meant that the difference between good and evil cannot be discovered. Many of the Sophists, therefore, taught that what we call good or evil, right or wrong, is a matter of arbitrary convention, of what you happen to feel at the moment, or of what is pleasant or unpleasant to you.

Similarly, in politics it is impossible to distinguish justice from injustice. Laws and conventions are chance, haphazard products of custom, climate, and self-interest, and might just as well be the opposite of the accepted versions. The Sophists easily persuaded their students, then, that since one answer is as good as another as far as right or wrong is concerned, man might just as well concentrate on a policy of self-interest. They used all the apparatus of their art to make their students capable of arguing with equal facility on either side of any question, with equal zeal for either side of any cause.

It is small wonder, therefore, that through the influence of these men the distinction between right and wrong in time became thoroughly blurred in both private and public life. Thucydides, the great historian of the Peloponnesian War, gives us an unforgettable picture of the moral cynicism which was to contribute fatally to the collapse of the high civilization of the Greeks:

"Words had to change their ordinary meaning and to take that which was now given them. Reckless audacity came to be considered the courage of a loyal ally; prudent hesitation, specious cowardice; moderation was held to be a cloak for unmanliness; ability to see all sides of a question, ineptness to act on any. Frantic violence became the attribute of manliness; cautious plotting, a justifiable means of self-defense. The advocate of extreme measures was always trustworthy; his opponent a man to be suspected. To succeed in a plot was to have a shrewd head, to divine a plot a still shrewder; but to try to provide against having to do either was to break up your party and to be afraid of your adversaries. . . . The fair proposals of an adversary were met with jealous precautions by the stronger of the two, and not with a generous confidence. Revenge also was held of more account than self-preservation. Oaths of reconciliation, being only proffered on either side to meet an immediate difficulty, only held good so long as no other weapon was at hand; but when opportunity offered, he who first ventured to seize it and to take his enemy off his guard, thought this perfidious vengeance sweeter than an open one, since, considerations of safety apart, success by treachery won him the palm of superior intelligence."[6]

The Fall of Athens

Faster even than the rise of Athens was her tragic fall. A twenty-year war with her neighbor Sparta exhausted her resources and drained her manpower. A pointless war which more than once could have been brought to honorable termination, it was prolonged and exploited by self-seeking politicians. Internal disorder paralyzed the government of Athens and fatally handicapped the conduct of the war. Weakened still further by a disastrous plague, Athens eventually succumbed to her enemies, going down to ignominious and total defeat.

Narrowly escaping total destruction (at the last moment even the prosaic Spartans shrank from razing the shrine of so much beauty), Athens, after a period of enemy occupation, was put under the rule of a group of compliant collaborators called the Thirty Tyrants. A brief resurgence of liberty and democratic self-rule was followed by final absorption into the empire of Philip of Macedon and his son Alexander the Great.

---

6 Thucydides, *History*, III, 82; Modern Library College Edition, p. 228. For the description of the sophist in Plato, read the *Republic*, Bk. I. Also the dialogue entitled *Sophist*; for an example of a sophistical argument, see *Theaetetus*, 151-187.

CHAPTER 5

Socrates

While I have life and strength I shall never cease from the practice and teaching of philosophy, exhorting everyone whom I meet.
SOCRATES, IN PLATO, APOLOGY, 29.

Among those who had foreseen the danger of collapse from internal decay of the high civilization of the Athenians was Socrates (470 B.C.-399 B.C.). For a generation the Sophists had taught the young men of Athens, as a consequence of their general denial of the possibility of knowing truth, that not justice but the best arguments are the important thing in the courts of law; not what is right or wrong, but what is most persuasive is what counts on the political rostrum. To succeed, no matter by what means, is the single goal that counts.

Socrates saw in this doctrine the corruption of the people of Athens and the destruction of the state. He felt that there really was such a thing as justice and injustice, right and wrong, truth and falsity, that they were supremely important, and that they could be known. Socrates set himself against the Sophists, therefore, and sought to find the means of combating their error.

The Appearance and Character of Socrates

Socrates must have been one of the more arresting sights of the Athens of his day. As his portrait has come down to us from Plato, Aristophanes, and Xenophon, we know that he was a strikingly ugly man, with a snub nose and "pop" eyes. He usually traveled around barefoot, and the playwright Aristophanes jeered that he strutted like a waterfowl. His friend Alcibiades described him as stalking like a pelican.

More sympathetically, he is compared to the carved statue of a grotesque satyr, which when opened discloses the image of a god.

He is described, again, as a torpedo fish, which benumbs everyone who comes near and touches it.

Socrates distinguished himself as a soldier in the Peloponnesian War, proving more than equal to the rugged life of the foot soldier, and on one occasion saving the life of his friend Alcibiades, who had been wounded. He was capable of great concentration, and the story is told of how one time in camp he stood lost in thought from early one morning until dawn of the next day, to the wonder of his curious fellow soldiers, who had set up their sleeping mats around him to see if he would stand in meditation all night.

Of not the least interest to his fellow townsmen of Athens was Socrates' "voice," which came to him often and which he called a divine oracle. This inner voice would warn Socrates, sometimes on the most trivial of occasions, putting him on his guard against some course of action. Socrates himself seemed imbued with the conviction that he had a kind of sacred mission in life to bring truth to his fellow citizens. He felt that if he could succeed in showing, against the Sophists, that expedience, selfishness, dishonesty, were in the long run self-defeating, he might yet turn Athens from its drift toward moral and political anarchy.

The Doctrine of Socrates

1. Knowledge Is Virtue

No man, Socrates pointed out, willingly suffers physical evil to himself without good reason. We know better than to blind ourselves or to jump off a high cliff, or to chop off our hands. Now Socrates held that although action of this kind would cause great hurt to a man, it would cause not nearly the damage that a lie or an act of injustice would cause. In the one case, the body would suffer damage but, in the second, the soul, which is much the more important part of man, is damaged or destroyed.

It is easy enough to recognize that it is foolish deliberately to harm the body, but it is even more foolish deliberately to harm the soul. If men could be taught that an injury to the soul is far more serious than the loss of an arm or a leg or an eye, they would be a good deal less likely to commit the sins and crimes which destroy them. In other words, if a man really saw things in their true light he would want to be virtuous and he would avoid evil in the same way that a man who knows that a drink is deadly poisonous will avoid that drink. That is what Socrates meant when he said that knowledge is virtue, and ignorance vice.

But how are we to teach men what is their true good? The Sophists said that even if there is good and evil it cannot be known. Socrates thought that it could be known and could be taught, and he set out to find the way to do so.

Deeply aware of the incompleteness of his own knowledge, Socrates decided that his best course would be to consult those members of the community who had the highest reputation for knowledge and learning.

In order to find out what justice is, he would ask those whose business it is to dispense justice—the magistrates, the lawyers, the lawmakers. To find out what religion is, he would ask the priests of the temples. He would find out what beauty is from the poets and the painters. Socrates accordingly went around the streets of Athens consulting the experts about their various specialties. He quickly found out that, although most of the people he questioned thought they knew what justice was, or democracy, or virtue, or piety, when they were pressed they could not give a clear answer.

This explained for Socrates why the Oracle at Delphi on one occasion had called him the wisest man in Athens. At first he had thought that the Oracle had made a mistake, for of all the men of Athens Socrates knew the least. But after he had questioned the supposed authorities and found that their assumption of knowledge really hid a deep ignorance, he concluded that possibly the Oracle was right after all: Socrates was the wisest man in Athens because he was the only one who knew that he did not know anything.

2. The Socratic Irony

A man who thinks he already has all the answers is not likely to make much of a search for the truth. The first step, therefore, on the road to knowledge, Socrates felt, was the recognition of our ignorance. This determination to make people realize their lack of knowledge is at the origin of what is called the Socratic Irony. Pleading his own ignorance, Socrates would ask the benefit of his hearer's wisdom. The latter was usually only too ready to display his superior knowledge and intelligence, but a few adroit questions from Socrates were generally enough to demonstrate that his informer knew even less about the matter than Socrates.

Sometimes this method succeeded in achieving its aim, which was to clear away the rubbish of error and prejudice and to bring about the necessary humility of the serious inquirer into truth. As often as not, however, it simply ended with Socrates making new enemies for himself.

3. The Socratic Dialectic

Socrates spared no one in the pursuit of his mission to stir people from their mental sloth (he called himself the "gadfly" of Athens). Going into the market place and other public gathering places, he would question anyone, high or low, rich or poor, friend or stranger, who would listen to him.

In order to lead up to more complicated problems, Socrates would often start off with deceptively simple questions about everyday affairs. For example, he would ask a carpenter how to make chairs and tables, an armorer how to make a set of armor, a shoemaker how to make a pair of shoes. "You are literally always talking of shoemakers and peddlers and cooks and doctors, as if this had anything to do with our argument," Callicles the Sophist protested to him.[1]

---

1 Plato, *Gorgias*, 491.

Socrates' aim, of course, was to appeal to the love of the Greeks for good craftsmanship. Here was something everyone understood—the need of the artist to know the rules of his craft and the limitations of his materials. With this as a starting point, it might be possible to demonstrate the same need of knowledge and skill in the leading of the good life.

4. The Method Illustrated

A good shoemaker, harnessmaker, carpenter, Socrates felt, would know what he was doing. To make a good set of harness you have to know what it is. To make a good pair of shoes, you have to know what a good pair of shoes is.

Can we find out what a good pair of shoes is? Do we know what a good pair of shoes is? If a shoemaker offered us a pair of shoes five sizes too small would we call them a good pair of shoes? If he offered us a pair of shoes made out of tissue paper would we call them a good pair of shoes? Suppose we want dancing slippers and he offers us hiking boots?

It does not take long to find out that what is a good pair of shoes for us need not be a good pair of shoes for somebody else; what is a good pair of shoes for one purpose is not a good pair of shoes for another. We have to take into account, then, in trying to find out what makes a good pair of shoes, such varying things as the individual for whom the shoes are intended and the purpose they are designed to fulfill.

It is not easy to give a definition of a pair of shoes, but we can recognize certain limits. We are, for example, restricted to certain materials and dimensions if we want a good pair of shoes. The limits are not easy to find, but once found they are binding on all shoemakers. And here is a point of very great importance. Once you have discovered the marks of a good pair of shoes, you have something that is binding on all shoemakers, on all without exception.

Suppose you went into a shoe store and asked the clerk for a pair of dress shoes. The clerk hands you a stone and says, "This is the latest model shoe." What would your reaction be? Suppose the same clerk pointed a gun at you while holding out the stone and said, "This is the latest model shoe. Isn't it a splendid pair of shoes?" You might answer "Yes," but you would know and the clerk, if he were sane, would know that it is not a pair of shoes.

Notice that it is not a matter of convention or custom or tradition. Shoes are shoes and stones are stones. No one—the dictator of Russia, the President of the United States, the King of England, the Pope in Rome—no one can make a stone be a pair of shoes. If every newspaper and radio in the world said that a stone was a pair of shoes you would know, and the world would know, that it was not a pair of shoes. A man may be otherwise the best shoemaker in the world but he cannot make a stone be a pair of shoes.

There are, then, certain limits, certain laws, which are binding on the shoemaker, and on the carpenter and on the harnessmaker, and no man can transgress these limits or laws without being a poor workman. Once more, let us recognize, *there are absolutely no exceptions.*

5. The Art of Good Living

Just as an artisan has to know the laws of his craft and obey them, so too in leading the life of a human being there are certain limits or laws which must be observed if we are to lead a good life. It is not easy to find out what these laws or limits are, any more than it is to find out what is a good pair of shoes, but once we have found these laws they will be binding on all men, just as the rules of good workmanship will be binding on all workmen.

What does it mean, for example, to be courageous? Would you call a soldier courageous who, instead of defending his country, drops his weapons and runs away at the first suspicion of danger? Would you call a man courageous who jumps off a twenty-story building to win a ten-cent bet? Somewhere within these limits we might find what courage is and, if we find it, it will hold good for all men without exception.

Again, to take another example, we can find within rough limits what temperance is. A man who gets drunk every night of the year would hardly be called temperate. Nor would we call temperate a man who destroyed his health by excessive austerity. And once more the important point is that once you have found the limits they hold good for everyone without exception. No matter how powerful the man, what his talents, his authority, his achievements, if he gets drunk every night he is not a temperate man.

The same applies for justice and the other virtues. Once find them and you have something which holds good for all men and for all times.

Now it is possible for a man to stumble along blindly imitating his forebears both as a workman and in his conduct as a human being. But we would hardly call that man a good craftsman who simply imitates through habit and custom what those before him have done. A good workman knows what he is doing and why he is doing it. He knows the rules of his craft.

Similarly, to lead a good life it is necessary to know what a good life is. We must know the rules of good living.

Commentary

Aristotle later on was to disagree with Socrates on this point, for he felt that Socrates was not taking into account sufficiently the irrational elements in man—the instincts, feelings, and passions. What we want, Aristotle would say, is to be courageous, not to know what courage is. And, Aristotle says, it just doesn't square with the facts that when a man knows, for example, what justice is he is therefore just.

It remains true, nevertheless, that with all the gaps and inadequacies Socrates deserves the credit of raising the study of morals to a scientific level and, indirectly, through the investigating techniques he developed, of paving the way for the profound philosophic explorations of Plato and Aristotle.

The Trial and Death of Socrates

For pathos and sublimity history offers few parallels to the trial and death of Socrates. In the grip of the fears and hatreds that followed the defeat of Athens by Sparta the Athenians succeeded in legally putting to death the best and noblest among them.

In his seventieth year, Socrates was brought to trial before a criminal court on the grounds that he did not believe in the gods of the city and that he was corrupting the youth of Athens. The real though unexpressed charge against Socrates seems to have been political. Socrates had been all too outspoken in his criticism of the follies and deceptions of the politicians. Nor did he hesitate to remind his fellow citizens in Athens that part of their trouble was due to their own ignorance and selfishness. It seems clear, at any rate, that the people wanted a scapegoat, and that they felt that here was a good opportunity to chasten and rebuke this irritating and non-compliant troublemaker.

Socrates' Apology for His Life

The trial of Socrates took place before the assemblage of his fellow citizens, some five hundred in number, who constituted the body of judges.

Socrates was anything but conciliatory toward his judges. He quickly reduced his accusers and their indictment to absurdity, and went on to insist that, far from his being a danger to Athens, Athens needed him.

Not even the fear of death—and Socrates reminded his listeners that he had faced death in battle more than once in defense of the city—could keep him from philosophizing. He must obey God rather than man: "for know that this is the command of God; and I believe that no greater good has ever happened in the state than my service to the God. For I do nothing but go about persuading you all, old and young alike, not to take thought for your persons or your properties, but first and chiefly to care about the greatest improvement of the soul. . . . This is my teaching, and if this is the doctrine which corrupts the youth, I am a mischievous person."[2]

Socrates then warns his audience that the person who commits

---

2 The quotations in this section are taken from the speech of Socrates at his trial as recorded in Plato's Apology.

injustice suffers a far greater injury than the one who receives the injustice, concluding this part of his defense: "And now, Athenians, I am not going to argue for my own sake, as you may think, but for yours, that you may not sin against the God by condemning me, who am his gift to you. For if you kill me you will not easily find a successor to me, who, if I may use such a ludicrous figure of speech, am a sort of gadfly, given to the state by God; and the state is a great and noble steed who is tardy with his motions owing to his very size, and requires to be stirred into life. I am that gadfly which God has attached to the state, and all day long and in all places am always fastening upon you, arousing and persuading and reproaching you. You will not easily find another like me, and therefore I advise you to spare me."

Socrates was found guilty by a small majority, and was asked to propose an alternative to the death sentence. The Athenian law said that a man condemned to death could propose another penalty, such as imprisonment or exile, and the jury had to choose between the two alternatives.

The jury probably expected Socrates to furnish them with an alternative that would spare him and, at the same time, satisfy their desire to humble him. However, after thanking those who had voted for his acquittal, Socrates told the judges that if he received his proper treatment from the Athenians they would honor him as they would a winner at the Olympic games and entertain him royally at the expense of the city as a public benefactor for the rest of his days.

This apparent contempt of Socrates for the jury angered them and, on a second vote, they condemned him to death with a greater majority than the first.

In his final speech Socrates warned the jury that they could not escape just judgment. "If you think that by killing men you can prevent some one from censuring your evil lives, you are mistaken; that is not a way of escape which is either possible or honorable; the easiest and noblest way is not to be disabling others, but to be improving yourselves."

Socrates affirmed his belief in a life after death, and then took leave of the unjust judges. "The hour of departure has arrived, and we go our ways—I to die, and you to live. Which is better God only knows."

The Last Days of Socrates

A month was to pass before the execution of Socrates, and part of the time was spent in conversation with his friends in his prison cell.

The story of the last hours of Socrates is given to us by Plato in the Phaedo, one of the great treasures of all literature. The theme of Socrates' last discussion with his friends is the immortality of the soul, and the blessing of death, which for the true philosopher represents the freeing from the shadows of unreality and the entrance into the realm where he can find wisdom in all her clarity and fullness.

The account of the last moments of Socrates, as the poison cup slowly takes its effect, is told with a dignity and poignancy which makes us share over the stretch of twenty-five centuries the grief and heartache of the friends and disciples of one of the noblest of mankind. "Such was the end," the dialogue closes, "of our friend; concerning whom I may truly say, that of all the men of his time whom I have known, he was the wisest and justest and best."[3]

---

3 Plato, Phaedo, 118 b.

CHAPTER 6

Plato

The safest general characterization of the European philosophical tradition is that it consists in a series of footnotes to Plato.
WHITEHEAD, PROCESS AND REALITY, P. 63

Life and Works

Plato as a young man stood high among the friends and intimates of Socrates. He was forced for his own safety to leave Athens for a time after the death of Socrates. He had loved Socrates as the wisest and most excellent of men, and the death of Socrates was, in Plato's eyes, a great disaster, not only for Athens but for mankind. Plato dedicated his life to the vindication of Socrates' memory and to keeping alive his teaching.

Plato, born in the year 427 B.C., came of a distinguished family, prominent in the affairs of Athens for many generations. Critias, an uncle of Plato, was one of the group called the Thirty Tyrants, an oligarchical council set up to rule Athens after the Peloponnesian War. Plato himself held aloof completely from the political life of Athens, in all likelihood because he thought it beyond hope of redemption.

After the death of Socrates, Plato spent several years in travel, visiting Asia Minor, Egypt, Southern Italy and Sicily, as well as various cities in Greece itself famous as centers of philosophic thought.

Plato lived for a while at the court of Dionysius I, the tyrant of

Syracuse, in Sicily. His outspokenness displeased the tyrant, and Plato was obliged to leave. He returned to Athens, where he founded a school of philosophy, the Academy. Named after Academus, the owner of the garden where it was established, the school was destined to have an unbroken life of over nine hundred years.

Plato returned a second time to Syracuse in the capacity of adviser and guide to Dionysius II, the son and successor of Dionysius I. Little came of the experiment of forming the philosopher-king, and Plato came back to Athens where, apart from a second brief trip to Syracuse, he spent the remainder of his life quietly teaching. He died in the year 347 B.C., at the age of eighty. He was eulogized by his pupil Aristotle as a man "whom bad men have not even the right to praise, and who showed in his life and teachings how to be happy and good at the same time."[1]

Most of Plato's works are in the form of dialogues and Socrates is usually the leading figure. The early dialogues mirror directly the teaching of Socrates. The later dialogues—the *Republic* is generally accepted as the dividing work—seem to give us more especially the thought of Plato himself.

In addition to the dialogues, some thirty-four in number, and the Apology of Socrates (Socrates' speech at his trial), seven and possibly eight of the Letters of Plato have come down to us. A number of spurious dialogues and letters have also been attributed to him. The dialogues were written for the general public, and Plato is supposed to have written, in addition, a number of prose treatises meant especially for the inner circle of his students. All of these have been lost.

The Platonic Dialectic

Socrates had contented himself with the investigation of moral problems. He was interested in making men lead better lives, rather than in knowledge for its own sake. Thus the big questions for

---

1   Rose, *Aristotelis Fragmenta* (Berlin, 1870), Fragment 623. Quoted by F. C. Copleston, *A History of Philosophy* (Westminster, Md.: The Newman Press, 1946), Vol. 1, p. 266.

Socrates were questions like, What is Justice? What is Temperance? What is Virtue? What is Goodness?

Plato went beyond this to ask questions like, What is Tree? What is Green? What is Triangle? What is Circle? What is Round? What is One? What is Ten? What is Number? What is Up? What is Down? What is Right? and What is Left? What is "Is" Itself?

Plato was especially interested in the question of meaning. Why do we give one name to some things and a different name to others?

What does it mean to give the *same* name to two *different* things?

In trying to answer the question, Why do we give the same name to two different things, let us recognize that it is the actual thing we are thinking of which is important, not the name we use for it. As we cannot see into one another's minds, we need signs to express what is in there. A name is just an agreed-on sign or sound for what we are thinking of. If I point to a triangle, for example, a man of France or of Germany or of ancient Rome or of ancient Greece would know what I had in mind, though all of them would have different oral signs, different spoken sounds, to signify this thing. It is the thing in our minds, then, and not the word, with which we are concerned.

Plato's Method Illustrated

When I say the paper on which I am writing is white and the snow outside is white, am I using the word "white" for one thing or for two things? What do I mean when I say the white of the paper and the white of the snow are the same, are alike? Why do I give them the same name? What does being the same, being alike, mean? Can two things be both the same and different at the same time and in the same way?

If it should snow tomorrow over half the world, would there be any difference in whiteness? Would there be more whiteness? Plato would say that if there is any difference—no matter how little —we should find another name for it. If there isn't any difference, if whiteness is the same after the snowfall as before, then quantity doesn't make any difference to whiteness.

Similarly, if the whiteness in any two white things is the same in both, place doesn't make any difference to it. Snow is the same kind of white in Attica as it is in America. Neither does time make any difference. When the Greeks, twenty-five hundred years ago, talked about white-capped Olympus, was the whiteness they were thinking of the same whiteness we think of? Whiteness, for Plato, is one single thing, and it is not affected by time, by place, by quantity.

If all the white things in the world were destroyed would there still be whiteness? Plato would say yes. If I destroy this piece of paper, I haven't affected whiteness. Similarly, if I destroyed every white thing whiteness would still stay the same. In other words, whiteness is not in this piece of paper or any other white thing in the world. If this world were destroyed, whiteness would still be the same. Whiteness, since it is not in any particular place, is not in this world.

This piece of paper is rectangular. Rectangularity is not in this piece of paper any more than it is in any other rectangular thing. Before this piece of paper was manufactured there was such a thing as rectangularity. And after this piece of paper is destroyed, rectangularity is still just the same. If all the rectangular things of the world were destroyed, there would be no difference to rectangularity.

What about numbers? Think of the answer to six plus six. Where is that number of which you are thinking? Is there any more of it since you have been thinking of it? Will there be any less of it when you stop thinking of it? If no one in the world were thinking of it, would there be such a thing as twelve? A ruler is twelve inches long. Is the twelve in the ruler or in your head? Is there one twelve or two twelves? If there are two twelves, how could we give them the same name?

Just as in the case of whiteness, we would find that twelve is not affected by quantity, or time, or place. It is not in any of the things that are called twelve, any more than it is in any other place.

This paper is thin. So is a newspaper. Is there one thinness or two thinnesses? If I destroy this piece of paper is there any difference in thinness? Thinness, we have to say, is not in this piece of paper any more than it is in any other place.

Consider again our piece of paper. It is white, but the whiteness is not in the piece of paper. It is thin, but the thinness is not in the piece of paper. What about paperness itself? If I destroy this piece of paper, have I made any change in paperness? If we follow our previous reasoning, paperness itself is not in the paper.

Our piece of paper seems to be slipping away beneath our very finger tips. Paperness is not in it. Rectangularity is not in it. None of the things we can say about it seem to belong to it. Notice, too, that we could substitute an identical piece of paper for it, and we would still have paperness, whiteness, number, although we need not know that a substitution has been made. In other words, whatever we can know in this piece of paper does not belong to it.

Is there anything at all there? Plato would answer yes, because the thing changes, and there must be something there which is the explanation of the change. "The philosopher," he says, "will include both the changeable and the unchangeable in his definition of being."[2] What is there, however, has so little reality that, except for the bare fact of its existence, it cannot be known.

Plato, it is apparent, has simply carried on Socrates' way of investigation into fields where Socrates did not venture. Just as there is only one Justice, one Temperance, one Virtue, unchanging, the same for all men and for all times, so too there is but one Whiteness, one Thinness, one Rectangularity, the same for all men in all times and in all places. If this world in which we live were destroyed, Plato held, very little worthwhile would be lost. Justice, Triangleness, Whiteness and the like would remain, eternal and unchanging.

Plato's Doctrine of the Two Worlds

Drawing out the consequences of his reasoning, Plato concluded that we are exposed, as it were, to two worlds at once. One is the world of unchanging things like Whiteness, Rectangularity, Justice—a world that is perfect, eternal, the source of whatever traces of perfection and goodness we find in the world around us. The other

---

2 *Sophist*, 249 d 3,

world is the changing, imperfect world of the senses. There is so little to this shadowy, transient world that all we know of it is that it is there, and is the source of change, multiplicity, and imperfection.

These two worlds are so mixed up together that only the rare person, the philosopher, ever comes to know that there are really two worlds. It is as though picture and sound were perfectly blended on a single strip of film, or as though two photographic negatives were skillfully superimposed to produce one composite picture.

With the eye of our body we see one world, the world of change, of movement, of imperfection. With reason, "the eye of our soul," as Plato calls it, we are in touch with the other world, the world of perfect, eternal, unchanging realities.

The "really real" world for Plato is not the changing world of the senses which, like the world of Heraclitus, is a flux of movement, a well of illusion, and can never be the source of real knowledge beyond the given fact of its existence. The real world, from which everything else draws its reality and which is the source of all our knowledge, is the world in which exist Whiteness, Triangularity, and the rest. To these things, Whiteness and Triangularity and so on, Plato gave the name Idea or Form.

The word Idea originally meant pattern and so, for Plato, the Idea is the pattern which runs through things which are alike. And these Ideas literally exist by themselves. If all the things of the world of sense were to disappear, if all human beings were to disappear, Whiteness, Treeness, Roundness, would continue to exist, unaffected, unchanged.

In trying to understand Plato's world of Ideas we must remember that he is using sense metaphors to describe a dimension of reality which has nothing to do with space or time. When he uses metaphors like "the place" of the Ideas or "off in the sky" we must remember that they are not meant to be taken literally any more than when we speak of "high" thoughts or "low" thoughts, or of being "up" in heaven and "down" in hell. What these words really express are statements of degree or comparison or value, and to give them a spatial or temporal interpretation is to distort their meaning entirely.

Similarly, when Plato speaks of the world of bodies being unreal, he is not arguing away their existence. He is emphasizing the fact that to the extent they are involved in change, are in a state of *becoming*, to that extent they fall short of *being*.

Plato knew that his teaching was a strange one and that people would laugh at him when he said the world we live in is not the real world. There are, furthermore, tremendous difficulties in his position which he could not solve. He was certain, however, that he had hit upon some truths of the highest importance and he was determined even at the expense of incompleteness and apparent inconsistency to cling to these insights.[3]

The Allegory of the Cave

To illustrate the doctrine that the world of our senses simply mirrors another and better world, Plato invented in the *Republic* the Myth of the Cave, one of the most famous of his explanatory allegories and a touching tribute to the memory of Socrates.[4]

According to this parable, the human race is like a tribe of people who have been chained generation after generation in a large cave, with their backs to the entrance. At the mouth of the cave there is a high wall, on the other side of which on a broad highway march a procession of people carrying statues representing all the objects of the world around us. The sun shining through the entrance of the cave casts the shadows of these statues on the back wall of the cave. These shadows, the "shadows of images," dim, shifting, and distorted, are the only things known to the people chained in the cave.

One day one of the prisoners of the cave is brought to the entrance and out into the sunshine. At first the strong light hurts his eyes, and he longs for the comforting darkness and familiar

3 For a very full discussion of what Plato meant by his doctrine of two worlds, see F. C. Copleston, *A History of Philosophy*, Vol. 1 (Westminster, Md.: The Newman Press, 1946), Part III. For an account of this general type of philosophical system and its way of explaining reality, see Stallknecht and Brumbaugh, *The Compass of Philosophy* (New York: Longmans, Green, and Co., 1954), Chap. 4, "Form and Field."

4 *Republic*, 514.

shadows of the cave. But as his eyes grow accustomed to the light, the beauty of the world around him floods in on him and he sees how much better, more real, more beautiful is the world outside. Thinking back with pity to the prisoners still chained in the cave, he feels that he cannot keep this knowledge to himself. Though he knows he will be laughed at, derided, even killed, the world of real things means so much that he must bring back the news of it. And so, sadly, the philosopher turns back from the world of light to re-enter the cave of shadows.

Plato's View of Man

Plato held that the true part of man is really his soul and that the souls of men once enjoyed a kind of existence in which they were in direct contact with the Ideas. Then for some reason man fell from his high estate and, as punishment for some crime, the soul was condemned to exist as a prisoner in the body. The body is the prison house of the soul, Plato said. But even in his fallen state, man remembers what he once was in the world of Ideas. What we call knowing is the remembering of what we once knew in our unencumbered state. (This teaching of Plato is called the doctrine of Reminiscence.)

Our knowledge is hazy and confused, Plato held, because our remembrance of the Ideas is dulled and entangled in the images which pour through our senses from the changing world of bodies outside us. The true philosopher will learn to separate these two worlds, to separate the true and certain knowledge of the unchanging Ideas from the opinion and probability which is all that the world of sense can give us. In Plato's own words:

"The soul when using the body as an instrument of perception, that is to say, when using the sense of sight or hearing or some other sense (for the meaning of perceiving through the body is perceiving through the senses) . . . is then dragged by the body into the region of the changeable, and wanders and is confused; the world spins round her, and she is like a drunkard, when she touches change. . . .

"But when returning into herself she reflects, then she passes into the other world, the region of purity, and eternity, and immortality, and unchangeableness, which are her kindred, and with them she ever lives, when she is by herself and is not let or hindered; then she ceases from her erring ways, and being in communion with the unchanging is unchanging. And this state of the soul is called wisdom."[5]

Conclusion

Plato, by way of Socrates, has brought us back to the old dilemma of Heraclitus and Parmenides. We still have the problem of reconciling permanence and change. Plato says that through our senses we are exposed to the world of bodies, the world of change or becoming. There is just enough reflection of stability and reality in this world to turn our minds to another realm, the realm of unchanging, immaterial being. This doesn't really solve the problem, however, for the separation between the two realms is still there, a chasm Plato never succeeded in bridging.

Plato has made, nevertheless, enormous contributions to the advance of knowledge. In raising the question, Why do we give the same name to different things, he has brought up the question of meaning: What do we mean by meaning? To answer this question, we must find out what we mean by thinking, and what a thought or an idea is. And these problems in turn are related to the problems of what man is and what kind of a world it is in which he lives.

Plato and Socrates, therefore, have not only raised some of the questions that are most important for philosophy but they also have taken us a long way down the road to answering them.

---

5 *Phaedo*, 79. Plato presented these views in the form of myths, "likely stories," as a way of indicating in symbolic fashion truths too dimly discerned for direct statement.

CHAPTER 7

Aristotle

Dear to me is Plato, but dearer still the truth.
ARISTOTLE.

Life And Works

Aristotle (384 B.C.-322 B.C.), the son of a renowned physician from Thrace, became a pupil at Plato's Academy at the age of seventeen, and remained there until Plato's death some twenty years later. In the year 343 B.C., Aristotle was called to the court of Philip of Macedon, where he was appointed tutor to Philip's son, the future Alexander the Great. During the reign of Alexander, Aristotle established a school in Athens called the Lyceum,[1] where he taught for the next twelve years. The name Peripatetic, "Walker," which is sometimes given to the philosophy or to the followers of Aristotle, came from Aristotle's habit of walking up and down while lecturing.

After the death of Alexander, Aristotle was forced by his political enemies to flee to Chalcis, in northern Greece. Referring to the death of Socrates, he refused, he said, to give Athens the chance to sin a second time against philosophy. In less than a year his exile ended with his death.

---

1   Aristotle's school was set up next to a temple dedicated to Apollo, one of whose names was Lycaeus.

Many of the philosophical writings of Aristotle have been lost. Like Plato, he wrote his philosophy in the form of dialogues which were meant for reading by the general public. These are known as the exoteric, or popular, works. All except a few fragments have been lost.

The prose treatises that have survived are known as esoteric works, written, that is, for initiates. Their understanding presupposes a thorough philosophical preparation, and they are apparently the notes based on Aristotle's lectures within the Lyceum. They have come down to us in somewhat mutilated form, and the wonder is that they survived at all, because for a century and a half the only complete edition lay buried and lost in a well where it had been hidden to avoid seizure during a time of war.

We probably possess most of the important prose works of Aristotle. These include a series of treatises on logic known collectively as the *Organon*—the tool or instrument of knowledge; treatises on the natural sciences, such as the *Meteorology* and the *History of Animals*, along with the *Physics*, a study of the philosophy of nature; the *Metaphysics*, or *First Philosophy*; and the ethical treatises including the *Nicomachean Ethics* and the *Politics*, to which can be added the *Poetics* and the *Rhetoric*.[2]

Aristotle's Relation to Plato

Aristotle was a devoted pupil of Plato and assuredly his most brilliant. Probably no one has ever known better the philosophy of Plato. Aristotle did not philosophize in opposition to his master, as is sometimes said, but rather brought the already rich and profound philosophy of his teacher to its magnificent fulfillment. On the key issue of the universals, Aristotle accepted the discoveries of Plato. Nevertheless, on one of the most fundamental points of

---

2 References to Aristotle's works are based on the pages, numbers, and lines of the standard Greek text of Bekker, 5 vols., Berlin, 1831-1870. Nearly all modern editions repeat these numbers. The pages are divided into two columns, a and b. Thus the reference *Meta.*, 985 a 15 (often referred to as "the Berlin number") means that the reference is to the *Metaphysics*, p. 985 of the Berlin edition, column 1. line 15.

his philosophy, the doctrine of the two worlds, the disciple parted company with the master: for Aristotle there is only one world, the world made apparent to us through our senses.

Aristotle agreed with Plato that there is only one Whiteness, one Treeness, one Triangularity, one Justice. They are not, however, in a world by themselves. Whiteness is in all white things, Treeness in all trees, Justice in all just actions. Instead of calling them Ideas Aristotle gave them the name Forms.

The Doctrine of Form and Matter

All the things in the world around us, he said, are made up of two principles. First, there is the *form*—that which makes them what they are, gives them their basic way of being: Manness, Treeness, and so on. Manness does not exist by itself, however; only individual men—Socrates, Plato, John, James, Peter—exist. Treeness does not exist by itself but only individual trees: this maple tree, that oak tree, and so on. Form alone, then, is not enough to explain the actually existing individual men, trees, and so on. There must be something else in things, something which limits them, which ties them down to this particular way of being, and not any other, to this particular time and place, to this quantity. There must, in short, be a second basic principle in things, a principle of limitation, a principle which limits *form*, restricts it, so to speak, which makes it individual, quantified, existing in a definite time and place. To this principle Aristotle gave the name *matter*.[3]

With this doctrine of the two basic principles at the heart of things, Aristotle is able to go a long way toward the reconciliation of some of the paradoxes of reality which perplexed earlier philosophers. He is able to account, for example, for the stability and permanence

---

3 It is important not to confuse Aristotle's matter with our modern notion of "stuff." The notion of matter is one which is arrived at as the result of a rational analysis; it is something we are led to as the result of an act of reasoning, and which cannot in any way be grasped by the senses. Similarly, the philosophic term "form" is not equivalent to the word form as it is used in everyday speech. The notion of form is also an intelligible principle, not reducible to anything that can be seen, touched, or imagined.

of things through the principle of form. Once given what a triangle is, you have something that holds good forever, and the intellect is able to know triangularity as separated from the conditions of change and imperfection—in other words, as something eternal, perfect, unchanging. Outside the intellect, however, forms exist only partially, imperfectly realized, coming to a relative completion only, through the successions of change, for form is never found separated from a second principle, the principle of matter. This second principle, which like form is never found existing by itself, is the principle which accounts for change, individuality, imperfection.

Act and Potency

Aristotle extended the notions by which he explained the composition of bodies to cover the whole range of reality—incorporeal as well as corporeal. In this wider usage he divided being into "the potential and the completely real."[4] Complete reality refers to the fullness of being, the actual existence of a thing as against its merely possible existence. "Actuality," Aristotle says, "means the existence of the thing not in the way which we express by potentially"; and he goes on to illustrate: "We say that potentially, for instance, a statue of Hermes is in the block of wood and the half-line is in the whole, because it might be separated out, and we call even the man who is not studying a man of science, if he is capable of actually studying a particular problem."[5]

The act of a being, then, is what is absolutely primary to it—the basic way of being itself. Aristotle calls this the "first act" of a thing; its operations beyond the bare fact of existence are called "second act." When referred to bodies, "first act" can also be called "form."[6]

---

4 *Metaphysics*, XI, 9; 1065 b 16. (All quotations from the *Metaphysics* are taken from the translation of W. D. Ross [Oxford: The Clarendon Press, 1928].)

5 *Ibid.*, IX, 6; 1048 a 30.

6 St. Thomas Aquinas would later on distinguish between "form" and "act," pointing out that the form itself is in potency to existence, "the supreme act of all that is." Cf. E. Gilson, *Being and Some Philosophers* (Toronto: Pontifical Institute of Mediaeval Studies, 1949), Chap. V.

The ways of being that are possible to a thing beyond what it is being at a given moment are its potentialities—or "matter," as referred to bodies.

The full reality of any being is what it actually is plus its potential ways of being. This is the truth which Parmenides missed, and the reason why he had to argue away the fact of change. For granted that a thing such as a possible statue is not *being* in the sense that an actual statue is *being*, nevertheless we cannot say that it is nothing. It is part of the reality of a block of stone that it can be carved into a statue; even though a builder is not building, he is capable of it, and that makes him something more than the man who is not able to build; even if I close my eyes, I am still capable of seeing, and that makes me different from the man who is blind.

If we are going to use the term *being* to stand for whatever is not nothing, then it will cover potentialities as well as actualities, and therefore we can say that all being is divided into act and potency. If a being has no possibilities in its make-up, then we say it is pure act; that is, it exhausts the full actuality of being. If it is not pure act, then it is composed of act and potency. Pure potency does not exist except as an abstraction, for a real possibility is always a possibility of something—has meaning, in other words, only in relation to some act.

The Explanation of Change

Aristotle's profound insight that the whole of reality included possible ways of being as well as actual beings came to him as the result of his effort to explain the mystery of change. Any existing thing is already all that it can be. (If it could be more, there is no reason why it should not be.) Therefore the explanation of change will not be found in what the thing actually is. Neither will the explanation be found in terms of what the thing will change into, for the goal of change does not yet exist, and what does not exist cannot be a positive factor in the explanation of anything. The explanation must be found then in the line of potency, in terms of what the thing is able to be under the influence of the appropriate external causes. Aristotle defines change, therefore, as "the actuality [or actualization] of the potential as such."[7]

Change is neither the potency of things nor their act, but something in between—an incomplete act, Aristotle says. It is incomplete because the reality toward which the change is moving is not yet fully realized, and the being undergoing change cannot be said to be changed until that new way of being is achieved. The intermediate stage between the starting point and the goal of change is, then, "actuality and not actuality"[8]—actuality in so far as it is on its way to realizing the new perfection, not actuality to the extent that it is short of the goal; "which is hard to detect," Aristotle says, "but capable of existing."[9]

The Explanation of Knowing

Not only do the concepts of matter and form enable Aristotle to explain the constitution of bodies and their changes without explaining away the world in which we find ourselves, but they also give him the key to the explanation of knowing. Although the things around us are constantly changing, nevertheless a true knowledge of the world of bodies is possible because the nature of things and the laws of change itself are unchanging. Man has two ways of knowing—through his senses and through his intellect, and their co-working is needed for complete knowledge of the world. Our senses carry to us the changing aspects of things, while the power of reason is required to put us in touch with their stable, unchanging elements.

Although whiteness, sweetness, triangularity, circularity, oneness, threeness, and all other ideas exist as universals only in the intellect (where they are known as eternally immutable and one) they nevertheless are drawn out of material things, where they exist as the formal element. Even though our world is a limited and changing

---

7 *Metaphysics*, XI, 9; 1065 b 17. For a further discussion of this definition, and of change in general, see below, Chap. 27.

8 *Ibid.*, 1066 a 26.

9 *Ibid.*, 1066 a 27.

one, therefore, it is real and knowable, not the insubstantial shadow world of Plato.

The Levels of Knowing

Aristotle goes on to explain how the light of the intellect is able to penetrate behind the panorama of change to deeper and deeper layers of reality, starting with the superficial aspects of things, their "surface" qualities, such as whiteness, sweetness, hardness, and so on, and penetrating to the deeper aspects of quantity, whereby we know things as having figure and able to be numbered.

The deepest thrust of all of which our intellect is capable is to the very heart of things—their being itself. Before a thing can be anything else it has simply to be, and this awareness of being, the awareness of what it means to exist, which the least of things can give to us, is the deepest knowlege of which the intellect is capable.

This deepest and most universal of all the things that can be known is the most basic study for the philosopher—a study which leads the intellect all the way from the contemplation of the unchanging aspects of changing bodies to their ultimate explanation in the *Unchanging Being Itself.* Aristotle gave the name *First Philosophy,* or *Theology,* to this branch of knowledge.

Aristotle's Doctrine of Man

Explaining knowledge as he did, Aristotle had to give a picture of man different from that of Plato. For Plato, the real man is the soul, and the body is a prison house which darkens and deadens the soul. But Aristotle, holding that all knowledge has its origin in the senses, had to hold that the body was just as much a part of man as the soul. Just as in all other bodies, there is in man a union of two principles, of form and matter. The soul of man is his form and that form exists limited, individuated. The mark or manifestation of that limitation is the body of man, and man would not be man if he did not exist as circumscribed, so to speak, as having this body and existing in this time and this place.

Plato held the doctrine of the pre-existence of souls and held, therefore, for the soul's immortality. Aristotle rejected the doctrine of the pre-existence of souls and, wary perhaps of the Platonic tendency to reject the world of bodies for some other world, practically ignored the problem of the soul's immortality. The few passages in his works which deal with this problem are ambiguous and inconclusive.

Aristotle's Completion of Socrates and Plato

Probably the most important single advance of Aristotle over Plato was his restoration of reality to the world we live in. Plato had held that the shadowy, changing world given to us by our senses could never be an object of real knowledge because it was always becoming something else even as we were in the act of being aware of it. By recognizing beneath the flux of sensation the unchangeable, enduring character of the forms of bodily things, Aristotle saw that real knowledge of bodies was possible and laid the foundation of the sciences of the external world.

In the fields of ethics and politics we find, again, that Aristotle brought to substantial completion the work so well started by Socrates and Plato. The most important contribution of Aristotle here is his distinction between the theoretical or speculative order and the practical order, the order of contemplation as against the order of action. Socrates had made knowledge the equivalent of virtue. Aristotle, however, emphasizes the fact that to know is not the same as to do. In the realm of acting the fact of free will makes it possible for us to choose in contradiction to what we know is right. He stressed, therefore, the importance of developing the virtues in man for the strengthening of the will and for the control of the animal appetites.

Along with some of the physical sciences, such as zoology, the science of logic received much of its content and its first formulation from the hands of Aristotle. Aesthetics, too, as a branch of philosophy, received its first systematic treatment from Aristotle.

The philosophy of Aristotle, in short, represents the glorious fruition of the work started by Socrates and carried on by Plato. In the words of Stace, the eminent historian of Greek philosophy, "It is the highest point reached in the philosophy of Greece. The flower of all previous thought, the essence and pure distillation of the Greek philosophic spirit, the gathering up of all that is good in his predecessors and the rejection of all that is faulty and worthless— such is the philosophy of Aristotle."[10]

Conclusion

The great significance of Aristotle for philosophy is that he brought it to completion; not in the sense that he finished it, but in the sense that he formulated it in its broad outlines, laying the secure foundation on which many future generations of philosophers could build. The philosophy of Plato incorporated the deeply profound and penetrating insights of a great philosophic genius, but his work is nevertheless incomplete. Where Plato threw intermittent flashes of light into the darkness of the unknown, Aristotle dissipated the darkness itself with a clear and enduring light whose rays stretched to the very horizons of man's ken. While the soaring genius of Plato raised philosophy to unequaled heights, winning priceless treasures of truth, Aristotle anchored philosophy to reality itself, insuring for it the stability, universality, and inexhaustibility which makes it the truly "perennial" philosophy.

"Plato's relation to the world," says Goethe[11]- "is that of a superior spirit, whose good pleasure it is to dwell in it for a time. It is not so much his concern to become acquainted with it—for the world and its nature are things which he presupposes—as kindly to communicate to it that which he brings with him, and of which it stands in so great need. He penetrates into its depths, more that he may replenish them from the fullness of his own nature, than

---

10 W. T. Stace, *A Critical History of Greek Philosophy* (London: The Macmillan Company, 1920), p. 332. (Reprinted with permission of The Macmillan Company.)

11 He is commenting on the famous painting of Raphael called "The School of Athens," where Plato is portrayed as pointing upward, whereas Aristotle is gazing earthward. This passage and the following paragraph are quoted by Ueberweg, *A History of Philosophy* (New York: Scribner's, 1872), pp. 103 and 139.

that he may fathom their mysteries. He scales its heights as one yearning after renewed participation in the source of his being. All that he utters has reference to something eternally complete, good, true, beautiful, whose furtherance he strives to promote in every bosom. Whatever of earthly knowledge he appropriates here and there, evaporates in his method and in his discourse. . . ."

"Aristotle stands to the world in the relation preeminently of a great architect. Here he is and here he must work and create. He informs himself about the surface of the earth, but only so far as is necessary to find a foundation for his structure, and from the surface to the centre all besides is to him indifferent. He draws an immense circle from the base of his building, collects materials from all sides, arranges them, piles them up in layers, and so rises in regular form, like a pyramid, toward the sky, while Plato seeks the heavens like an obelisk, or better, like a pointed flame."

Conclusion to Part I

With the full flowering of Greek philosophy in the work of Aristotle we bring our historical study to a close. The principles elaborated, refined, and organized by Aristotle were destined to become the foundations of what is called the perennial philosophy, the enduring philosophy, the one philosophy which, renewing itself over and over again through all the vicissitudes of time and history, offers to each new generation the unchanging key to the mysteries of reality. Our historical survey makes no pretense to completeness. Its purpose has been twofold: to introduce the reader to the problems of philosophy in what seems to us the easiest and most interesting way, and to elaborate certain basic concepts which we can now use as tools or instruments in a more direct probing of the mysteries of reality. In the chapters which follow we shall endeavor to expose in broad perspective the truths about man and the universe in which he finds himself, as they have been elaborated by the cooperative efforts of countless thinkers following down through the centuries in the footsteps and in the spirit of Aristotle.

PART II

THE MEANING OF MAN

CHAPTER 8

The Nature of Man

Man is but a reed, the weakest in nature, but he is a thinking reed.
PASCAL, PENSEES, II, 3.

The motto "Know Thyself" which was placed over the door of
Plato's Academy marked an important change of emphasis in
Greek philosophy. The first philosophers had been interested in
the mysteries of the world in which man finds himself. They asked
questions about the sun and the moon and the stars and about the
stuff out of which everything is made. But with Socrates, Plato,
and Aristotle, the nature of man himself, rather than the physical
universe, became the most important mystery for the study of the
philosopher.

The philosophers of the Middle Ages, while not ignoring the
world around them, also stressed the study of man above the problems of the physical world. And although there are sharp differences in the outlook of the ancient world and the world of the
Middle Ages, there was substantial agreement on the all-important
point, which the Greeks had been the first to justify on grounds of
reason, that man is different from the rest of the animals in that he
possesses the distinctive powers of reason and free will.

Through all the diversity and historical accidents of the past
twenty-five hundred years, this concept of man as responsible and
rational has exerted a continuing and profound influence on the
political and social thinking and institutions of the West. Yet, in

our own times, probably no element in our cultural inheritance has been more called in question. And since the answer to this question affects us so profoundly even in practical, everyday affairs, we shall start our systematic study of philosophy with the problem of man himself and his destiny. In the latter part of our systematic study we shall consider the world in which man finds himself.

The View of Man Changes

Probably the most widely held view of man today in opposition to the older, traditional view is that man is simply one more of the brute animals—a superior animal, to be sure, but still just an animal, with the same questionable and transitory value of any other animal. And just as animals in general are creatures of instinct, with no real control over their instinctive drives or over the pull on their senses from the outside, so too man is impelled purely by the attraction of sense goods and by the blind drive of instinct.

A still grosser view of man sees him as a kind of machine, a bundle of conditioned reflexes which respond as necessarily to the impersonal laws of mechanics and physics as the leaf falling from the tree. Manipulate the physical stimuli which act on man and you can control both the individual and society as surely as you can control machinery: given the proper stimulus, the reflex will be mechanic, automatic, and foreseeable.

Common to both these doctrines is the view that man is a freakish, haphazard, evanescent appearance in an ever evolving universe, a chance collection of atoms, an insignificant dot destined to last but the flash of an instant in the vast perspective of time unending: a being without meaning, without destiny, without hope.

"Ideas Have Consequences"

Many philosophers and psychologists over the past two hundred years and more have taught this and similar doctrines about the nature of man. For a long time the consequences of this teaching were not too apparent, for the leavening process of ideas is a slow one. We have reached the point in our own day, however, when large parts of the world are controlled by men who apply literally the teachings that yesterday belonged to the lecture hall. As a result we see today the manipulation of whole populations as though they were herds of cattle; we see people used in slave labor camps and their worth calculated at what it costs to feed them; we see the human personality assaulted and shattered by the identical techniques used by the Russian scientist Pavlov in his experiments on the conditioned reflexes of brute animals. And no one can be sure that in some "Brave New World" of tomorrow he will not be the victim of inhuman state technicians. There are few questions, then, whose right answer is so important to us as this question, What is the nature of man?

Man Is Different

Philosophers and scientists are right when they insist on the strength and importance of man's instincts and sense appetites, and when they assert that he is deeply immersed within the impersonal forces of the physical universe. For man is, of course, an animal, and as such a part of the physical universe. As a material being, he is obedient to the laws of physical nature. If he puts his hand in fire his hand will burn. If he goes out in the rain he will get wet. If he doesn't breathe or eat he will die.

But to make this side of man the whole man is as erroneous as to say that a Rembrandt portrait is a mixture of colors on two square feet of canvas, or that a sonnet of Shakespeare consists of some splashes of ink on a small strip of paper. For just as something shines out of the picture or the sonnet which is more than a mere arrangement of physical elements, so too something shines out of man which is more than the sum total of any possible arrangement of the physical elements which go into the make-up of his body.

Besides being an animal, man has a power—the power of reason—which in itself makes him different in kind from the rest of the animals. Man can see the sameness in difference which runs through things, the oneness in many, the enduring reality behind outward change. He knows meaning and law and purpose and, through his power of free choice, he can choose between the various alternatives which are presented to him by his intellect. In short, man is a being altogether unique as compared with the rest of the physical universe, because in knowing and judging he rises above the inexorable law and rigidity of the realm of matter.

Many philosophers have been tempted to deny reason to man, thinking thereby to make it easier to explain him. Our university libraries are full of books which compare the activities of man with those of other animals such as guinea pigs and monkeys. The usual implication is that there is no real difference beyond a rising scale of complexity.

Since man is an animal with a body, sense powers, feelings, and emotions just as are the other animals, it would be very surprising if there were not many and deep correspondences between animal and human behavior. But the really important fact, which many psychologists ignore, is that man has a whole range of activities for which there is no parallel in the rest of the animal kingdom—activities which are explainable as the product of reason and unexplainable otherwise. Not until the ape and the guinea pig also start performing these activities can the student of animal psychology legitimately assert that there is no difference between man and the rest of the animal kingdom.

Deny Reason, And What Follows?

Deny reason and you deny science and philosophy, for you cannot deny reason and then proceed to use it. Only man has scientific knowledge of himself, of the other animals, of nature itself. Only man can philosophize, because only man can see meaning in the universe and ask questions about it. If man, like the other animals, had only senses whereby he could acquire knowledge, then he would have to end up by denying knowledge itself, for the sciences and philosophy are concerned with what does not change, with what is enduring behind the everlasting flux of sense appearances.

Not only would those painfully built up bodies of knowledge which we call science and philosophy disappear, but the simplest statement of knowledge of any kind, such as "John is my brother," would lose its meaning if, like the animals, we had only sense knowledge. Words like "John" and "brother" imply a reality which endures, which remains the same, and to which we can continue to apply the same name. No two sensations, however, even in successive instants, are ever *exactly* the same. Every sensation takes place at a moment in time which vanishes forever as soon as the sensation is completed. Every sensation, too, involves a unique, irrevocable change in the physical organ—the effect of light waves on the eye, sound waves on the ear, and so on. To this we must add the fact that the outward appearances of physical things and the conditions under which they are sensed are also subject to the universal law of change, as Heraclitus and his followers pointed out.

If all we know, then, is endlessly changing sense experience, then reality is becoming something else at the precise moment we experience it. Even language loses its meaning. Each new sense experience, since it is totally new in relation to every preceding one, would need whole new sets of words for its expression.

Yet everyday experience tells us that we know the same reality throughout all its different appearances. Our words continue to indicate the same thing through its successive changes, and the power which penetrates beyond surface changes to the enduring reality of things is the power of reason.

Comparison of Animal and Human Knowing

Why does man have the arts, whereas the animals do not? Because man knows beauty and can re-create the *patterns* of beauty, imposing new *forms* on matter. No animal stops to admire a symphony, a painting, or a sunset. The animal does not make tools or decorate its dwelling places. It does not develop schools of architecture, fashions in dress, styles in cooking. It does not "try out new ideas."

Animal speech is without conscious order, without grammar. The animal does not write poetry or read books or keep historical records. It does not learn new languages or reconstruct lost ones or invent Esperantos.

The brute animal does not judge itself. It does not laugh and it does not pray. It does not have remorse of conscience, New Year's resolutions, maxims of good conduct. It does not have codes of law, does not develop schools of oratory, does not conspire to overthrow old forms of government or experiment with new.

All these things become explainable only on the basis that man has reason, the power to penetrate beyond the surface of things to their meaning, their understandability, the secret of their inner being, which we call their idea. Deny to man this power and man becomes infinitely more difficult to explain—in fact, impossible to explain, as so many fruitless attempts in the history of philosophy clearly tell us.

The evidence is overwhelming, then, that there is something in man which sets him apart as a new kind of being from the rest of the animals. We shall make it our next concern to examine in closer detail that "something else" in man which makes him properly human.

Summary

The traditional culture of the West which rests on the belief that man is rational and free is threatened by a new view of man which sees him as simply one more of the animals, different in degree, possibly, but not in kind. Man is a material being, and therefore subject to the laws of the physical universe. He is also an animal, and therefore displays many traits in common with the animals. But a comparison of the activities of men and the rest of the animals reveals a range of specifically human activities, such as the arts and the sciences, the conscious ordering of self and society, for which there is no parallel in the animal kingdom. The differences between the rational and free activities of man and purely animal activities are so great that the similarities are trivial in comparison. We conclude therefore that man is different in kind from all other animals.

CHAPTER 9

The Nature of Knowing

Knowledge is the food of the soul.
PLATO, PROTAGORAS, 313

One clue to the difference which sets man apart from the rest of material creation is what we might call his "expansiveness"— the superior range of his activities and the width of his horizons as compared with all other beings on this earth. Since "a thing is received according to the nature of the receiver," the more perfect way of assimilation which we find in man points to a more perfect nature or more perfect mode of existence.

The Kinds of Communication

The communication between lifeless bodies is limited strictly to an immediate physical impact, a momentary instant of contact —an entirely surface communication. A purely physical being receives another being only in the most superficial manner—as a cup takes in water or a pail, sand. Any more intimate communication means that physical things lose their identity, becoming something else; the union of hydrogen and oxygen, for example, results in a third thing, water.

The being of a plant is richer than the being of a lifeless body, for the plant can take in other substances and make them its own without losing its identity. It can grow and reproduce itself. Its world is still a lonely and a private one, however, for like the lifeless body its range is limited to the area of direct physical contact. To the imme-diate moment, too, for there is no past or future for plants—no past, for the past is no longer; no future, for the future too is not physically present.

The horizon begins to expand when we reach the level of ani-mal consciousness, of sensation. The animal is affected not only by those bodies with which it has immediate physical contact, but it is also in intimate relationship with other things at a distance. It can see food across the meadow and walk toward it. It can see an enemy in the distance and run away from it

The way an animal receives things is vastly superior to the mere physical taking in of plants and inert bodies, but the animal's world is still a private and a closed world. Its horizon is bounded by the physical range of the senses—the limits of vision, sound, smell, the particularities of sense memory; it is submerged, too, in the sea of feeling and instinct.

Only in the case of man do we find the limitations of physi-cal existence transcended. Because man in knowing can take in the forms of other beings, not only in their mere surface aspects, but in their inner reality, his own being is enlarged, enriched both by the whole universe of bodies to which he gives a new existence in the act of knowing, and by the realm of the spiritual itself, which he reaches through the twin powers of intellect and will. Nor is man enclosed in the particular moment, for the past lives in his memory and he gives the future a kind of being by anticipation. (This is dimly foreshadowed in the higher forms of animal knowing.)

The nature of man is such, then, that he is able to take in the whole universe and make it his own, without at the same time losing his own identity. "Beings that know," says St. Thomas, "are superior to beings that do not know because beings that do not know have only their own forms, while the being that knows is such that it is able to receive the form of the other."[1]

---

1 St. Thomas Aquinas, *Summa Theologiae*, I, 14, 1. (The *Summa Theologiae* of St. Thomas is divided into three Parts; the second of these is divided in turn into two more parts. The first figure of the reference, given in Roman numerals, refers to the number of the Part.

The Change Involved In Knowing Is an Immaterial Change

Here we have a very great mystery—the fact that the soul can become, as Aristotle says, all things, while at the same time remaining itself. For in the act of knowing we make the things we know part of ourselves—not in any physical way, in the manner, for example, in which we make food a part of ourselves, but in a way which leaves unchanged both our own physical being and that of the object known. The kind of union that takes place between the knower and the thing known is different from any physical union, represents a kind of change for which there is no counterpart in the world of bodies.

Change in material things below the level of animals, as we have seen, always means some new physical determination which did not exist before—a new third thing, the product of the union of matter with a new form. The change that takes place in knowing, on the other hand, does not result in any new physical determination, either on the part of the thing known or of the knower. I know the fire of the sun, for example, without myself being on fire. Nor is the fire changed by my knowing it. Since the change brought about by the knowledge is not, then, something physical or material, we have to term it nonmaterial or immaterial.

The Knower Becomes the Thing Known

The soul of man rises above the limitations of matter and hence can become the other, the thing known, without being physically changed—can know stones without being petrified, cats without becoming feline, fire without becoming hot. By the same token

Each Part is divided into Questions. The second number, in Arabic numerals, refers to the Question. Each Question is divided into from two to a score of Articles, and the third and last number of the reference refers to the Article. Each Article, in turn, contains a number of objections, an argument taken from authority and stated in the *Sed Contra*, the development of St. Thomas' own thought in the body, and answers to the various objections, indicated by the expressions *ad* 1, *ad* 2, etc. Thus our reference here reads, Part I, Question 14, body of Article 1.)

we can know contraries at the same time—sweet and sour, hard and soft, black and white; and we can know ourselves—can stand off to one side, so to speak, and see ourselves both as knower and thing known.

The first assimilation of form without matter is found in sense knowing, where the sensible forms—color, sound, consistency, temperature, and so on—are received immaterially; we receive the color of gold, for example, without receiving gold itself. But although the sensible forms are thus separated from matter, they are received under the conditions of matter, for sensation is always the act of a bodily organ upon whose physical alteration it is dependent. This dependence on the material sense organ is reflected in the character of sense knowledge which is always particular and individual.

Intellectual knowledge, in contrast to sense knowledge, is of the universal, because the intellect raises the things it knows to its own level, giving them a share in its own unalloyed immateriality and thereby giving them a new kind of existence. It gives them a new existence without robbing them of their old. For what happens in the act of knowing is that the same thing, identically the same thing, exists in the intellect as exists outside. To know a thing is to live it, to give it a new birth; it is literally to be that thing, in the way of being proper to the intellect.

Intentional Existence

How is it possible for us to be another thing, a tree, for example, and still retain our identity as human beings? St. Thomas explains that this is possible because the same form is capable of existing in more than one way. Besides the existence of nature by which form is united with matter in the act of physical existence, there is another kind of existence which St. Thomas calls intentional existence—a nonphysical existence, a kind of superexistence which the intellect gives to things when it knows them.

Thus it is not a mere copy or image of the thing that we know. If that were the case we would never be sure that the image or representation was exactly like the object it was supposed to represent.

We would know images, not things. What I know is the form itself of the thing, present in me not in a physical way but in an immaterial mode of existence. In union with the principle of matter, the form constitutes this concrete, individual oak tree. Joined to the intellect, the same form becomes the abstract, immaterial "treeness."

In other words, what the thing is is the same in the intellect and in the thing, though the kind of existence is different. St. Thomas, using the nature of man as an example, points out that, strictly speaking, there is implied in the nature of man just those notes which express the ultimate structure of this nature—animality and rationality. Neither individuality nor universality is implied in the nature of man. The pure essence, so to speak, of man is indifferent as to whether it is found in the concrete individual human being, or in the universal idea of man in the intellect. "The nature of man absolutely considered abstracts from any kind of existence, in such a way however that it does not exclude any of them," St. Thomas says.[2]

Thus, by distinguishing between *what* a thing is, or its essence, and its "is-ness," or that whereby it exercises the act of existence, we can say that the same reality is both in the external object in its physical, material mode of existence and in the intellect in its universal, immaterial mode of existence.

"The Problem of the Universals"

The doctrine of intentional existence gives us the solution of Aristotle and St. Thomas to what has come to be called in the history of philosophy the problem of the universals. The answer to the question, What is the nature of ideas? is one of the most important and revealing that can be asked of any philosopher, for it is the key not only to what he holds about the nature of thought but also to his teaching on man and the universe. Philosophies can be classified according to their answer to this question, although the modifications of the basic positions are innumerable.

---

2 On Being and Essence, Chap. 5.

1. Moderate Realism

The view of philosophers in the tradition of Aristotle and St. Thomas is that what is known exists as universal in the intellect, but as individual outside the mind. This position is called *Moderate Realism*. It is called realism because the universals really do exist in the intellect; moderate, because their existence stops there. Since the form universalized in the intellect is identical with the form individuated in the thing, we can say, following the traditional formula, that our ideas are universal in the intellect only, but have a foundation in things.

Implied in this view of the nature of the idea is the spirituality of the intellect (otherwise the universal could not exist there) and the matter and form composition of all corporeal substances, including man.

2. Absolute Realism

The position of Plato and his followers, where the universals are real things existing by themselves, is called *Absolute Realism*, because the universals have a real existence in themselves. This doctrine is also termed Platonic Realism. Some of those who disagree with the position call it also Exaggerated Realism or Extreme Realism because they believe that it gives too much reality to the ideas.

This view implies a radical separation between the world of ideas and the world of bodies. According to it, man is a soul imprisoned in a body, or else soul and body are two separate substances. Reality is referred so exclusively to the ideas that the world of bodies is an indigestible fact or else it is dismissed as illusion.

3. Conceptualism

A modification of the Absolute Realist doctrine is found in the German philosopher Kant and his disciples. Rather than maintaining that the idea or universal is a spiritual reality existing independently of man, the same whether or not man exists at all, Kant placed the universal idea in the mind as a "form" or category, a structural necessity of thought itself, a kind of mold into which our thoughts are cast. Thus we must think things as though they were universal, but this is due solely to the way the mind is constructed, and there is no relation of the idea to whatever may be outside the mind. Since universals exist as mental concepts only, this doctrine is given the name *Conceptualism*.

The nature of the outside world, the "thing-in-itself," is unknowable for the conceptualist, since what comes into the mind is re-cast according to the configuration of the mind itself. The end product of this constructive activity of the mind is called the *Phenomenon*.

The unknowable "something" outside mind is called the *Noumenon*. Some of Kant's followers went beyond him and said that there is nothing whatever outside the mind itself. They are called *Idealists*, since they reduce all reality to the nature of mind and idea.

4. Nominalism

It is possible, finally, to deny that there are any universals at all, either in the mind or outside the mind. What we call ideas are simply sense impressions. This position is called *Nominalism*. The name comes from an eleventh-century philosopher called Roscelin who said that ideas are just names (*nomina*), "puffs of breath," standing for nothing.

Since there are only sensations and no ideas, the nominalist is forced to admit only one kind of reality. Either he is a *Materialist*, and admits the existence of bodies only, or he is an *Idealist*, who says that what we call sensations are mental modifications, which along with mind constitute the whole of reality.

Summary

Knowing implies the following truths:
1. There is some kind of communication between the knower and the thing known.
2. Things communicate in accordance with their nature.
3. Change in material beings always means a new physical determination.

4. The change of knowing is an immaterial change.
5. Sensible forms are received immaterially, but under the conditions of matter. Sense knowledge is therefore always individual in its mode.
6. Intelligible forms are received immaterially and apart from the conditions of matter, since there is no matter in the intellect. Intellectual knowledge is therefore always universal in its mode.
7. The knower becomes the thing known, taking in the form according to the conditions proper to existence in sense power or intellect (intentional as against physical existence).
8. The form of the thing known is universal in the intellect but individual in the object. This position is known as Moderate Realism. Opposed positions are called Absolute Realism, Conceptualism, and Nominalism.

CHAPTER 10

The Kinds of Knowing

The human soul is on the boundary line of corporeal and spiritual creatures, and therefore the powers of each come together in it.
ST. THOMAS AQUINAS, *SUMMA THEOLOGIAE*, I, 77, 2.

Although we can isolate the component parts of man's consciousness in order to study them, the very fact that they are found existing together, reciprocally influencing each other, is itself one of the elements which we must take into account. We must remember, for example, that man is a feeling as well as a knowing being, and the process of knowing always takes place against a background of feeling and emotion. Similarly, although we study sense knowing and intellectual knowing as separate processes, in man they are never found in isolation from one another. "Properly speaking," says St. Thomas, "neither sense nor intellect knows, but man through both."[1]

Sense Knowing

According to philosophers like Aristotle and St. Thomas all human knowledge has its starting point in sensation. The external senses— seeing, hearing, tasting, smelling, touching—are the channels, the avenues through which the things outside man come into him.

The start of the process of sensation is some stimulus from the

---

1 *Truth*, 2, 6.

world of physical objects: light waves for the eye, sound waves for the ear, and so on. The stimulus causes some modification of the sense organ: the light waves are focused on the retina of the eye, the tympanum of the ear vibrates, and so on; and in all instances of sensation nerve impulses are sent to the brain, where further physiological changes take place.

These elements, necessary as they are, are only the mechanical accompaniments of the act of sensation, which is a vital action. If this were the sum total of sensation—as some philosophers hold —all that would happen would be a physical change in the body. But a physical change alone is not enough to explain knowledge. Otherwise the film in the camera could know the image imprinted on it.

The important element that is missed in this purely mechanical explanation of knowing is that the sense organ is a living organism. The form which affects the sense organ is taken into the very being of the knower who becomes one with the thing known—not in its physical existence (the eye does not become physically red when it knows the color red)—but in its intentional, immaterial mode of existence.

It is this vital union of the knower and the thing known which constitutes the act of knowing. The same form, as we have seen in the preceding chapter, is present in the sensible thing and in the knower, but under different conditions of existence. In the physical thing it exists in union with a material principle which circumscribes it, fixes it, so to speak, in the concrete, individual thing. The function of the knowing power is to disengage the form, to free it from matter.

Since, however, the act of sensation is the act of a bodily organ, the sensible form is still individualized, for wherever there is body there is matter, and wherever there is matter there is individuation. For the same reason the senses are necessarily blind to the treasures of existence and intelligibility which remain hidden beneath the opaque cloak of matter.

The different aspects of things brought in by the external senses are coordinated by a power called the unifying sense,[2] and are stored up by the sense memory. Other powers which deal with the material presented by the external senses are the imagination, which brings back into consciousness the images of concrete individuals not present to the senses, and the estimative power, a kind of inborn wisdom, which alerts the organism to what is harmful or useful.[3]

These last powers are called internal senses. They are so termed because there is no visible organ by which they operate, as in the case of the external senses. (They do have a physical basis in certain areas of the brain.) Although they do not have any visually observable organ, we know that they exist because of the operations they perform. They are called sense powers because they deal with the particular, individual aspects of things.

Intellectual Knowing

We have seen that man has a kind of knowing different from sense knowing, for otherwise man would not be able to act in any ways different from the other animals. To sense and to understand are not the same thing. To hear a foreign language, for example, is not to understand it. A dog can look at a signpost and receive the same picture on the retina of its eye as a man. But the human being understands the sign whereas the animal does not.

Yet we say, following Aristotle and St. Thomas, that nothing comes into man other than by way of the senses. How then account for this something in man beyond the mere animal awareness?

It is obvious that there must be some power of knowing which is different in kind from the sense powers. This power is called the intellect (from the Latin, *intus* and *legere*—to read within) and its

---

2   This is also called the central sense and the common sense. The latter term is a direct transliteration of the Latin *sensus communis*. It is too liable, however, to confusion both with our everyday expression "common sense" and the historical use of this phrase in recent philosophy. (See the last chapter for a discussion of these other uses.)

3   In man the estimative power is also called the particular reason, since it operates under the influence of the intellect.

nature must be such as to account for two facts. First, the intellect does not know to start with; it is in potency to knowledge. Second, although it is dependent on the world of bodies for what it knows—since it needs the senses as the sole channel by which things can come to it—nevertheless what comes into the intellect has an immaterial rather than a material mode of existence. To account for the second fact, we must posit as part of our intellectual equipment a power in man which lights up the sense data and reveals something there which is opaque to the animal consciousness—the inner natures, the secret depths of things. This is the power, in other words, which raises the forms of things from the conditions of materiality in which they are found in sense knowing to the level of immateriality proper to the intellect. Aristotle called this power the agent intellect.[4]

The intellect as it receives the forms of things raised to intelligible luminosity by the active intellect, as it is in potency to knowledge—for at first it is like a blank page, as Aristotle says —is called the possible intellect.[5] The function of the agent intellect is preparatory. It raises the intelligible forms to the level of immateriality which makes them capable of being assimilated. The actual knowing begins with the joining of the form to the possible intellect in the vital unity of a single act of intentional existence, the act whereby the knower becomes the thing known. This is but the beginning of the complex process which continues with the acts of judging and reasoning. We will briefly analyze these successive steps.

---

4 Other names commonly used to designate this power: active intellect, acting intellect, illuminating intellect, active reason. Whether Aristotle held that there was an agent intellect in each individual human being or but one agent intellect in which the whole human race shared is not clear from the texts. Generally speaking, the medieval Arabian commentators of Aristotle held for the latter interpretation, the Christian Aristotelians the former. St. Augustine, and many medieval philosophers following him, placed the illuminating intellect in God. The One Teacher, God, illuminates all mankind with a kind of spiritual light, just as the one sun in the sky illuminates all the parts of the earth.

5 Passive intellect and passive reason are the other names given to it.

1. Simple Apprehension and the Concept

The marriage of the intentional form with the intellect bears fruit in the formation of the concept, the spiritual likeness of the object made present in the act of knowing. The concept is sometimes called "the mental word," as though the intellect spoke the thing to itself so as to clarify it for itself, just as we sometimes say a difficult thing aloud to help ourselves understand it better. Besides "mental word," other names given to the concept are idea, notion, universal, intention, species.

There are many kinds of concepts and it is part of the business of logic and philosophy to discover and put in order all the different kinds of concepts that are possible.

It is important to recognize that while the concept is necessary to rational knowing, it is only *a means by which* we know, and not *that which* we know. It is a necessary means, just as eyeglasses may be necessary for me to see with; yet just as it is really the table I see and not the lenses of my eyeglasses, so too it is really the thing itself I know and not my concept of it. To say that the objects of my knowing are concepts rather than things would be to fall into the trap of those philosophers called Idealists. For if all we ever know is always idea, then we can never know whether or not there is anything existing outside our mind corresponding to our ideas. Thus, following the Idealists, all reality would consist of minds and the thoughts they think.

The operation by which the intellect grasps the intelligible form of something in this first act of knowing is called the act of simple apprehension: apprehension, because it lays hold of the thing mentally; simple, because the intellect simply takes the thing in, without affirming or denying anything about it.

2. The Judgment

The act of simple apprehension singles out, separates, divides, for things come to us under many forms, many individual intelligible aspects. It is the function of the judgment to reintegrate these forms, to restore the dynamic unity and wholeness of the world of natural things. Our knowledge is not complete until we refer our concepts back to the source from which they came, to see whether or not we have declared them to be as they really are in the world of things which exist independently of our thoughts.

In the act of judging we unite two concepts and affirm or deny that this is the way they are found in the world of things outside the mind—or whatever the appropriate realm of existence may be: the realm of legend, of logic, of grammar, of mathematics, and so on.[6]

This return to the original source of our knowledge—ultimately in one way or another always to the world of the senses—is necessary because things have an existence in the intellect different from what they have outside. In the intellect things exist as immaterial and universal. They can be separated and joined in ways that are not possible in the physical world. I can isolate the intelligible note "redness" or "sweetness" in my intellect, for example, though I can never find red or sweet in isolation outside the intellect. I can think of a flying red horse, though I have never seen one in the world of physical things.

Since then it is possible for me to think things in a way different from what they are outside the mind, to make sure that what I judge to be the case is really so, I have to return to the source from which all my knowledge ultimately comes. Being itself, existence itself, is the touchstone by which I verify my judgments.

3. Reasoning

The activity of the intellect does not stop with the judgment, for by means of truths previously possessed the intellect can progress to the knowledge of new truths. This step-by-step advance in the acquisition of truth is called reasoning.

Reasoning may be of two kinds. The intellect can take as its

---

6 Dragons exist in the realm of legend or grand opera, for example; nouns exist in the world of grammar, surds in the realm of mathematics, etc.

starting point the data presented to it by the senses. From a sufficiently repeated number of sense experiences, it may come to see the intelligible lines of a thing with sufficient clarity to be able to isolate its essential structure. For example, after a sufficient number of experiments which indicate that metals conduct electricity, the intellect sees clearly enough into the nature of metals to be able to affirm that this kind of being is such that wherever you find it you will have something that conducts electricity. This kind of reasoning is called induction.

Because of this power of the intellect to penetrate intelligibly to the inner heart of things, it becomes possible for us sometimes to be able to say "all" or "every" of a certain nature or class of thing even though we have not experienced every possible member of that class. Thus, for example, we know human nature sufficiently well to recognize that wherever you have this kind of being you have mortality, so that without having to see all human beings die, we can say "Every man is mortal."

In order to test the truth of our inductions, we have to refer them back to the realm of evident fact. This reverse process whereby we return from the plane of the universal idea to the plane of the senses is also called induction.

The second kind of reasoning starts from the self-evident first principles of being, such as the principle of non-contradiction —the principle that the same thing cannot at one and the same time exist and not exist—or from more complex judgments whose truth has been proved, and draws out further implications from these previously known truths or resolves more complex judgments back into simpler ones. This kind of reasoning is called deductive or syllogistic reasoning.

It is possible to discover the laws of thought by which we can test whether or not we have formulated correctly our inductions, or whether or not we have passed correctly from one set of judgments to a further one in the act of syllogistic reasoning. The body of knowledge which concerns itself with the study of this universe of thought, with the life and forms peculiar to it, is called the science of formal logic.

Formal logic concerns itself primarily with the correctness rather than the truth of thought. To be able to reason correctly is not necessarily the same as to reason truthfully, for it may be that our correct reasoning starts from a wrong assumption; the insane asylums after all are full of people who reason with admirable logic from wrong starting points.

People, too, were able to reason correctly long before Aristotle came along to constitute the science of logic, and the student today learns to reason correctly before he has begun the study of logic. The science of logic, in short, is simply man's reflexive knowledge about how he thinks when he thinks correctly. It helps, in the avoidance of error, to know these laws of correct thinking, but just as there is a natural ability to strike a ball with a club or racket before any professional instruction begins, so too there is a spontaneous capacity of the intellect for correct reasoning, which is there from the beginning.

Connatural Knowing

Besides the knowledge characteristic of the sciences and philosophy, knowledge by means of distinct concepts and the pathways of induction and deduction, we must recognize still other ways of knowing, the kind of knowing characterized by St. Thomas as connatural. This is the knowledge which follows on the lived experience of the truth, the living contact of the intellect with reality itself, a knowledge which is not always given expression in concepts, which may be obscure to the knower and overlaid with elements from the affective or feeling side of man's nature.

The knowledge we gain through love is an example of knowledge by connaturality, by sympathy, by "fellow feeling." The lover sees more in the loved one, the fond parent sees more deeply into the nature of the child, than the rest of the world does (granted that it is a precarious knowledge and one especially susceptible to error). The case pre-eminent of knowledge through love is that of the mystic, who knows God through the union of charity better than any philosopher or theologian, yet in a way beyond expression through concepts or words; "known as though unknown," in the words of St. Thomas.[7]

The truths of the moral life can be known either in the abstract doctrine of moral science or in the lived experience. "I would rather feel compunction than know how to define it," says Thomas a Kempis.[8] Many a person who could not give you a definition of justice or temperance can tell you unerringly whether a given action is just or unjust, temperate or intemperate. Although he may not know anything about the science of ethics, he is just and temperate in his own life, he embodies the virtues and can judge an action by his own predisposition or propensity: "The virtuous man is the rule and measure of human actions," says Aristotle.[9]

Let us take as a final example of knowledge by connaturality the knowledge of the artist. The making of a work of art has to do with the practical order, but it presupposes knowledge on the part of the artist—the artist's peculiar vision of reality, and his expression of it in a poem, a painting, a musical composition. The poet or the novelist is not a sociologist or psychologist, yet he may have a deeper insight into the nature of man or society than the erudite scholar: a Shakespeare or a Goethe, for example, a Dickens or a Dostoevski. Were the artist obliged to express his insights through the ordinary form of rational discourse he would probably be rendered inarticulate, mute, for his knowledge finds expression in the work itself, the painting, the statue, the poem, rather than in concepts. "Such knowledge knows not in order to know, but in order to produce. It is towards creation that it tends."[10]

Summary

Man's knowing is a complex of sense awareness and intellectual

---

7   *Summa Theologiae*, I, 1, 6.

8   *Following of Christ*, I, 1, 3.

9   *Nicomachean Ethics*, X, 5. (All quotations from the *Nicomachean Ethics* are taken from the translation of J. A. Smith [Oxford: The Clarendon Press, 1925].)

10   J. Maritain, *Creative Intuition in Art and Poetry* (New York: Pantheon, 1953), p. 124.

insight against a background of feeling and emotion. Sensation has both material and immaterial aspects: material in as much as it is the act of a bodily organ, immaterial because it is the exercise of a vital power. Intellectual insight has both a passive and an active character. The active power which raises the sense data to the level of immateriality necessary for intellectual assimilation is called the agent intellect. The passive, receptive power which takes in the forms of things known is called the possible intellect. The steps discernible in the act of reasoning are three: the act of simple apprehension, which results in the production of a concept; the act of judging, which re-establishes in the judgment the original unity of the thing known; the act of reasoning, inductive or deductive, by which the intellect advances to new knowledge from old. Non-conceptual ways of knowing, such as the knowledge of the mystic and the artist, are called connatural: knowledge, that is, by way of sympathy, fellow feeling.

CHAPTER 11

The Truth Of Knowing

Philosophers who refuse to philosophize.
WEISS, NATURE AND MAN, P. 82.

Philosophy almost from its beginning has had the task of defending itself not only against those who deny its very possibility but, even further, the possibility of any knowledge whatsoever. In modern times, the preoccupation with this problem, particularly in the thought of Descartes, Hume, and Kant, has become so great that what was formerly a comparatively minor part of philosophy has been elevated into the status of a whole new branch of philosophy. Utilizing elements from metaphysics, psychology, and material logic, this new branch of philosophy concerns itself with the basic problem of whether we can know any truth at all, and the marks by which we can tell the truth when we have it.

Different names are given to this discipline: *Criteriology* and *Critics*, since it investigates the criteria of truth; *Epistemology* and sometimes, more rarely, *Noetics* because it studies the nature and validity of knowledge; or again, the *Science of First Principles*.

The Primordial Certitudes

Just as formal logic codifies and clarifies the laws of correct thinking as reflected by the actual working of the human reason, so too, on an even deeper level, philosophy must reflect on, clarify, and justify the spontaneous certitudes of common sense. By common sense we mean our native capacity to know certain fundamental, immediate, and self-evident aspects of reality which lie open to our senses and intellect—aspects of reality so clear and evident that they do not need demonstration. It would be contradictory, in fact, to try to prove them, since they are implied in all proof.[1]

The first of these primordial certitudes is the fact of existence, which is given to us through an absolutely fundamental intuition of the senses and the intellect—of the intellect in the senses, so to speak. Before we know *what* a thing is, we know *that* it is; and we know this not necessarily by conscious reflection but implicitly, as taken for granted in all our concepts and judgments.

Furthermore, in any being that comes into the understanding, the intellect perceives certain intelligible aspects which are called the first principles of being. These primordial certitudes of the intellect are called the first principles of being because they declare what a thing has to be in order to be at all; they are called the first principles of the understanding because they are the absolutely primary, ultimate insights of the intellect into the structure of reality, because they are the starting point of all our knowledge.

The most fundamental of the self-evident first principles of the understanding is the *principle of identity*, which says that what is, is, or that each thing is what it is. The principle of identity is the philosophical formulation of the spontaneous knowledge that there are certain fundamental consistencies of being which are ultimate, and which common sense expresses in such statements as, "Eggs are eggs," or "A tree is a tree."[2]

The *principle of non-contradiction* is the negative statement of the principle of identity, and states that a thing cannot be and not be at the same time and in the same respect. Common sense says that "A tree is not an egg," or "You can't go downstairs and meet yourself coming up at the same time."

---

1 For a further discussion of common sense see Chapter 10.
2 See St. Thomas, *Summa Theologiae*, I—II, 94, 2.

The *principle of the excluded middle* is still a further elaboration of the first two, and says that a thing either is or it isn't, that no middle ground is possible. Other self-evident first principles, which cannot be denied except at the expense of absurdity, are the *principle of sufficient reason*, which states that each thing must have a sufficient reason for its being, and the *principle of causality*, a particular application of the principle of sufficient reason which declares that every being which comes into existence must have part of its reason of being outside itself. We speak also of subordinate orders of first principles, such as the first principles of arithmetic, of physics and so on, which are first in their particular order, but which depend ultimately on the first principles of being.

The Nature of Truth

In the initial apprehension of reality by both the senses and the intellect there is no possibility of error. For the first step in knowing is a simple receiving, without any affirmation or denial of what is taken in. Both the senses and the intellect just take in what is given to them according as they are equipped to do, according, that is, to their strength or weakness, the medium in which they operate, and other attendant circumstances.

Even in the extreme case of a mirage before the senses there is no question of error, for the senses do no more than report what is the actual appearance of things at that moment. Error here is no more possible than in the case of a camera, for example, which simply registers what affects it according to the circumstances of the moment. Not until we make a judgment about what is brought in—that the mirage is a reality, for instance—does the possibility of error arise.

Since it is possible for the intellect to understand things in a way different from what they are outside the mind, our judgments, if they are to declare accurately the nature of things as they are, are profoundly and inescapably dependent upon the world of actually existing things. The truth of knowing depends on the accurate correspondence of my judgments to the way things are independently of my thoughts.[3]

If what I have joined or separated in my intellect in the act of judgment corresponds to what is really existing independently of my intellect, I say that my judgment is a true one. Thus when I say, "A dog is an animal," this is a true judgment if I can determine, by returning to sense experience, that the inclusion of dog under animal is actually verified by the world of physical beings.

Following the classical definition of truth used by St. Thomas, we say that truth is the conformity of the intellect with the thing.

This relationship of the intellect with things is called logical truth, or the truth of knowing. We say, furthermore, that truth is objective because the term (term-ination) of the truth relationship is found outside the intellect in the thing or object.

Error, or logical falsity, is the lack of conformity between our intellect and reality. The intellect, that is, affirms things to be one way when they are actually another. We say that our judgments in this case are false.

The Denial of Truth

In his defense of the truth of knowing, the philosopher in the Aristotelian-Thomist tradition meets two main groups of adversaries, the skeptics and the subjectivists—the one denying any possibility of knowledge, the other making knowledge so dependent on the individual intellect, so private, as to destroy its meaning.

1. Skepticism

Common sense frequently says it is skeptical, but it means simply that it demands to be shown the evidence—a position not only commendable but necessary for the true philosopher. When we say "skeptical" in the philosophical sense, however, we are referring to those who refuse to accept even the first principles of the understanding, even the very existence of the self, as evident and knowable.

To demonstrate the error of skepticism to the skeptic is impossible

---

3 See above, Chapter 10, on the nature of the judgment.

because the skeptic refuses to accept the principles which make demonstration possible. It is no use saying to the skeptic, "At least you are certain of one thing, and that is that you are not certain of anything," or "At least you know that you do not know anything." All such propositions imply the validity of the principle of non-contradiction, which the skeptic refuses to accept.

It is verbally possible to doubt everything forever. Whether it is actually possible to have a living, real doubt of everything is a deeper question, and to answer it we must penetrate behind the barrier of language.

The real problem of skepticism is not whether it is verbally possible to doubt everything but whether it is psychologically possible; whether, that is, a human being can actually be what the absolute skeptic says he is. It is not necessary to question the sincerity of the person who calls himself a skeptic but it is legitimate to remind him of the difference between a verbal doubt and a real doubt and of what is implied by real doubt.

Real doubt paralyzes activity. If you had a *real* doubt whether or not your food was poisoned you would not eat it. If you had a *real* doubt of the safety of the elevator you would walk. If you had a *real* doubt of the destination of your train, you would get out and ask. Of course, if you had a *real* doubt of everything you would doubt the very existence of the food, of the elevator, of the train. You would also doubt, *really* doubt, the existence of other people, of your own past, of the immediate future. If a person *really* doubted all the evidence of his senses and intellect, he would be able only to lift his little finger, as Aristotle puts it. The absolute skeptic is reduced, in short, to the existence of a vegetable.

This is one check, then, that can be made against the absolute skeptic. Does he really act as though he had a real doubt of everything? For if someone asserts a philosophical position as true, it is legitimate to ask whether he acts in accordance with his asserted philosophy.[4]

---

4 Cf. Bertrand Russell: "Scepticism, while logically impeccable, is psychologically

We may ask, furthermore, whether the intellect has time to reject the evidence which leaps into it on its first awareness of being, any more than the eye has time to reject the light which flashes into it. For before the intellect even has the chance to formulate the doubt of being, the intellect rests in the certainty of existence. It cannot destroy this certainty just by asking a question about it. I can put square and circle together in words and concepts, and say that they are identical. I can assert it forever, but can I really think in the depths of my thought that they are one? Does not my initial intuition of their irreconcilable difference persist behind any possible denial? Once more, the heart of this problem is not what is mechanically possible to speech, but what is possible in the world of lived thought.

2. Subjectivism

The French philosopher Descartes, in an effort to make proof doubly sure, demanded that we prove the existence of things outside the mind. We might be dreaming, he said, when we think we know the world of physical things, and there is no sure way of knowing the difference between the waking state and the state of dreaming.

Modern philosophy has in general followed Descartes on this point, demanding that we start from inside our own mind and prove both the existence of the world and of other human beings. This position is called subjectivism because it is based on the consciousness of the thinking subject, making the objects of knowledge a part of the thinking subject himself, his ideas, feelings and so forth, so that there is no objective, external test of truth.

Descartes, when he demanded proof for the existence of the outside world, started a false problem which gave rise in modern philosophy to innumerable errors: a false problem because the question is asked in such a way that no answer is possible, as though we

---

impossible, and there is an element of frivolous insincerity in any philosophy which pretends to accept it." Human Knowledge (New York: Simon and Schuster, 1948), p. xi.

were to say, "Prove that Julius Caesar was the third President of the United States." The fact of the existence of the outside world is not an abstract truth. It is not a necessary truth, for any number of possible worlds other than our own is conceivable. The existence of the world of bodies of which we are a part is no more necessary than my existence or yours. It could have not been, just as we might have not been. That it exists at all is something that we discover, not prove.

Let us take a further look at the point, for it is of crucial importance.

All the beings we know by direct experience, including ourselves, are contingent existences; that is, they need not have existed, and they can go out of existence. To know that they exist *in fact* is to experience that existence directly, here and now. To know that the wall is brown, for example, I have to sense it immediately. I cannot take it on faith. If I take your word for it, a painter may be changing its color to green while you are telling me that it is brown. Similarly it cannot be proved syllogistically. In the very act of stating the syllogism that leads to this conclusion, the color of the room could be changed. We do not invent, or create the existences which form the field of our knowledge. We *discover* these existences, and there is no possible way of knowing what has, in fact, been given existence other than to discover it (many other kinds of existences than the ones we know could have been brought into being).

For the philosopher to ask proof of the actual existence of contingent things, including his own existence, is to betray the evidence of the fundamental intuition of his senses and intellect. It is to ask proof for what does not need proof, for what indeed cannot be proved, since it is prior to proof and is implied in all demonstration.

"The one reason why we state that we exist and that London is in England is because reality is that way. Being is the lord of the intellect and whenever we make a judgment that we know is true and certain, it is because being is so presented to the intellect that reality determines, forces and constrains us to assent to it. There can be no turning back at this point because in the field of knowledge-content the intellect is the servant, reality the master, and it is reality which dictates to the intellect, not vice-versa."[5]

The Problem of the Dreamer

Suppose I am dreaming? The question was not new with Descartes. St. Thomas answered it with the admonition, "Consult your senses."[6] The very question implies the knowledge of the difference between the state of conscious awareness and the state of dreaming.

What if I only know the modifications of my own nervous system, as so many philosophers and psychologists of our own day maintain? Here again the question itself implies that we have the direct experience of the existence of our nervous systems.

We may conclude by affirming that when the subjectivist asks you to prove the existence of the world of bodies, he is refusing to accept the evidence in the only place where it can be found—in the world of bodies itself. In fact, this is the only conceivable place where it can be found, since it is a contingent existence not made by us or brought into existence by our thought. The arbitrary refusal of the subjectivist to accept the evidence in the only place where it can be found precludes beforehand the possibility of any answer, as in the classical example of the man who asks what numbers make up twelve, but prohibits you from using twice six, or three times four, or twelve times one.[7]

The Meaning of Evidence

As against the doubt of the skeptic and the relativism of the subjectivist, the philosophy of being offers as the anchor for our judgments the intelligible consistency of the thing itself as grounded in existence. The test or criterion of truth is not something private or

---

5   Hassett, Mitchell, and Monan, *The Philosophy of Human Knowing* (Westminster, Md.: The Newman Press, 1953), p. 81.

6   *Truth*, 1, 1.

7   See Plato, *Republic*, I, 337.

individual or beyond reach. It is the natures of things themselves as they are disclosed to us when we know them. It is, in short, the *evidence* of their being.

The word "evidence" is a term which we have taken over from the world of sense knowledge. Just as a bodily object is evident to the sense of sight when it can be clearly seen, so too something is evident to the intellect when the intellect sees within it adequate grounds for making a judgment about it. When we understand a thing well, we say we "see" it clearly. We speak of "bright" ideas, and so on. In other words, we have to use language borrowed from sense experience to explain operations which are not sensible and not material. (These metaphors, nevertheless, stand for realities which are not reducible to sense experience.)

The capacity that things have, then, of delivering themselves up to the intellect in the act of knowing—their "clarity," their "understandability"—is their evidence, and is both the reason for the truth of the judgment, and also its test or criterion.[8]

Modern philosophy differs profoundly from the philosophy of being in that it generally places the basis of truth in the clarity of ideas or perceptions. Evidence for modern philosophy then does not refer to the knowability of things outside the intellect, but rather to the clearness of ideas or perceptions which are already in the mind and therefore known basically as states of consciousness. This kind of philosophy says, "Ideas are evident"; the philosophy of being says, "Things are evident."

Summary

The branch of philosophy which vindicates the truth-value of knowledge against its enemies is called epistemology. Reflection on and analysis of the act of knowing reveals the evident character of being and the first principles of being. The foundation of truth is in the world of beings to which the intellect conforms itself. The

---

8 See St. Thomas Aquinas, *Summa Theologiae*, I, 108, 1; *Summa Contra Gentiles*, III, 154; Truth, 9, 2.

skeptic denies any possibility of knowledge, although he has to philosophize to justify his denial. The *subjectivist* denies the objectivity of knowledge, setting up an impenetrable curtain of ideas between himself and the world apart from himself. Evidence, the criterion of truth, is the intelligible clarity of reality as it manifests itself to the intellect.

CHAPTER 12

The Nature of Desire

An inclination follows upon every form.
ST. THOMAS AQUINAS, *SUMMA THEOLOGIAE*, I, 80, 1.

One of the strongest thirsts in man is the thirst for knowledge whereby, taking the world of things into the immateriality of the intellect, each person becomes a kind of universe in miniature.

But there is another drive in man which reverses, as it were, the procedure of knowing: instead of taking things into himself, man is drawn to things outside himself. This drive by which man tends to something other than himself is called appetite or desire and it may exist on a purely natural, insensitive level, on a sensory level, or on an intellectual level.

Desire in man is a special case of the tendency of all being to seek its own completion, its own fulfillment or perfection—a thing is said to be perfect of its kind when it is complete. The philosophers of old expressed this in the axiom, "All things desire their own perfection."[1] As long as a thing has certain capacities of development we say it wants or needs such things.

Like every other being in the universe, man too tends toward what he needs for his fulfillment. But we must distinguish in the case of man between natural desire, which corresponds to the inner, natural striving of all beings to achieve their own perfection, and conscious

---

1   See St. Thomas Aquinas, *Summa Theologiae*, I, 5, 1. 88

desire, which is the desire that follows on some kind of knowledge. These two different kinds of drive in man are rooted in the two kinds of form found in man: the natural form (manness) which is the source of the inner desire toward self-perfection; and the intentional forms whose presence in the knower draws him out toward the object made inwardly present by the intentional form.

In the case of man, then, there are two distinct factors in the make-up of desire: first, the general tendency toward good which is characteristic of all being; and second, the conscious impulse toward the good as apprehended by some knowing power—either the individual good apprehended by sense, in which case we speak of sense appetite, or the universal good apprehended by intellect, which we call rational appetite. (It is doubtful in the case of man whether sense desire and intellectual desire, any more than sense knowing and intellectual knowing, are ever found in complete separation from each other; we can isolate them only in thought.)

Many philosophers would restrict the use of the term "desire" to its conscious manifestation, although popular speech persists in extending it, at least in a metaphorical sense, even to non-conscious beings; thus we say the flower "desires" sunlight, water "seeks" its own level, the stone "wants" to fall. We will limit our own study to desire on the conscious level.

Sense Appetite and the Passions

The movements of the sense appetite are known in the terminology of St. Thomas as *passions*. Passion—from the Latin, *pati* —to suffer change—in its widest sense means any change from potency to act, the thing changed being considered as receiving action from something else. The term is narrowed here to stand for those changes which take place in man when he becomes aware of things which are seen as good or bad for the life of the body.[2] It is in this sense that St. Thomas says that "acts of the sense appetite, since they are linked with bodily change, are called passions."[3]

The movement of the passions begins with the desire which follows on sense awareness. The awareness of the thing sensed as good or evil is followed by an impulse toward or away from the thing perceived. (This is called the conative element in desire, from the Latin, *conari*—to try.) The physical change which is part of the movement of passion—increased pulse beat, higher rate of respiration, glandular changes, etc.—is a consequence both of the profound unity of the two principles, spiritual and material, in man and of the fact that the operation of sense desire is completed only by physical movement toward the thing desired. The whole man, in short, is involved in the process of desire.

The Classification of the Passions

St. Thomas distinguishes between two sets of desire on the sense level, each with its own characteristic set of responses. Some objects which the senses present as good or evil are easy to obtain or avoid, and these give rise to the simple responses of desire or aversion. These are the everyday desires connected with the more or less immediate feelings of pain and pleasure. The name concupiscible appetite is given to the source of these mild desires.

When the object of sense desire becomes difficult or impossible of attainment, the passional response has a different character. Since the good apprehended is now linked up with some evil in the form of danger or difficulty, the response called for takes on the

---

2 The term "passion" has become radically restricted in its everyday usage, standing usually for any intense and prolonged feeling. To charactcrize mild desires many philosophcrs and psychologists would substitute the word "emotion" for "passion." These terms, "emotion" and "passion," are also substituted for the somewhat cumbersome expressions, "concupiscible appetite" and "irascible appetite." Since, however, the contemporary usage of these terms is so variable we shall hold to the older terminology, which though awkward-sounding to modern ears has at least the merit of precision.

3 *Summa Theologiae*, I, 20, 1, ad 1.

character of an emergency reaction; the source of knowledge here shifts to the instincts and memory, and the resultant reactions are closely allied to the absolute biological necessities of the organism. Once again the stimulus is recognized as favorable or unfavorable, but this time as difficult to attain or avoid. Passions of this category are called irascible.

This classification of the passions into concupiscible and irascible, since it is based on the changes within the subject that feels, is called subjective. The passions can also be classified—less satisfactorily—according to the classes of objects which give rise to the emotion: whether the object is beneficial or harmful, for example. The attempt has been made in recent times to classify the passions according to the different kinds of physiological response. Much progress has been made in the observing and measuring of the physical changes accompanying emotional states, but the method fails as a way of classifying the emotions because it is difficult if not impossible to distinguish between the physiological responses called up even by radically different passions.

Passions of the Concupiscible Appetite

According as the object which gives rise to desire is favorable or unfavorable, our emotional response is one of love or hate. These primitive reactions of love and hate are at the root of all our passions—one of the few points all psychologists, ancient and modern, seem to be agreed on.

The movement of desire does not stop with the initial apprehension of something advantageous or harmful. If the object is present and obtainable the emotions of desire and joy follow respectively upon aspiration and attainment. If the object is harmful, the emotion which succeeds hate is one of aversion. If the unpleasant object cannot be avoided, sorrow is felt.

We can group these passions then according as the thing apprehended is good or evil, absent or present:

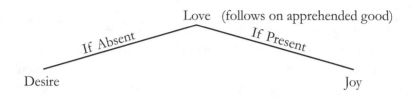

Love   (follows on apprehended good)

If Absent   If Present

Desire   Joy

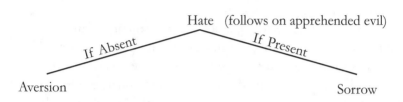

Hate   (follows on apprehended evil)

If Absent   If Present

Aversion   Sorrow

We should recognize that the initial love or hate for the object persists through all the other passions and that there are innumerable shades and nuances of emotional reactions throughout the passage from love to joy or from hate to sorrow.

Passions of the Irascible Appetite

When obstacles are placed in the way of our realizing the good apprehended by sense, our response becomes a mixed one. We still experience love and hate for things sensed as good and evil but the difficulty or danger which hinders the attaining of the good or the avoiding of the evil adds a whole new set of responses which, since anger seems to be the dominant note, are called irascible passions (from the Latin, *ira*—anger).

The irascible appetite and its passions differ essentially from the concupiscible appetite and passions. This is evident from the fact that the two are sometimes found in opposition; an animal, for example, will fight in spite of the pain which his concupiscible appetite tells him to avoid. Nevertheless, the movement of the irascible appetite implies the initial love and hate of the concupiscible appetite and the irascible appetite can be considered from this point of view as a kind of reinforcement of the concupiscible appetite. "The irascible appetite," St. Thomas says, "is a kind of champion and defender of the concupiscible appetite when it rebels against what hinders things agreeable to the concupiscible appetite or fights against the harmful things the concupiscible appetite shuns."[4]

The passions of the irascible appetite are also divided into two groups according as the object is apprehended as a good difficult to obtain or an evil difficult to avoid. A further division follows according as the difficulty is seen as within the agent's power or as beyond the agent's capacity.

The passion which accompanies the movement toward a difficult good which is also seen as within the agent's power is hope. If the good is seen as beyond the agent's power, the response is the passion of despair. When the difficult object is obtained, the resultant passion of joy belongs to the concupiscible order, since there is nothing arduous about the possession of good.

Daring is the response to a great evil not yet possessed, if the evil is seen as within the agent's power. Daring gives way to fear if the evil threatens to become overwhelming. If the agent acquiesces in the presence of some difficult evil, the resultant passion is sorrow, a concupiscible passion, since the note of struggle is no longer present. If the struggle continues, the accompanying passion is anger, which seeks revenge against the evil. An unstable passion, anger issues either in joy, when the revenge is achieved, or sorrow, when the evil is finally accepted.

---

4 *Summa Theologiae*, I, 81, 2.

We can classify the passions of the irascible appetite as follows:

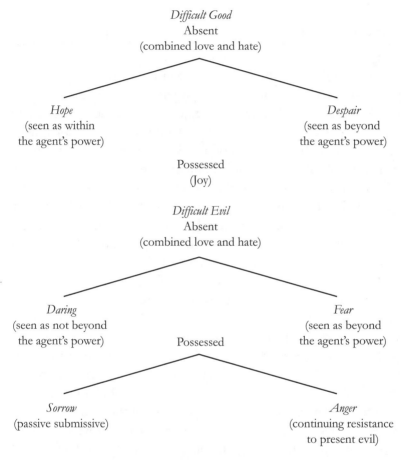

Difficult Good
Absent
(combined love and hate)

Hope
(seen as within
the agent's power)

Despair
(seen as beyond
the agent's power)

Possessed
(Joy)

Difficult Evil
Absent
(combined love and hate)

Daring
(seen as not beyond
the agent's power)

Possessed

Fear
(seen as beyond
the agent's power)

Sorrow
(passive submissive)

Anger
(continuing resistance
to present evil)

Let us remark again that the passions of the irascible appetite begin in the primitive love and hate of the concupiscible appetite and that they may also conclude in the concupiscible passions of joy or sorrow according as the terminus of desire is good or evil. The various passions we have enumerated, too, are often found in a mixed state. Joy for example may be felt in the very desiring of an object, and in the case of the irascible appetite we find love and hate persisting together through the various passional states: love being felt for the good which is desired, hate for the obstacle which stands in its way. Man's passional life, in short, is complicated and difficult to analyze.

Rational Desire

In addition to the whole range of sensible desires which man shares with the rest of the animal kingdom, he possesses a further power of desire for which there is no apparent counterpart in the rest of the animals. For just as he can rise above the horizon of the senses because he possesses reason, so too through rational desire he can choose the universal good and thereby rise above the sea of individual sensible goods which pull on him.

Like every other being in the universe, man must desire his own good. This is the natural urge toward perfection that he has in common with all creatures. But, unlike every other material being in the universe, man can know his ultimate goal and cooperate in its attainment by choosing among the multiplicity of means which can lead to it. (Hence the importance of knowing what man is. To know what is good for man we have to know what man is.)

The power of rational desire in man is called the will. It is of the very nature of the will to love the good. It finds its rest only in the perfect, unlimited good, and this it has to love. From this point of view, therefore, the activity of the will is a necessary activity.[5] But the very fact that only the good-in-general will fulfill his nature frees man from being committed to any particular good. This is the origin in man of free choice. "A human being can be in love with anything," says Father Martin D'Arcy, "because he is in love despite himself with the end and consummation of all loveliness, God. Being content with nothing but the best he is not determined to this or that and he can never be constrained by the magnetism of any object he

---

5   In everyday speech the words "voluntary" and "free" are used interchangeably. When we say "voluntarily" or "willingly" we mean "freely." This convention of everyday language can, however, be a source of error in understanding the nature of the will, for although all actions of the will can be called "voluntary," i.e., belonging to the will, not all voluntary actions are free.

beholds. It satisfies him in part, but it always has a rival."[6]

The Freedom of the Will

The acts of the will, let us repeat, fall into two categories: the necessary and the free. Man *must* will the good, for that is the way the will has been made—that is its nature. It is drawn to the good in general, the universal good, because it is a power of rational desire, and the good known by the intellect is not this or that particular good but goodness in general—good in its universal aspect.

It is a matter of fact however that we are never in this life confronted with the direct, immediate choice of goodness in general, but only of this or that particular, finite, limited good. It is in this direction that we find the area of free choice. In the words of St. Thomas, "Whatever beings have a judgment that is not determined to one thing by nature must have free choice. Such are all intellectual beings. For the intellect apprehends not only this or that good, but good itself in general. And so . . . the will of an intellectual substance will not be determined by nature except to the good in general. And so it is possible for the will to incline toward whatever may be offered to it under the aspect of good, since there is no natural determination to the contrary to prevent it. Therefore all intellectual beings have a free will, resulting from the judgment of the intellect."[7]

The will of man, then, is free with respect to any particular good because the only thing that can command it is the good in general.

---

6 M. C. D'Arcy, *Christian Morals* (London: Longmans, Green, and Co., 1937), p. 118. For the problem of man's last end, see below, Chapter 17. We might note here the following: Only infinite good can satisfy the will, and the infinite good is God. Therefore the will tends of its nature toward God. However man does not always realize that the all-satisfying good can only be God, and so he often puts his happiness in something else. In the words of St. Thomas, "Before the necessary connection [between happiness and God] is made evident in the beatific vision, the will does not adhere to God of necessity" (*Summa Theologiae*, I, 82, 2).

7 *Summa Contra Gentiles*, II, 48. (All quotations from the *Summa Contra Gentiles* are taken from the translation of the Dominican Fathers of the English Province [London: Burns, Oates, and Washbourn, 1924].)

(This is known as the freedom of specification.) It is also free with respect to its own activity. Since it cannot be compelled by any one particular good, therefore it can always either will it or not will it; that is, it can freely choose or freely refrain from choosing. (This is known as the freedom of exercise.)

Confirmatory Evidence of Free Will

The analysis of the nature of will discloses that under man's present conditions of existence there is necessarily an area of indetermination and therefore an area in which choice is non-necessary. This analysis of reason is confirmed by the experience of everyday life. Making all the concessions necessary to the influence of educational, environmental, and temperamental factors, we are nevertheless conscious of frequent occasions when we actively dominate a situation by our individual choices, when we can say, often against the pull of pleasure or selfish interest, "I am determined to do this," or "I will not do this." Even the person who denies in theory the freedom of the will acts as though he were free, and will, indeed, protest as vigorously as the next person when his freedom of action is interfered with.

We may note, finally, that the whole pattern of man's existence, if it has any meaning at all, implies free choice. If there is no free choice, then all responsibility and obligation disappear. The whole elaborate structure of laws, moral codes, political institutions by which man guides his life are meaningless if man is not free. "Man has free choice," says St. Thomas, "otherwise advice, admonishment, commands, prohibitions, rewards, and punishment would be to no purpose."[8]

Summary

The tendency in man by which he is drawn toward things in order to possess them is called desire. This is manifested both in the general

---

8 *Summa Theologiae*, I, 83, 1. For a further discussion of what the denial of morality implies, see Chapter 18.

tendency toward good which is characteristic of all being, and in the conscious striving for good things. On a sense level desire gives rise to feelings and passions; on an intellectual level, to will-acts. The passions which accompany sense desire are classified according to their origin and intensity as concupiscible or irascible. Rational desire is the pull toward the good as reason knows it. Man naturally desires the good-in-general, but has to choose among the particular goods which are the means that lead to it. Thus the willing of man's last end is necessary, but the willing of the means is free.

CHAPTER 13 ◈

Freedom And Liberty

The good man, although he is a slave, is free; but the bad man, even if he reigns, is a slave, and a slave not of just one man but, what is far more grievous, of as many masters as he has vices.
ST. AUGUSTINE, THE CITY OF GOD, IV, 3.

The will, as we have seen, is a kind of corollary of reason. If we can know the good in general we can never be completely satisfied by partial, finite goods. Nevertheless the only choices with which we are immediately confronted are partial goods. These limited goods and the power of choosing them are a kind of means to an end. The end is man's self-fulfillment, whereby he identifies himself with the all-good.[1] In the Christian tradition this means the ultimate union of man with God, and following the terminology of St. Paul and St. Augustine, the higher, fulfilling freedom is called "liberty." The freedom of choice, then, as the mechanism by means of which our freedom is realized, must be distinguished from the state of liberty, which is the willing of our true end, the goal which fulfills our nature. Since the word "freedom" may thus be employed in widely different contexts, it is important to clarify its usages.

The Kinds of Freedom

1. Freedom of Non-Coercion

For those who characterize man as a pure animal the only kind

---

1 See Chapter 17.

of desire is sense desire, and therefore the only meaning the word freedom can have is the freedom of not being interfered with in the working out of natural and necessary tendencies. In this sense we say that an animal is free if it is not caged up, or even that a stone is "free" to fall if the hand that supports it is withdrawn. It is in this elementary sense of the word freedom that we say anyone who is not in jail is "free" or that a tramp or a child is "care-free."

2. Freedom of Choice

Even when there is agreement on what the last aim of man should be, there may still be a wide variance in the paths that lead to this end. Man's ability to choose among the various means open to him in the achievement of his destiny is called his power of free choice.

The tendency today is to restrict the use of the word freedom to those who have the widest potentiality of choice. Thus for many people the free man is the man of wealth, the financial tycoon, the captain of industry. Or again the free man is exemplified by the great generals of history, or the kingly potentates of past times, or the all-powerful dictators of the present day.

There is a sense in which it is true to say that all these men are more free than other men. A tyrannical dictator may be the only man who is politically free in his country. The man of wealth is free to travel, free to change his dwelling place, free from the hampering restrictions of poverty. The general of the army is freer than the private who takes everybody's orders.

In another sense the men we have instanced are less free than others. The millionaire has the ceaseless task of guarding his wealth. The dictator is the slave of the fears engendered by his own tyrannical rule. The general of the army shoulders the weighty cares of his office.

None of these freedoms, in other words, is absolute. To choose something means to commit oneself. The very act of choosing is a limiting act. If you choose the career of a lawyer you usually close yourself off from the other professions. If you choose marriage you gain the benefits of family life but lose the advantages of the single state. No matter what you choose as your end in life, you cut yourself off from the contraries of that choice.

It is possible to make free choice an end itself, turning it into a kind of god. Paradoxically, for one who makes free choice itself the supreme good, real choice becomes impossible. Such a person refuses to choose a definite profession, because it "ties him down." He refuses marriage because it binds him. He refuses the commitment of any kind of duty or love because of the restrictions it may place on him. A person of this kind who spends his life refusing to make choices in order to preserve his freedom actually dissipates his freedom in anarchy or indecision. In saving his freedom he loses it.

3. Liberty, or the Freedom of Self-Realization

Free choice is not an end in itself but rather is given to us in order that we may realize our full potentialities as human beings. Men do not all agree, however, on what makes for the truly human fulfillment. Some place their fulfillment in wealth, some in power, some in sense pleasure, some in beauty, some in virtue, some in God. Some place their fulfillment, in short, in self-aggrandizement, others in self-giving: a false liberty may be set against true liberty.

Only if man uses his freedom of choice rightly will he enjoy true liberty—the freedom of self-realization, the freedom of autonomy or self-rule, as the Greeks called it. For although man is free to choose, he cannot free himself from the laws of the universe of which he is a part and cannot therefore escape the consequences of his choice. If someone chooses to jump out the window, he is free to do so, but he is not free to float in the atmosphere independent of the law of gravity. If a man chooses to make drunkenness his chief good in life he is free to do so, but he must accept the ravages to his health and fortune that such a choice entails.

The highest freedom, then, depends on a person choosing rightly in terms of what a human being should be. True liberty will not be found in the libertine, who enslaves himself to his animal instincts. It will not be found in the men who refuse commitment for fear of losing their freedom, for these men have already chosen, and what they have chosen is nothingness. Neither will it be found in the men who have chosen wealth and power as their fulfillment, for history tells us how easy it is for them to pervert their freedom to egoistic and vicious ends, so that while outwardly free, they are inwardly slaves to vice, greed, pride, ambition.

True freedom is found only in the man who has mastered himself, so that neither the constraint of instinct from within nor the pressure of force from without can make him deviate from the line of his conscience; it is the freedom of the man who has freed himself from the chains of ignorance and vice.

History gives us sublime examples of men who have realized the highest freedom through giving themselves to some ideal—to justice, to truth, to beauty: a Socrates, for example, who prefers the poisoned cup to injustice, a Regulus who chooses torture over dishonor, a Rembrandt who accepts an old age of poverty rather than betray his talent. But where we undoubtedly find the supreme examples of the men and women who are truly free is in the lives of the saints. In the words of Barbara Ward: "As I look back across the years, again and again I come upon personalities of overpowering beauty and attraction. Now it is St. Francis of Assisi loving the world so passionately that not only men but even animals were tamed by the quality of his peace making. Now it is a Father Damien dying among the lepers, a St. John Bosco gathering the orphan children of Italy around him, a Mother Cabrini laboring among the outcast poor of New York. All these men and women have in common a warmth, a generosity, a largeness of heart, a lack of constraint and limitation which sets them apart from our ordinary blind and imprisoned humanity and proclaims the intensity of their freedom. In the saints and mystics it is almost as though we saw, for the first time, the true stature of man. This is what men look like when the command 'Love thy neighbor' becomes not an impossible perfection but a daily reality. This is what is truly meant by 'the glorious liberty of the Sons of God.' "[2]

Freedom and Society

The manner in which we employ our freedom determines the kind of persons we are. "We are our loves," says St. Augustine, who saw society itself divided into two camps according to the basic choices men made: "Two cities have been formed by two loves: the earthly by the love of self, even to the contempt of God; the heavenly by the love of God, even to the contempt of self."[3]

The controlling principle of the moral life of the individual and of society is the same. If a society is united in the love of good, it will be a good society; if its aims are evil or misconceived it will be a bad society. Society thus is a kind of mirror which reflects on a magnified scale the ideals of those who compose it. In this mirror we can see manifested the political philosophies which stem from the different concepts of freedom, their emphasis, their distortion, their balance.

1. The Slave State

The equation of freedom with natural necessity, the "freedom" of the stone to obey the law of its nature, of the animal to follow instinct, gives rise to the dictator state conceived as the product of the inexorable working out of the forces of nature. "Freedom is necessity," says Engels, one of the co-founders of the Marxist philosophy. Freedom in this context means the freedom to consent to what you have to do anyhow.

2. The Laissez-Faire State

Social life built on the idea of freedom which limits it to the too narrow concept of freedom of choice results in the 'liberal,'

---

2 From a speech delivered in New York before the Herald Tribune Forum. Quoted in the New York *Herald Tribune*, October 26, 1947.

3 *The City of God*, XIV, 28. (All quotations from *The City of God* are from the translation of Marcus Dods as found in *The Basic Writings of St. Augustine*, edited by J. Whitney Oates [New York: Random House, 1948].)

laissez-faire state. The purpose of the state is conceived to be the safeguarding of the freedom of the citizen to do as he likes with as little restriction as possible. The role of the state is that of the traffic policeman.

The concern for freedom which this philosophy manifests is often hypocritical. Its freedom is the freedom of the fox in the chicken coop. In actual fact such a doctrine, which denies the concept of social justice and the common good, has never been realized except at the cost of exploitation, and its issue is either in some form of economic totalitarianism or in social anarchy. Both these tendencies are compensated for (since men have to live) by such a complicated series of social structures—laws, price controls, cartels, trade unions, employer associations, government bureaus, etc.—that in time the citizen becomes a slave to the very machinery set up to ensure his freedom.

3. The Superstate

Social life may reflect a distortion of the freedom of autonomy, of self-realization. The goal of freedom may be conceived as power, achievement, glory, realized through the State, the Class, the Empire, the Leader, which the citizen sees as an extension of himself. Freedom in such a society is the service of the common task or of the Leader.

Such a freedom is again hypocritical and self-destructive, since it despises free choice, the root of man's freedom, crushing the individual for the glorification of the deified Hero or the juggernaut State, and ignores man's true end, substituting Caesar for God.

4. The Just State

The social philosophy which embodies the true conception of man and his destiny sees the state as meant for man and not man for the state: the life of man is for eternity, the most powerful state will some day come to an end.

The purpose of the state is to foster the common good: both the material well-being of the community, and also the spiritual climate under which each person can freely strive for the realization of the highest freedom, the freedom of self-mastery. Not merely the freedom to live, but the freedom to live well is the concern of the just state.

Summary

The liberty whereby the will freely adheres to the supreme good must be distinguished from the freedom of choice, which is the means by which we reach the state of liberty. Different aspects of freedom are illustrated in different kinds of lives, from the superficial freedom of the careless and irresponsible, through the relative freedom of a life rich in scope for enterprise, to the highest freedom of self-fulfillment, where the deepest potentialities of human nature come to fruition. These lives are mirrored within society itself, which may be the slave society of the anthill or the beehive, the community of rugged individuals or of supermen, or finally the well-ordered commonwealth of responsible persons.

CHAPTER 14

Liberty and Love

The law of liberty is the law of love.
St. Augustine, Letter 167, Vi, 15.

The primary impulse, by which our power of willing is set in motion, the impulse by which we are drawn toward objects which we perceive as good for us, is given the name of "love." Love is thus at the heart of our freedom; it is the mainspring of desire, so that the choices we make are the fruit of our love. *Pondus meum, amor meus*, says St. Augustine: My weight is my love—I gravitate toward what I love.[1]

We can be weighted in the direction of things in different ways. We can want other things, such as food and drink, solely for our own benefit, because they are useful to us. We can love persons, our friends, our husbands and wives, for their own sake, not selfishly, but as a kind of second self. Christianity adds to these a third dimension, the love of charity, the love by which we are able to love God, and all other things in Him, with the supernatural love of charity.

---

1 Confessions, XIII, 9. (All quotations from the Confessions are taken from the Pusey translation, Everyman edition [London and New York: J. M. Dent and E. P. Dutton, 1950]).

Love is thus a kind of genus, of which there are three species:

$$\text{Love } (amor) \begin{cases} \text{desire } (delectatio) \\ \text{friendship } (amicitia) \\ \text{charity } (caritas) \end{cases}$$

Selfish Love

Selfish love is the lowest and most elementary form of love. It is the love of desire by which we want things in order to fill up some lack or deficiency within ourselves. In this kind of love we are drawn toward things only so that we can make them a part of ourselves, increasing ourselves at their expense, so to speak. If you love lobster, for example, it is at the expense of the lobster, which is destroyed as the result of your love.

St. Thomas called this love the love of concupiscence[2] or desire. It is not a bad love as long as it is well ordered, since man needs lesser goods to perfect his own nature.

Altruistic Love

A higher form of love is what Aristotle called the love of friendship.[3] This is the love proper to human beings and implies a factor which can never be found in the love proper to lesser things—the return of love. The love of friendship implies a certain relation of equality. I may love my dog, but my dog cannot love me back with the same kind of love; friendship in the strict sense is not possible because the gap between the animal and the man is too great for any real sharing to take place.

Aristotle enumerates three kinds of friendship. The lowest kind is the intercourse based on reciprocal self-interest—the friendship of people who profit from their association in a business or political way, for example. This is a friendship which vanishes as soon

---

2 See *Summa Theologiae*, I–II, 28, 4. This meaning of the word "concupiscence" must be distinguished clearly from its meaning in theology, where it refers to the disorder consequent upon original sin.

3 See *Nicomachean Ethics*, VIII, 2; 1155 b 16-1158 a 5.

as the occasion for profit disappears. The second kind of friendship is that based on the love of some superficial characteristic of the person, such as good looks, wit, charm. On this basis people are friends because they take pleasure in one another's company. Friendships of this kind, though more solidly based, are also apt to be transitory, for tastes may change, or the traits on which they are based may disappear.

But neither of these two kinds of friendship meet the requirements of friendship in the strict sense, for the love of perfect friendship is a disinterested love. The other is loved not because he is useful, or a source of pleasure—good-looking or well-mannered, "good company"—but because he is seen to embody values, perfections, which make him worth loving for his own sake.

His good is desired in the same way that we desire our own. To love or desire people as objects to be used and exploited, to sacrifice their good to our private good, is a serious derangement of the right order of things, since it is to love them with the love proper to inanimate things rather than to human beings.[4]

The Love of Charity

The love of charity is something we know about through revelation. Because we have reason and will, it is possible for us to know God and return His love for us. But because of the inconceivable disproportion between the finite and the infinite, intimate friendship with God is not naturally possible. Revelation tells us, however, that God gave to man the gift over and above nature of returning His love with the love of friendship—to love God as God loves Himself in the Blessed Trinity. This capacity for divine love, lost through the Fall, has been restored to man through the Redemption, the act whereby Christ, true God and true man, regained for the human race the intimate friendship of God, so that when we love it is with God's love: "In this is charity, not that we have loved

---

4   Note the correspondence of the three kinds of friendship to the three basic categories of good, the three reasons, that is, why we love things: the good that is useful, the good that is pleasurable, and the good that is worthy. (See below, Chapter 26.)

God, but that he has first loved us, and sent his Son a propitiation for our sins" (1 Jn. 4:10). And St. Paul says, "It is now no longer I that live, but Christ lives in me" (Gal. 2:20).

The love of charity interpenetrates and transfigures the lower forms of love. If we love God with the love proper to God, we will love all creatures because they come from His hand. Even the little things of creation, we will love with a love like that of St. Francis, which sees them not as mere objects to be used selfishly but as reflections of God's perfection, and therefore to be used reverently and temperately. Much more will our love for our fellow man be transformed, since man, created in the image and likeness of God, is now known as a brother in Christ Himself: "the fellowship of man with the Father and with his Son, Jesus Christ," St. John says (1 Jn. 1:3).

The Love of Friendship in the Social Group

Friendship, for Aristotle, is the moral bond of society. "For in every community," he says, "there is thought to be some form of justice, and friendship too; at least men address as friends their fellow travellers and fellow soldiers, and so too those associated with them in any other kind of community."[5]

The kinds of society which men form will reflect the same reasons for which they form individual friendships. Thus some societies will be organized simply for reasons of utility, because the members find it mutually advantageous to be associated in such an organization. Many commercial and labor groups are of this kind.

Another kind of society is formed for the sake of pleasure. Here the bond of friendship is the pleasure which the members take in each other's company. Lodges and clubs are usually of this character.

A third, and the highest, kind of society is that which is based on the love of the good itself, in this case the common good, which becomes as it were the soul of the community. The love which

---

5 *Nicomachean Ethics,* VIII, 9, 1; 1159 b 25.

informs such communities—the love of family, the love of country—was exalted by the Greeks and Romans into one of the highest of the virtues.

It is possible, of course, for the same society to reflect more than one of these loves. Profit and pleasure may be equally found in a single social group, and any of them can be ennobled by reference to the larger good of the community.

A nation in which only the lower kinds of friendship are fostered, a nation in which the dominant ties are those of profit and pleasure, will be an essentially unstable society. Unless the various elements in society subordinate private interest and pleasure to the love of the common good, the community will decompose, as the demands of self-interest and faction multiply into an explosive mixture of mutually repelling atoms. We see this happen whenever various "special interest" groups within a country set their own good against the good of the community as a whole, when class sets itself against class—military against civilian, capital against labor, agriculture against industry; or when section sets itself against section—province against province, race against race, religion against religion.

If the multitude of different goods and interests which the various classes and segments of society represent are to be reconciled, it must be by transcending self-interest in the highest friendship, where the common good of the community is seen as so worthy of being loved as to make the highest sacrifices worth while. Only in the strength of this true and proper love of community can an organic and enduring unity be realized.

But friendship, as we have seen, implies a certain equality, since it is of the essence of real friendship that the other person is loved as though he were our very own self. Hence any widespread inequality or disproportion in society will be a source of strain and weakness, a solvent of the friendship that is the soul of the community. Thus, the institution of slavery ran like a great flaw through the heart of ancient society, for the gap between master and slave was beyond bridging.

Christianity, with its revelation of the love of charity, closed the gap even between freeman and slave. "There is neither Jew nor Greek," says St. Paul, "there is neither slave nor freeman; there is neither male nor female. For you are all one in Christ" (Gal. 3:27). Thus the base of friendship is widened and strengthened, so that a deeper bond for society is made possible. "Men are one, now, in a new association whose common good is no longer merely temporal and earthly, but spiritual and heavenly. . . . All men without exception are united in that common life, and every human institution, natural or voluntary, is embraced within that higher life of the supernatural society of men with God.[6]

Summary

Love is at the root of all desires. It is realized in man on three levels: the selfish love of concupiscence, natural to all animal beings; the altruistic love of friendship, characteristic of beings possessing intellect; and the love of charity, which is a supernatural gift. Friendship is the love of another person according as he is useful, pleasant, or virtuous. Man's social structures mirror all these levels of friendship. The deepest bond of union possible is the love of charity, which levels every natural barrier to the friendship of man for man.

6 Gerald B. Phelan, "Justice and Friendship," in the Maritain volume of *The Thomist* (Jan., 1943), p. 167 ff.

CHAPTER 15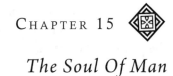

The Soul Of Man

Man is not his soul.
ST. THOMAS AQUINAS, COMM. IN I COR. XV, LECT. 2.

The Meaning of Soul

The basic meaning of the word "soul" is that of vitalizing principle, the principle, that is, by which a thing is able to perform the activities which we associate with "being alive." Common sense sees it as the power of self-movement as, for example, when a child pokes a strange object with a stick to see if it will move. The philosopher narrows down the minimum functions of vital activity to the powers of nutrition, growth, and reproduction. In certain marginal beings, as in the case of the virus, it is difficult to tell whether all or only some of these functions are realized, so that there is argument as to whether or not they should be called alive. In other words, the dividing line between living and nonliving is not precisely clear to us.

In the sense of "vitalizing principle," then, it is proper to say that plants, animals, and men have souls, though not of the same kind. The animal soul differs from the plant soul in that it adds to the minimum of vital functions the powers of sensation and of movement from place to place. The human soul differs from the animal in that it adds the powers of intellect and will to the animal powers.

The Existence of the Soul

By studying the powers of the soul we learn about the nature of the soul itself as the ground and origin of these powers. The powers themselves cannot be the soul, because they are not always in act. We do not think, for example, when we are asleep or unconscious. We do not see when our eyes are closed. Yet the power to think and the power to see remain. There must be some anterior reality, then, in which these powers are seated.

Because we do not have immediate, firsthand knowledge of the soul but have to learn about it indirectly through its activities, some philosophers have denied its existence. No one has ever seen a soul, they say, or photographed one, or isolated one in a test tube, or weighed one in a laboratory.

The fact that we cannot sense a thing does not mean, of course, that it does not exist. I cannot see or touch the national debt, or my right to vote, or my neighbor's love for his children, yet no one seriously doubts the existence of these things. We know that the soul exists as an inference which follows necessarily from certain observed facts, in the same way, for example, that an astronomer may know there is a certain body in the heavens, even though he cannot see it with his telescope; he knows it because the movements of other heavenly bodies which he can see make the presence of the unseen heavenly body necessary as the only possible explanation. Similarly in the case of man, certain activities are performed which cannot be explained merely as the response of inert matter to physical forces. These activities differ in kind from purely material activities, and therefore we have to conclude that there is a special way of being which is the ground and explanation of these activities. This principle of being we call the soul.

The Soul of Man

Man is first of all a bodily substance, existing among other bodily substances. By a substance we mean a being capable of existing on its own—unlike a color, or a taste, for example, which have to be in something else in order to be at all. Following the terminology of Aristotle, we say that if man is a substance he has a substantial form. This means that man has a certain basic way of being which gives him his particular kind of being as against other basic kinds of being—"man" as against "tree," for example. Since man is a corporeal substance, his substantial form is limited by the principle of matter. Otherwise we would not have individual human beings but only "manness." Man therefore is a being made up of matter and form.

Matter and form, as we already know, are complementary principles. One could not come into existence without the other. This means that in the case of man the soul could not have come into existence except as the form of the human body. It means also that to speak of the body is to speak at the same time of the soul, for without the rational soul which makes it alive it is not a human body. In brief, the unity of man is so profound that it is wrong to think of soul and body as though they were two separate beings. They are rather two distinct aspects, each implying the other, of the same being man.[1]

The root of man's activities is in his form. (It could not be matter, which is merely an indeterminate and limiting principle.) The primary act of the form is the activity of being alive. Therefore we give it the name "soul," and we say that the soul of man is the substantial form of man.

The soul of man is also the root of those secondary powers which range from the elemental activities of nutrition, growth, and reproduction which are found also on the plant level up through the animal powers to the specifically human powers. (See Chart on page 114.)

What is the role of the principle of matter in the human composite? Matter is the principle which limits, circumscribes, gives

---

1 Although as we shall see later the soul of man, once it has come into existence, can exist apart from the body which it informs, its separated existence is nevertheless an incomplete, imperfect existence. See St. Thomas Aquinas, Summa Theologise, I–II, 4, 5, ad 5; also *Summa Contra Gentiles*, IV, 79.

quantity, dimensions, and thus makes the form *individual*, causing it to be the form of *this particular body*. Thus it is that the form exists in time and in space—when I sit down my thoughts sit down with me, Montaigne says—so that we have the strange mystery of a spirit which because it informs a body "acquires a whole biological, psychological and social individuality."

When all is said, however, it remains true that the formal and material aspects of man—the soul and body aspects—are different, and one cannot be reduced to the other. "They are in opposition in that one is a principle of unity and concentration, and the other a principle of dispersion and multiplicity. Their unity is one of tension, of polarized opposition, involving a possibility of conflict, of antagonism and, at the limit, of disaggregation."[2]

The Spirituality of the Soul

One way of knowing the nature of a thing is from the way it acts. We know, for example, that the soul of an animal differs from the soul of a plant because the animal can sense things whereas the plant cannot. In the same way we learn about our own souls by studying the operations we perform. (We do not have a direct knowledge of our soul because it does not fall under our senses; we have to infer its nature from the observation of what it does.) Now although a great many of the operations of man, the vegetative and sensible activities, for example, are such that they could not take place except as the acts of a body, there is one set of operations, the activities of understanding and willing, which do not basically depend upon anything material.

In the act of intellectual knowing, as we have seen, the forms of things exist in man as universal, and therefore as nonmaterial. This means that the intellect must be nonmaterial, for something material could not be the receptacle of the immaterial any more than a tin can could contain the idea of patriotism or any other abstract

---

2 Jean Mouroux, *The Meaning of Man* (New York: Sheed and Ward, Inc., 1948), Chap. 4, p. 65.

idea. If, in other words, there were matter in the intellect, the forms that are joined to it in the act of knowing could not be universal because where there is matter there is quantity, dimension, individuality. The intellectual activity of man, then, is intrinsically independent of matter. The act of the will is similarly independent of matter, for its object is always something known under the aspect of the universal good.

Since the actions of knowing and willing are independent of matter, the principle or ground of these activities, the soul, must be independent of matter. If it is independent of matter for its activities, it must be equally independent of matter for its existence. Therefore we can call the soul of man a spirit as well as a soul, for this is what being a spirit means: to be independent of matter both as to existence and operation.[3]

The soul of man is an "incomplete" spirit, however, for it can come into existence in the first place only in union with the principle of matter, as the soul of a body. Furthermore many of its activities, such as sensing, are basically dependent on the body which it animates. There is an accidental dependence on the informed body even for the acts of knowing and willing, because the soul would remain "a blank tablet" without the sensible channels of information. The soul separated from the body which it animates will therefore be an incomplete substance, for it is still its nature to be the form of a body.[4]

Other Views of the Soul

Opposed to the Aristotelian-Thomist view of the soul as the substantial form of the body is the doctrine that the soul is a substance separate and distinct from the body. We have met this concept in Plato, who characterizes man as a soul imprisoned in a body "like

---

3 For a complete treatment of this problem see the work of Renard and Vaske, *The Philosophy of Man,* rev. ed. (Milwaukee: The Bruce Publishing Company, 1958).

4 Cf. St. Thomas: "To be separated from the body is not in accordance with the soul's nature" (*Summa Theologiae,* I, 89, 1).

an oyster in his shell."[5] St. Augustine, following in the Platonic tradition, defined man as a rational soul using a body.[6]

Plato's view, in effect, reduces man to his soul, and the body of man becomes a hindrance, something alien and antagonistic to the true being of man. St. Augustine, as a Christian who believed in the resurrection of the whole man, body and soul, had to find room for the body as well as the soul in his definition of man. Even St. Augustine's definition, however, leaves the body of man as a kind of awkward appendage to the soul, as though only the soul were really man. St. Augustine's view, in other words, still left endangered the unity of man and, as such, was hard to reconcile with the Christian doctrine of man.[7]

The French philosopher Descartes, whose philosophy has been so influential that he is frequently called the Father of Modern Philosophy, made man a kind of machine—the body—with an independent driver—the soul. All animal bodies are pure automatons: a dog or a canary, for example, is simply an elaborate piece of machinery. When the dog barks or the canary sings, it is simply a noise that the machinery makes, no different than the "squealing" of brakes or the "screech" of a saw. The human body or machine differs from the animal machine only in that it has a conscious spirit tied to it as a kind of superintendent.

Descartes made soul or mind and body so distinct and independent of each other that both he and his followers never quite succeeded in getting them together again. This problem of bridging the gap between soul and body has been called in modern philosophy "the mind-body problem."[8]

---

5 Phaedrus, 250.

6 *De moribus Ecclesiae*, I, 27.

7 It was this inadequacy in St. Augustine's concept of the nature of man which turned the eyes of St. Thomas toward Aristotle, as offering a philosophy of man more compatible with Christian truth.

8 To ask how two dissimilar things like soul and body can act on each other is to raise a false problem. Man, as we have seen, is not made up of two dissimilar parts, soul and body, but is a composite of form and matter which together make up a single being. It is not soul and body that act, but man, who manifests both material and immaterial

Other modern philosophers, such as David Hume and John Stuart Mill, either deny the existence of a specifically human soul, or deny that it can be known. They make the activities of man completely dependent upon bodily functions. The activities of knowing and willing are explained away as forms of brute animal sensation and desire. These philosophers are called phenomenalists, because they reduce reality to the appearances (phenomena) open to the senses, denying any reality behind these appearances, or because for them the knowing activities of man are mere passing phenomena of his physical body.

We may cite, finally, those modern philosophers and psychologists who say the soul of man is simply nonexistent. La Mettrie, an eighteenth-century follower of Descartes, bluntly termed man a machine. Man is just Descartes's machine-body which has lost its driver. The twentieth-century version of this doctrine is seen best in the behaviorist school of psychology, which denies consciousness itself as "a belief [that] goes back to the ancient days of superstition and magic."[9]

The Origin of the Soul

The soul of man, we have seen, must be spiritual since some of its activities are of a spiritual nature—independent, that is, of the limitations of matter, of quantity, dimension, time, space. We have, then, in the case of man, the existence of spiritual forms in a material universe. What is the origin of these spiritual beings?

We cannot say with the mechanists and materialists that the soul of man comes from bodies, because the gap between the material and the spiritual is too great to be crossed. A thing cannot produce something greater than itself, any more than a stone can burst into song, or the Atlantic Ocean gush from a teacup.

We cannot say, either, that one soul comes from another (spiritual traducianism) because what is spiritual cannot be divided; you

---

aspects in the act of being.

9   John B. Watson, *Behaviorism* (New York: W. W. Norton, 1925), p. 1.

cannot, for example, cut an idea in two. Although our bodies come from our parents, we cannot say the same for our souls.

The only explanation left to us is that the soul is directly created— that a new soul comes into being with each new human being. Since the soul is spiritual, it is not contained in any of the potentialities of matter. Since it comes into being, it could not create itself. It must therefore have its origin in some spiritual being who has the power of creating new beings. And the spiritual being who has the power to create new beings out of nothing is the being whom we call God.

The Immortality of the Soul

Once the human soul has come into existence it cannot be destroyed. In other words, it is immortal.

A substance can be destroyed in two ways. First, from the inside, so to speak, through the disunion of its essential parts. This is what happens in the destruction of any bodily being, when the form is separated from the matter. (Matter is always potentially able to receive new substantial forms, and therefore all bodily beings are naturally corruptible.) But, as we have seen, the soul of man is the form of the body and therefore is not itself composed of form and matter. Since it is not made up of parts it cannot be separated into parts and therefore cannot be broken down from within.

The second way a substance can be destroyed is from the out- side—through some external factor such as the destruction of some other being without which it cannot function. This is what happens in the case of the forms or souls of plants and animals. The entire act of these forms is bound up with the bodies of which they are the animating principle. Those bodies are of course capable of disintegration, and when they are destroyed, the soul which ani- mated them and which was totally dependent on them disappears. But this does not hold true in the case of the human soul, since as we have seen it is a spirit as well as a soul; that is, it has activities— understanding and willing—which, being intrinsically independent of the body for their exercise, indicate an act of existence equally independent of the body.

There is, then, no principle of death in the soul, for neither can it be broken up into parts nor is it vitally dependent upon some other being whose destruction it would share. The only conceivable way the soul could go out of existence is by annihilation, and this would mean an act of destruction by the Creator of the soul, and for this philosophy can envisage no good reason.

The famous positivist philosopher Comte has popularized in modern times the doctrine of what is called "subjective immortality." According to this point of view, man finds his immortality through the continuing effect of his works, through his books, his paintings and so on, and in the memory of his loved ones. Such a doctrine of immortality—proper perhaps in a metaphorical sense to material things—is a mockery to the man who faces the fact that all the works of man are destined one day to be swallowed up in the cold silence of the stars. The immortality to which man really aspires, the only one which makes sense, is the immortality of unending conscious existence.

Confirmation of the Philosophical Argument

The cold and abstract argument of the philosopher for the immortality of the soul finds corroboration in the spontaneous convictions of common sense—in the instinctive sureness that man has of his survival, as expressed for example in the mythologies of primitive man; in the burial remains from earliest times, where such things as food and weapons are nearly always provided for the journey beyond the grave; in the casualness with which men often risk their lives for even trivial reasons—in automobile races, mountain climbing, bullfights, for example, as though they were subconsciously aware that life continues beyond physical death; in the natural thirst for unending existence which is so deeply embedded in man's heart as to imply immortality.

Further corroboration is found in certain insights based on the moral life of man—experiences of a uniquely important and profound character which would lose all meaning apart from their relation to a transearthly existence. For at least once or twice in the life of every mature person there arises the necessity of a choice which in the depths of that person's feelings he knows is the right choice—to give up one's life for one's fellow man, for example, or to sacrifice fortune rather than honor—choices which have meaning if man is immortal, but which make a mockery of his most sublime aspirations if his life is to perish with his body.

The Inadequacy of the Philosopher's Knowledge

The immortality of which philosophy speaks is an immortality of the soul. But the soul is not the whole of man, for man is body as well as soul. Of the survival of the whole man, body and soul, philosophy has little to say. The separated soul is not the whole person, for the human soul needs the body for the full exercise of its powers. Philosophy can assert the continuing desire of the soul for union with the body, but it cannot envisage the satisfaction of that desire. Neither can it envisage the satisfaction of the soul's desire for an eternal union with God, for this is not within the power of nature, but is a supernatural gift. Strong as was the thirst for immortality of the great philosophers of antiquity, such as Plato and Aristotle, deep as was their nostalgia for God, it seems as though they hardly dared to hope, and they turned from the problem as though with regret, acknowledging the unsatisfactoriness of the philosophical answers.

The Religious Knowledge of Immortality

One kind of religious answer to this problem is the doctrine of the transmigration of souls, which holds that the soul passes through a series of animal and human bodies, working out the consequences of reward or punishment for the activities of its preceding lives. Such a doctrine envisages usually an eventual release of the soul from the wheel of successive lives, and reabsorption into the ultimate principle of all things. True personal immortality disappears, of course, in a doctrine of this kind.

The Christian tradition teaches the survival not only of the soul of man, which is the most reason can attain to, but of the body also. The whole man, soul and body, works out his destiny, for good and evil, in a single existence, and the whole man, soul and body, lives for eternity the kind of existence he has freely chosen. That the body is immortal along with the soul is possible, of course, through the omnipotence of God.

Revelation tells us that God is not a remote, impersonal force or principle, but a Person, and that the eventual explanation of the immortal existence of man is the great goodness of God, who wills to share His existence with His creatures, not destroying but fulfilling their personality.

Summary

The existence of the soul is known through its activities. It is primarily a principle of life, secondarily the source of the various powers of the living body. The soul of man is spiritual because it performs operations which are independent of matter. For Aristotle and St. Thomas the soul is the substantial form of the body, as against philosophers like Plato and Descartes for whom the soul is a separate substance independent of the body to which it is accidentally united, or as against philosophers like David Hume and John B. Watson for whom the soul either is unknowable or does not exist.

As spiritual, the soul of man must be the product of a direct Creation. It must also be immortal, for there is no principle of dissolution in a spiritual being.

CHAPTER 16

Human Personality

As individuals, we are subject to the stars. As persons, we rule them.
MARITAIN, THREE REFORMERS, P. 21.

The Individual and the Person

Man as both body and soul is the link between the world of matter and the world of spirit, the bridge between the temporal and the eternal. On this rests the classical distinction between the individual and the person.

From his physical aspect man is an individual, a very small part of the great physical universe, immersed in it, and subject to its laws—the "frail reed" of Pascal. From his spiritual aspect, however, man is a creature who escapes the laws of matter, a being self-knowing, self-directed, with an eternal destiny, a person. From this point of view, "there are no *ordinary* people. You have never talked to a mere mortal. Nations, cultures, arts, civilization—these are mortal, and their life is to ours as the life of a gnat. But it is immortals whom we joke with, work with, marry, snub and exploit."[1]

There is a dynamic tension in man between the two sides to his nature, and he must strive constantly to secure the right balance and proportion between the physical and spiritual. If in the search for riches, pleasure, power, security, he fosters the material side of his

---

1 C. S. Lewis, *The Weight of Glory* (New York: The Macmillan Company, 1949), p. 14.

nature, to that extent he weakens what is truly personal within him. If in the struggle for virtue, knowledge, beauty, he refuses the due claims of the material he equally distorts his nature. For man is so truly one that to do violence to either soul or body is to do violence to the other at the same time. If you do not give a man enough to eat, says St. Thomas, you cannot expect him to practice virtue. Deny him the food of the soul, dignity, justice, truth, and neither again will he be fully human.

The Person and Society

Man as an individual in the species needs society, both to secure the material conditions under which he can realize his destiny as a person, and to secure the good which is open to the whole race of men working in communion. From the standpoint of his individuality, then, man is subordinate to the community, which may legitimately call on him to sacrifice his time, his wealth, even on occasion life itself. These demands are justified because the common good reflects eternal values in so far as it relates indirectly to the last end of man. But there are sacrifices which the state cannot demand and which man cannot give. If the state demands injustice, falsehood, the renunciation of fundamental rights, it is assaulting personality itself, the very thing which it exists to serve.

Most of the ills of society today have their source in the sacrifice of man's personality to his individuality—of the spiritual side of his nature to the material. In the words of Jacques Maritain: "In the social order, the modern city sacrifices the *person* to the *individual*; it gives universal suffrage, equal rights, liberty of opinion, to the *individual*, and delivers the *person*, isolated, naked, with no social framework to support and protect it, to all the devouring powers which threaten the soul's life, to the pitiless actions and reactions of conflicting interests and appetites. . . . It is a homicidal civilization."[2]

Just as in the case of the individual, the community may reflect either an excessive regard for material things or an inhuman

---

2 J. Maritain, *Three Reformers* (New York: Charles Scribner's Sons, 1929), p. 21.

contempt for them; in either case to the denial of man's true nature, of his personality. The civilization that overvalues material things takes as its end pleasure, comfort, security, the accumulation of physical wealth, and sacrifices honor, dignity, truth, the values which make man truly a person, to these subhuman values. The civilization which barbarously despises material values equally shows contempt for human nature, dissipating the physical heritage, the courage, the life itself of its citizens for the inhuman ends of power and domination.

A sound civilization neither despises nor overvalues material means, but relates them to values which are higher than anything earthly. It does not treat its citizens as means, but regards each as an end in himself. It protects and fosters the material conditions for the well-being of the citizen, but does not shrink to sacrifice them if a higher value demands it. The good civilization will, in short, reflect the qualities of the virtuous citizen: temperate in its pursuit and use of material goods, valiant in its defense of what is right, wise in governance, it will order all things in the light of the worth, the dignity, the immortal destiny of the person.

PART III

THE MAKING OF MAN

CHAPTER 17

In Search of Happiness

Thou madest us for Thyself and our heart is restless until it rests in Thee.
ST. AUGUSTINE, CONFESSIONS, I, 1.

On this earth only man escapes the prison of physical deter-minism which confines all other bodily creatures. The growth of the acorn into the oak, the thrust of the plant toward the light, the drive of the animal toward food—all these impulses are blind, determined from without. Though we sometimes speak of a plant or an animal as bad, or imperfect, or not all it should be, there can be no sense of "ought" in the sense of "duty" for these creatures. The case is different with man. Although man too has a natural tendency within him which points him toward his goal, he also possesses intellect and will by means of which he can knowingly and freely co-operate in the full realization of what his nature ought to be.

It is a plain fact of everyday life, however, that man is not always what he could or should be. It is possible for him to choose erro-neously or perversely, frustrating the inborn impulse toward self-fulfillment. It is necessary for him therefore to search out the con-ditions and rules of the good life. The study which is concerned with the ideal fulfillment of the life of man is called the science of morals or ethics.[1] It has been succinctly summed up as "the science

---

1 From the Latin *mos* (*moris*), custom, and the Greek *ethos*, pattern of conduct.

of what a man ought to be by reason of what he is."[2]

Happiness As the Goal of Man

What is the final goal toward which man should strive? Clearly it must be whatever will best complete his nature. (It could hardly be what would frustrate or pervert his nature.) Different names can be given to this final end, this ultimate good of man. Aristotle called it happiness, a name he took from everyday speech. When the man on the street says "I'm happy," he usually means that he feels pleased because he is satisfied.

A man may make money his principal desire in life. If you ask him why, he will say he does so because it makes him happy. Or he may spend his life in the pursuit of knowledge, health, or pleasure. The reason for this conduct is that he finds his happiness in these things. If you ask him why he wants happiness, you have come to the root of the whole problem of ethics. Of all the things man can desire, happiness alone is desired for its own sake. Happiness in its ultimate meaning, then, is the state that follows the fulfillment of desire.

The Nature of Happiness

A happy life is a life which has a good ending. A life may have much tragedy and still be called a happy life, just as a play which has a happy ending is called a comedy rather than a tragedy although the characters may experience many troubles. A life may be a very happy one while it lasts, but if it is cut off before its prime—when, for example, the brilliant young scientist or the gifted artist dies with his promise before him—we say it has a tragic end.

In this life, then, happiness and unhappiness are relative terms, denoting the dominant tendency of a life, a truth often reflected in everyday expressions. Happiness in this life is something becoming, something being achieved, something toward which man tends. The final "set" of a man's life is for eternity, and only in this perspective

---

2 A. D. Sertillanges, *Foundations of Thomistic Philosophy* (St. Louis: B. Herder Book Company, 1931), p. 234.

can he be said to be finally happy or unhappy. "Call no man happy until you know the nature of his death," said Herodotus.[3]

One thing implied by happiness, then, is final fulfillment. This leads us to a second consideration: full or final happiness cannot be the possession of some goods to the exclusion of others. I cannot be finally happy if my ultimate choice excludes other good things, leaving me with unsatisfied desires. Real happiness must be exhaustive of all desire—it must mean the sure possession of everything I can call good.

It is obvious, however, that the possession of some of the goods that make men happy excludes the possession of others—or at least seems to. If, for example, I find my joy in a life of bustling activity, I am excluded from the delights of the contemplative life; if I make drunkenness my principal good in life I cannot enjoy the good of sound health. If our definition of happiness as the possession of all good things is to stand, we must recognize that there is an order of good things, that some things are better than others, and that the man who wants to be happy must choose these goods according to their proportionate value, not emphasizing one at the expense of others.

There are many different kinds of goods for man because he has many different capacities to be filled. The expression "all good things" does not refer to the sum total of all particular goods—all the money in the world, for example—but to goods of every kind which are needed for man's fulfillment.

Although it is the nature of man to choose his own good—choose happiness, in other words—he can misconceive the nature of the good suitable for him and therefore err in his choice of the goods which he thinks will give him total happiness. The man who wants to be happy will then, if he is wise, investigate goods of various types and try to put them in their right order.

---

3 Herodotus, *Clio*, I, 32.

The Order of Goods

1. Means and Ends

A quick survey of the things men actually desire shows a wide variety of things called good. We say oranges are good, a long walk is good, popularity is good, solitude is good, knowledge is good, and so on. Nor do we always name a thing good for the same reason. I may say oranges are good because they contain vitamin C and therefore insure good health. Someone else may say oranges are good because they taste sweet. One person may say that it is a good thing to see a play so that he can discuss it intelligently with other people. Another person will find the same play good just for its own sake, just because he enjoys it.

One fact that clearly emerges is that the principal value of some things is that they lead to the possession of others which are more valuable. Money; for example, gold, silver, or paper, is principally valuable according as it can be exchanged for such things as food and shelter. Food and shelter themselves take on additional value according as they make possible the good things of life in society.

Some things, on the other hand, are chosen just for their own sake, because they are good in themselves—a concert or a play, a book or a poem, the view from a high mountaintop. In short, some goods are primarily desired as means or instruments. Others are desired as ends, for their own sake and not as means to something else. If man is to lead a good life, he must put these goods in their right order, not choosing means as ends or ends as means.

2. The Goods of Fortune

One big class of good things—the goods Aristotle called the goods of fortune—clearly bears the character of means rather than ends. This class comprises such things as food, clothing, shelter, and money as the means to buy them. Some men do in fact make such things their supreme good in life, but theirs is a false and disappointing choice. St. Thomas gives four reasons why this must be so.[4]

---

4 *Summa Theologiae*, I-II, 2, 4.

First of all, man's last end, if it is to make him truly happy, must be completely dissociated from evil. But the goods of fortune are found among both good men and bad. The supreme good of man, however, could not be such as to leave its possessor in an evil state. Second, man's last end must be able to satisfy *all* his desires, and the possession of physical goods leaves unfulfilled many of man's possibilities—one can be rich and lack knowledge and virtue, for example. The third reason, according to St. Thomas, why the goods of fortune cannot be the final goal of man is that the last end must be such that no evil can come from it. Physical possessions, however, may make a man a target for envy and violence. Finally, man's last end must flow from his nature; to put man's happiness solely in external things is to put his fulfillment in something less than himself. We deride the "clotheshorse," or the man who "lives to eat."

3. The Goods of the Body

For the same reasons that St. Thomas rejects the goods of fortune as the last end of man, we must say that the goods of the body —health, strength, sense pleasures, leisure, and so forth—cannot be the last end of man.

Of all the lower goods that can be wrongly chosen as man's last end, pleasure stands out as the one most frequently adopted. The doctrine that makes pleasure the final end of man is called hedonism. (The name comes from the Greek word for pleasure.) The great blunder of the hedonist is to confuse the pleasure which follows on the satisfaction of certain desires with the object of desire itself. In other words, we always choose some thing, which may or may not bring pleasure with it. The error of the hedonist is to choose the pleasure itself, separating the pleasure from the act that brings the pleasure. "This is the reason for the so-called hedonist paradox: no one is apt to end in such misery as the consistent hedonist who becomes so obsessed with the golden egg that he forgets the goose that lays it."[5]

---

5 John Wild, *Introduction to Realistic Philosophy* (New York: Harper & Brothers, 1948), p. 43.

4. Social Goods

Higher in the scale of values are the social goods—such things as friendship, social status, political honor, fame, power, the state itself and its welfare. These goods, too, like the goods of fortune, can be lost and can be abused. They, too, if they are made into the highest of all goods, subordinate man to something lower in the scale of values than his own nature.

The modern cult of the all-powerful state is an example of a good of this class that has been wrongly exalted to the status of a final end. More subtle versions of this error are found in the French philosopher Comte's deification of humanity or John Stuart Mill's doctrine of utilitarianism. Mill makes "the greatest good of the greatest number," that is, the general usefulness of our actions to the community, the ultimate criterion of human conduct. Such a standard fails to recognize that certain values attaching to the individual person belong to an order which towers over that of the general civic welfare. It is wrong, for example, to subject one person to injustice so that the community as a whole can benefit, as though to repeat the cry that it is expedient for one man to die "instead of the whole nation perishing." While Mill's axiom has all the appearance of being nobly altruistic, it has for its net effect the total subordination of the person to the community; to something, in other words, less in the scale of values than itself.

The important truth which both utilitarianism and humanitarianism try to emphasize but in fact only distort is that man, by nature social, cannot achieve his fulfillment in isolation. Capable of love, it is man's nature to be self-giving, self-communicating. His happiness, his fulfillment will be realized only in sympathy and union with his fellow man. None the less, he cannot advance the general good by wrong means, for if the means are evil, the effect which they bring about will also in the long run be evil.

5. Goods of the Soul

The goods of the soul are the habits or virtues, intellectual and moral, by which man perfects himself.[6] Certainly growth in virtue takes man part of the way toward his fulfillment. A man strong in virtue is better than the same man without any virtues; it is better for a man to be wise than stupid, brave than cowardly. Furthermore, since the virtues are possessed inwardly, they cannot be lost through the ill-wind of fortune—that is one reason why the Stoics made the acquisition of virtue the end of man.

Nevertheless the soul is capable of many virtues which can never be realized—much knowledge that will never be acquired, capacities for courage, justice, and other virtuous actions that will never come to fruition. Action, too, is better than the possibility of action, and yet we know that it is impossible for a human being to act always at the peak of his capacity.

Thus, though the virtues are necessary for a fuller life—and therefore for a happy life—they do not bestow the fullness of life. The acquisition of virtue does not of itself realize the conditions necessary for full happiness.

6. The Supreme Good

None of the goods we have so far enumerated give man happiness. Neither can any of them be excluded from happiness, since each corresponds to some capacity of man's nature. The will recognizes each as good, but it is finally drawn not to this good thing or that good thing, but to goodness itself, which alone can exhaust its capacity. In short, the word *good*, when we are speaking of man, may refer either to the particular goods we have been considering, or it may refer to *the* good, the being to which these partial goods lead, and for whose sake they are called good. No created thing or combination of things could constitute *the* good, which as the supreme good must be eternal, perfect, all-inclusive. The only being that meets this description is God.

---

6 See Chapter 19.

The Last End of Man for the Philosopher

If God exists He is the last end, the total fulfillment of man. Only the infinite goodness of the Being who is good by essence can satisfy the will's limitless desire for good.

The philosopher knows that God exists. But can He be possessed? In what way can He be the last end of my existence?

Aristotle's answer is instructive. God is a being so perfect that He is infinitely remote from man. The best that is open to man is the imperfect and precarious possession of God through natural knowledge. The happy life for Aristotle, then, in so far as it is possible to man, is the life according to the intellect, the life of wisdom, spent in the undeviating contemplation of truth. This is the activity which comes closest to fulfilling the conditions of happiness, since it brings into the fullest and most harmonious realization all the powers of man, culminating in the exercise at its highest capacity of the noblest power, reason.

Yet it is not possible for man to spend more than brief periods of his life in this highest of activities, for fatigue and the interruptions of daily life call him down from this exalted peak. A life spent in the contemplation of truth implies, too, some dependence on the goods of fortune, since it is hard to pursue a detached interest in truth in the face of, for example, starvation or grave illness.

Aristotle concluded that, in the light of these qualifications, the ideally perfect life is possible only for the very few, and then only in part. A life spent as much as possible in the search for and contemplation of truth, accompanied by a reasonable sufficiency of external goods, is the most man can hope for.

A Difficulty

A further factor intervenes to complicate the calculations of the philosophers. There occur situations in which a life according to virtue demands total sacrifice—when the soldier must give up his life in defense of his country, the citizen prefer death to the political lie, when we must give up our life for our friends. What meaning can the happy life have when life itself is cut off?

Since he can prove the immortality of the soul, the philosopher has part of the answer. The life of the soul continues beyond the life of the body. And "if the soul is really immortal," as Socrates says, "what care should be taken of her, not only in respect of the portion of time which is called life, but of eternity."[7]

The philosopher can also prove the existence of a God who can reward and punish in the life that continues beyond the earthly life. Any consideration of man's happiness must take into account this further possibility.[8]

The Incompleteness of the Philosophical Answer

The philosopher's answers about the last end of man are unsatisfactory. He can, for example, prove the immortality of the soul, but not of the body. As far as philosophy is concerned, therefore, this continuing existence of man is an imperfect existence. Similarly, although man can know God as the absolute, all-embracing Good, the possession of this infinite Good is beyond the natural powers of man, for there is no proportion between the infinite and the finite.

The philosopher can know, then, that the all-satisfying object of desire does exist, but he knows too that it is an object which so far transcends human nature as to be beyond reach. It is possible, of course, that God as an infinitely powerful being could intervene in the order of nature, helping man to attain what is beyond his natural powers, but whether or not He does so is beyond the investigation of the philosopher.

Philosophical contemplation reaches at this point the limits of its capacity. To learn whether or not this help which takes man beyond what is naturally possible to him has actually been given, the philosopher has to turn to an examination of religion. Where God as known by philosophy falters, remaining hidden behind the impenetrable clouds of mystery, God as known through revelation

---

7   *Phaedo*, 107 b.
8   For the philosophical arguments for the existence of God see Chapter 28.

intervenes and answers the question raised but not answered by philosophy. "These great geniuses [Aristotle, Alexander of Aphrodisiac, Averroes the Arab] suffered from being straitened on every side," says St. Thomas, whose large heart well understood their anguish. "We, however, will avoid these straits if we suppose, in accordance with the foregoing arguments, that man is able to reach perfect happiness after this life, since man has an immortal soul; and that in that state he will understand [God] in the same way as separate substances understand [Him]."[9]

Summary

Man alone of earthly creatures participates in the shaping of his own destiny. To gain his true goal, however, he must know where he is going and how to get there. This is the subject matter of ethics, the science of morals.

Happiness as descriptive of man's fulfillment is the name given to his goal. Man must will happiness, but he can be mistaken about what constitutes his real happiness. He must properly evaluate, therefore, the different classes of goods and put them in their right order.

Through the experience of partial and imperfect goods man is led to the knowledge of the supreme good as the only thing which can totally satisfy his desire, the only thing therefore that can bring him complete happiness. Whether God as the Supreme Good can actually be possessed by man is a problem beyond the scope of the philosopher, who has to turn to religion for the answer.

---

9 *Summa Comtra Gentiles*, III, 48.

CHAPTER 18

The Road to Happiness

Morality knows nothing of geographical boundaries or distinctions of race.
HERBERT SPENCER, THE EVANESCENCE OF EVIL.

If he does really thimk that there is no distinction between virtue and vice, why sir,
when he leaves our house let us count our spoons.
DR. JOHNSON, IN BOSWELL, LIFE OF JOHNSON, ANNO 1789.

Relativity in Morals

When the ancient Greeks first set about extending their commercial and maritime empire around the shores of the Mediterranean,
they were shocked to find different codes of manners and morals
among the various peoples with whom they came in contact. Things
which were held abominable in Athens were deemed praiseworthy
in Carthage. In one place the ability to lie well and to cheat skillfully
were virtues to be cultivated; in another they were regarded as dis-
honorable. To care for the aged was a sacred duty in one country; in
another it was a social duty to get rid of them.

The scandal of these conflicting ideas of right and wrong forced
the Greeks to a rational examination of the foundations of morals.
Hence the conflict between the sophists, who claimed that morals
were an invention of man, and therefore subject to arbitrary change,
and philosophers like Socrates who maintained that, in spite of surface differences, the laws of moral nature were just as objective and

changeless as the laws of physical nature.

Today in our own culture the situation is not dissimilar. Anthropologists and sociologists have ranged the wide world over, collecting examples of strange manners and customs, different and sometimes conflicting ideas of moral behavior. Many, perhaps the majority, of our professional philosophers and moralists are today on the side of the sophists. They teach that the principles of morals are not a matter of knowledge but of opinion, and that one man's opinion is as good as another's. Moral beliefs are explained away variously: they are mere social conventions, an invention of the weak to protect themselves against the strong, or a fiction of the clever to dupe the foolish; or, again, they are emotional biases stemming from local prejudice, instinctual inclination, temperamental predisposition. In short, morals are purely arbitrary, subjective, capricious.

The True and False of Moral Relativism

It is a fact that people do differ about moral practice, but the differences are superficial rather than profound. People differ because it is not always easy to know right from wrong, and men have sometimes come up with different answers to the same moral problem just as they have in physics or in mathematics. Individuals and nations alike are affected by the circumstances in which they make their decisions, and we know that in matters where self-interest and survival are concerned moral judgment is easily warped. It is true too that peoples as well as individuals grow in the knowledge of what is right and wrong and a culture that is young may sanction practices which in the light of accumulated experience would be condemned as wrong.

It is not true to say that because some people have customs and laws different from others that they have different moralities. They may have different ideas of what is right and wrong about *some* things, but the differences are reflected against a broad background of agreement. A *really* different morality would be one, for example, in which it would be just and right to praise a man for murder; ingratitude would merit heartfelt thanks; robbery, cruelty, calumny, would be civic virtues; children would be taught tales in school about the heroes of old who stole from the blind and poisoned their parents; the honest cashier would be a scandal, the brave soldier a traitor; the atheist would be praised from the pulpit, the virtuous warned to mend their manners. This is what a *really* different code of morality would mean.

Moral Relativism Cannot Be Lived

The case of the skeptic in morals closely parallels that of the absolute skeptic in general—it is in practice impossible for him to live the doctrine he claims to hold—the doctrine, namely, that there is no fundamental difference between right and wrong, that the words have no meaning, or that if they do they can't be known. The moral skeptic cannot help but lead his life as though there were standards universally agreed to—that his wife will not whimsically put arsenic in his food, that his cronies will not cheat him at cards, that his employer will not steal his salary.

Even the moral relativist will strive to defend himself against a charge of unfairness, will appeal to some standard by which he justifies himself. If he is maliciously labeled a child beater or a blackmailer he is more likely to sue for libel than shrug it off with the reflection that standards vary or that terms are relative. He will react indignantly if he is accused of fascism or communism, although logically political morality should be just as fictitious and arbitrary as individual morality. The complete moral relativist, in short, is not found outside books and classrooms.

Moral Standards

When people disagree on what is right and wrong, how are we to decide who has the right answer? What is to be our test or standard of judgment? A number of answers have been given: the amount of pleasure an act will bring us, whether it will help us make money, or become a leader of society, or build the perfect state, and so on. We have seen, however, that the purpose of human life is realized in none of these partial goods but only in the possession of

God, the Being who is all-good. An action is called right or wrong, good or evil, according as it takes us toward or away from our goal, according as the well-being of our nature is benefited or frustrated. To judge rightly of human actions, therefore, we have to know what human nature is and its place in the scheme of things. Human nature, then, as seen by reason in its right relation to all reality, will be the test or standard by which we judge the morality of our actions. And because reality is an ordered whole and human nature the same in all men, the standards of morality will therefore be the same for all men.

Knowing our destination does not solve our problems. We can still make mistakes about how to get there, choosing what is bad for us when we think we are choosing what is good. To help us find the right road nature has given us two guides—one external, the other inward. Our outer guide to good conduct is the natural law, the given order of nature, including human nature, to which man must conform himself, and which he knows by reason. The inner guide to good conduct is conscience, man's individual reason telling him how to harmonize his individual choices with the right pattern of things.[1]

Natural Law, The Exterior Guide to Conduct

If a rock falls from a cliff and hits us on the head we do not punish it. We do not blame the pig for being greedy or reproach the leopard for its cruelty. It is their nature to be that way. It is the law of their being. But when a human being strikes us, or is greedy or cruel, we blame him and say he should act differently. For the law of man's nature is not the same as the law of a stone or an animal. The stone and the animal must act the way they do. Man could act differently. The stone and the animal have a built-in drive toward the goal proper to their natures. Man's nature is open, he can determine his own goal, he is free.

---

1 To these the theologian would add the grace of God and the law of God as revealed in a way much more sure and much more complete than in the natural law.

Man's freedom is not a blind freedom. He is given the power of reason by means of which he can discern the overall order of things to which he *should* conform himself. The overall order of things is the law of the universe, the law by which God regulates all creation. Man's law is to put himself through his free actions in conformity with what reason tells him is his true end. This is what is meant by the natural or moral law: man's rational and free participation in the overall order established by God. It may be defined as *the eternal law or disposition of things as known by reason, to which man must conform himself if he is to realize his end.*[2]

The natural law, then, is not made by man, but is based on the structure of reality itself. It is, therefore, the same for all men and all times, an unchanging rule or pattern which is there for us to discover, and by means of which we can rationally guide ourselves to our goal.

The Knowledge of the Natural Law

Man has a connatural, lived knowledge of the natural law long before he makes it explicit in codes and formulas.[3] When people make appeal to fair play, demand square treatment, apply the golden rule, they are spontaneously invoking the natural law. When St. Paul speaks of "the law written in the hearts of men," he is referring to our native capacity to know the natural law. The "unwritten law" of the Greeks is the natural law, the law invoked by Antigone in her proud defiance of the Theban King:

For me it was not Zeus who made that order.
Nor did that Justice who lives with the gods below mark out such laws
    to hold among mankind.
Nor did I think your orders were so strong that you, a mortal man,
    could over-run the gods' unwritten and unfailing laws.

---

2 Cf. St. Thomas, *Summa Theologiae*, I—II, 91, 2: "The natural law is the sharing of the rational creature in the eternal law." See also Maritain, *The Rights of Man and Natural Law* (New York: Charles Scribner's Sons, 1947), p. 61.

3 On the knowledge of connaturality see above, Chapter 10.

Nor now, nor yesterday's, they always live,
    and no one knows their origin in time.
So not through fear of any man's proud spirit would I be likely to neglect
    these laws, draw on myself the gods' sure punishment.[4]

Man's reflection on his own conduct gives rise to the explicit formulation of the precepts of the natural law. And just as there are
absolutely basic, self-evident first principles of the speculative intellect, so too there are self-evident first principles of the practical
intellect. The rock bottom evidence for the intellect in its practical
activity, the most evident principle, and the one from which flow all
the principles of the natural law, is the principle "Do good"; that
is, do what is right in order to attain the goal of human nature. Put
negatively it becomes the principle of non-contradiction, as it were,
of the practical order: "Avoid evil"; that is, do not perform activities
that will frustrate or destroy your nature.

The primary principles of the natural law are those which follow immediately on the awareness of what is radically good or evil
for our nature, so that, as St. Thomas says, "Whatever is a means
of preserving human life or of preventing destruction pertains to
the natural law."[5] And similarly with the means of preserving the
species and the realization of our rational and social nature. These
principles are spelled out in such rules as the Ten Commandments
and are so basic as to be evident to all men.

Besides these most common principles of the natural law there
are "secondary and more particular precepts which are like proximate conclusions of the first principles."[6] These more remote
implications of the primary principles find expression in such precepts as those regarding the education of children, the stability of
family life, the demands of hospitality, and the prohibition of their
contraries, such as the neglect of children, divorce or polygamy,

---

4 Sophocles, *Antigone*, II, 450-460. Trans. by Elizabeth WcKoff. (Chicago: University of
   Chicago Press, 1954.)
5 *Summa Theologiae*, I—II, 94, 2.
6 *Ibid.*, 6.

wanton injury to others.

Although men cannot help but know, once they reach the use of reason, that they should do good and avoid evil, nevertheless the force of circumstance—inherited bad customs, poor instruction, low cultural level, for example—can be such that when it comes to the knowledge of the less immediate implications of the natural law, it is possible to find variations in the answers they give. Anthropologists and historians, for example, have made it clear that primitive man's knowledge of the natural law was often confused, often mixed up with magical rites and tribal taboos. Just as it took man a long time to separate out and clarify the laws of physical nature, so too for the laws of moral nature. Only with the passage of time have some of the more profound implications of the natural law become apparent. Slavery, for instance, is now recognized as wrong, though it was once regarded as a normal and natural thing. Judicial torture, once universally employed, is looked on with horror when it appears again in human society.

These growing sensitivities do not mean of course that there is any change in the natural law. It simply means that with the slow growth in knowledge through the centuries, with the accumulated wisdom of human experience, more profound and subtle implications of the natural law are laid open to our understanding.

Rights and Duties

Because he can know and co-operate in the attainment of his own proper end, man has the *duty*, the moral obligation, to do those things which will lead him to his goal and to avoid those things which will take him away from it. Since it is his duty to strive for that goal, he has the *right*, the moral right, to demand those things which are the necessary means to his final end.[7]

Some rights are more basic than others; the right of survival, for example, is more fundamental than the right of ownership and would therefore take priority over it. Thus, a man starving to death

---

7 For a discussion of the foundations of rights and duties, see Chapter 22.

would have the right in justice to the surplus food of his neighbor. A distinction is made, too, between natural moral duties, based on the natural law, and positive moral duties, which are based on positive law. Similarly we distinguish between natural rights, such as the right to educate our children, and civil rights, such as the right to vote, the right to a jury trial, and so on.

Moral duties based on the positive law of the land are binding if they are not in conflict with the natural law. Our civil rights are similarly related to the natural law, as flowing from it. So deep is this dependence of positive law on natural law that a law of the state which goes against the natural law is not binding on the citizen. In the words of St. Augustine, "an unjust law is no law."[8]

Conscience, The Interior Guide to Conduct

The natural law is known to us in the form of broad general precepts: Honor your father and mother, Do not kill, and so on. But our immediate choices are always made in a world of particular, concrete, individual things. We have to know then how to fit the general law to the demands of the unique occasion.

The natural law is meant for all men, but no two men ever find themselves in exactly the same situations in life. The moral problems of the soldier are not those of a doctor; those of the businessman differ from those of the schoolteacher. The moral climate of a dictatorship is not that of a democracy. The path of right conduct is not laid out in the same way in a concentration camp as in a monastery. No one can predict the circumstances under which he will have to apply the precepts of the natural law tomorrow. There is need therefore of an interior guide to conduct, a means of determining how the natural law should be applied in these particular, concrete circumstances by this particular, unique individual. The practical judgment by which we decide whether or not in the light of the natural law a particular action should be taken is called the judgment of conscience. Conscience therefore may be defined as

---

8 *De libero arbitrio*, I, 5.

the judgment by which the practical reason applies our knowledge of the moral law to each particular human act.[9]

Can Conscience Err?

Reason, then, directed toward moral action, is the internal rule of man's conduct. It cannot err about the self-evident first principles of morality—do good and avoid evil—any more than the speculative intellect can err about the self-evident first principles of being. When we are obliged, however, to apply these principles in the complicated and unpredictable conditions of everyday life, error is always possible. Thus we find people in all good conscience making different, even contradictory moral judgments about the same thing.

This does not invalidate the moral law any more than a mistake in arithmetic invalidates the laws of mathematics. It simply means that it is sometimes difficult to know what is right and wrong. It is for this very reason, we might observe, that we are given external aids in the form of the revealed laws of God and the positive laws of human society, both of which spell out, as it were, the implications of the natural law.

Conscience and Feeling

Conscience is sometimes confused with the feelings and passions that accompany the act of choosing. But while our feelings and passions usually reinforce the judgment of conscience, they are not an infallible guide. Our feelings sometimes run contrary to what we know to be right or wrong. It is possible, for example, to have strong feelings of antipathy toward people of a different race or color simply because they are different in race or color, yet reason tells us that judgments and actions based on such feelings are foolish and immoral.

If these feelings were our guide to morality, then morality would be truly subjective, and the same thing could be right and wrong

---

9 See St. Thomas Aquinas, *Summa Theologiae*, I, 79, 13.

simultaneously. But a little reflection will indicate to us that morality is not a matter of blind feeling. The so-called "voice" of conscience is none other than the directing and ordering power of reason telling us in the light of objective moral principle what we should or should not do.

Summary

An investigation of the rational foundations of morality reveals that the differences among people about what is right and wrong are on a comparatively superficial level. There is both an objective and a subjective aspect to morality. The moral law has an objective foundation because the laws of nature, including human nature, are the same for all men. There is a subjective factor in moral choice because the fulfillment of the individual involves applying the moral law under unique and particularized conditions. The external guide to conduct is the natural law, man's rational insight into his place in the over-all order of things. The internal guide by which we apply the natural law to our particular, individual situation is conscience, the judgment of reason about what should be done here and now.

CHAPTER 19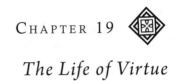

The Life of Virtue

Virtue solely is the sum of glory
And fashions man with true nobility.
MARLOWE, TAMBURLAINE, I, 1941.

Morality is not just a set of rules, a collection of do's and don'ts imposed on us from the outside, but rather a way of life, the way by which we fulfill the possibilities of our nature. The law, whether the natural law or the revealed law, has to be interiorized before the life of morality really begins. We have to make the law our own, willing it according to the light of our own intellect, making it part and parcel of our very being. The interior means by which we do this are those general habits of right behavior which we call the virtues, a kind of "second nature" which is grafted onto and completes the original endowment of nature.

The Meaning of Virtue

The word *virtue* tends today to have a much more restricted meaning than it had in the past. In popular usage it has even come to have a faintly derisive connotation, as though there were something soft or effeminate about it. Yet for the man of the renaissance, virtue was synonymous with qualities of strength and vigor. (Our expression "strength of character" comes pretty close to expressing what the renaissance man meant by "virtue.") The English word "virtue" comes from the Latin *virtus*, which is rooted in the word vir (man), and for the Romans virtue signified actions that were manly and heroic. The Greek word meaning virtue (*areté*) had an even wider application, and referred to all kinds of excellence. Socrates and Plato, with their deep interest in the problems of human conduct, were the first to explore the meaning of virtue and its role in the formation of character. Aristotle, relating virtue to habit, gave the concept its philosophical precision.

Virtue As a Habit

According to Aristotle and St. Thomas, virtue is a species of habit. A habit may be defined as "a permanent quality according to which a subject is well or badly disposed in regard to either its being or its operation."[1] Those habits which modify the being itself of the person—habits such as health or beauty—are called entitative habits. The second kind of habit affects the operations or powers of man and it is this class of habit which has to do with virtue and vice.

Some of man's powers, such as the agent intellect and certain physical powers, breathing, for example, are always active, capable of always operating at their peak when called upon. Other powers are purely passive, needing the constant stimulus of some outside agent before they can function; our sense of sight is an example. There are some powers, however, which are midway between these two—capable of some activity from the beginning, but capable also of more perfect operation. This last class of powers can, with repeated exercise, acquire permanent dispositions which enable them to act with greater facility and exactitude. The permanent dispositions thus acquired are called habits or virtues. The powers capable of being perfected in this way are four in number:

1. The possible intellect
2. The will
3. The concupiscible appetite
4. The irascible appetite

---

1 B. Wuellner, Dictionary of Scholastic Philosophy (Milwaukee: The Bruce Publishing Company, 1956), p. 54. See also St. Thomas Aquinas, *Summa Theologiae*, I—II, 49, 1.

The first two are spiritual powers. The other two, though rooted in the sensible sphere, are under the guidance and control of the intellect and will and therefore share, as it were, in their spirituality.

Virtue Defined

Virtue as defined by St. Thomas is *a good quality or habit of the rational powers which renders them capable of acting rightly, and which cannot be used badly.*[2] Virtue is termed a quality or habit because it is a kind of increase or growth within the power, a super-excellence or perfection of the power. Virtues are called habits *of the rational powers* because they refer to specifically human powers of the soul as against instinctive responses or physical mannerisms, which are not habits in the strict sense. (One of the common psychological errors of our day is to explain virtue as a kind of physical conditioning.) Since the virtues strengthen the powers, they *render them capable of acting rightly* (as against the vices). The phrase *which cannot be used badly* distinguishes the virtue from natural dispositions, which are capable of being turned in the direction of either good or evil. The virtues cannot be used badly because there is nothing arbitrary or capricious about them. They are the ways a human being must be if human nature is to be fulfilled.

The Kinds of Virtue

The virtues are either intellectual or moral, according as they perfect man's knowing or appetitive powers. (See Table, p. 149.)

The intellectual virtues fall into two classes: those which perfect the intellect in its *speculative* activity, and those which perfect it in its *practical* activity.

The primary virtues of the speculative intellect are threefold. First, *the habit of first principles*, which perfects the intellect in the initial intuitive activity by which it seizes things in their existential reality. Implicit in the first judgment of existence is the awareness of those intelligible veins which radiate through the core of being

---

2 See *Summa Theologiae*, I—II, 55, 4.

and which we designate as the first principles of being—the principles of identity, non-contradiction, and so on. Since the intellect can be made more and more sensitive to the evidence of these principles and their ramifications, we can therefore speak of a habit of first principles.

The second habit of the intellect is the habit of *science*, whereby the intellect possesses in a habitual way the knowledge which expresses the necessary, intelligible connections of things in the world around us: thus, arithmetic, biology, physics, would all be habits of science. There is third the habit of *wisdom*, whereby the intellect has habitual knowledge of the deeper, ultimate intelligible structures of things. This is the habit of philosophy.

The primary virtues of the practical intellect are *art* and *prudence*. These are the basic habits of the practical order, the realms of making and doing. The virtue of art is the habitual right reasoning about things to be made. The various divisions within art, the useful arts as well as the fine arts, are examples of the artistic habit. The virtue of prudence is the habitual right thinking about things that have to be done in the moral order. Although, strictly speaking, prudence is an intellectual virtue, it is perhaps more commonly called a moral virtue, since it is directed toward moral matters.

The moral virtues are fourfold if we include prudence. Besides prudence the other three are justice, temperance, and fortitude. Justice is the virtue which perfects the will, enabling it to order our acts rightly in relation to our fellow man. Fortitude is the virtue which helps us to act rightly and easily in the realm of the irascible appetite. Temperance is the virtue which strengthens and orders the passions of the concupiscible appetite.

The Interrelation of the Cardinal Virtues

The moral virtues, prudence, justice, temperance, and fortitude, are called cardinal (from the Latin word meaning "hinge") because they are the virtues "on which the moral life turns and is founded."

It was a point of controversy among the Greeks whether the moral virtues were one or many. Aristotle held that the virtues are manifold because they perfect different powers: the practical intellect, rational desire, and the different sense desires. The interdependence of the virtues is such, nevertheless, that both Aristotle and St. Thomas held that it would be impossible to find one in separation from the others.

St. Thomas illustrates this interpenetration of the virtues by pointing out that there are four intrinsic factors within each virtue, corresponding to the four cardinal virtues. Thus, to be virtuous, every action must be done knowingly and with right reason; in other words, it must be prudent. Second, since all our actions have repercussions on the environment in which we find ourselves, they must be rightly ordered with regard to the other persons to whom we are related—to our neighbor and to society; and the virtue that rightly orders our actions in relation to our fellow human beings is the virtue of justice. Third, we must persist in the face of sensible obstacles if our actions are to be carried through, and for this we must be strengthened by the virtue of fortitude. Finally, since we make our choices through the medium of individual sensible goods to which we are attracted, our choices must be tempered, moderated, well regulated, in relation to sensible goods. This is the work of the virtue of temperance.[3]

To understand the interdependence of the virtues, we must distinguish between the virtue itself which is the relatively permanent, undeviating habit rooted in the soul, the habit of acting temperately, for example, and a virtuous tendency, such as a natural disposition toward acting temperately, which could be the source of many temperate actions and still not be the virtue of temperance. We must distinguish too between isolated choices and the habit itself. It is possible for a coward to perform just actions, and a drunkard may perform courageous actions. Yet the lack of any one of the virtues will make the possession of any of the others unstable, and to that extent, therefore, they will be short of being habits. The cowardly

---

3 "The virtues separated from another cannot realize the full measure of virtue, for that is not true prudence which is not also just and temperate and firm." St. Thomas Aquinas, *Summa Theologiae*, I—II, 65, 1.

man may be a very just judge, for example, until moral pressure is exerted on him, making him give a biased judgment; lacking fortitude, in other words, he ceases to be just. Similarly, a man who is intemperate will sooner or later sacrifice prudence or justice to satisfy his intemperate demands—the drunkard, for example, will make his family suffer to satisfy his thirst.

In short, the moral life is a whole life, and it cannot be lived in parts, some good and some bad, any more than your breakfast egg can be partly good and partly bad. It is man himself, not his powers taken separately, who in the last analysis is morally good or evil. The virtuous man is the whole man, the well-balanced man, who is most fully human because he lives with his human powers of mind and of will, developed to the peak of their possible perfection.

The Meaning of Vice

Just as virtue signifies the perfecting, the fulfillment of human nature, so does vice mean a falling away from, a degradation, of human nature. Whereas the habit of virtue implies a growth, a further perfection of man, the habit of vice indicates a relatively permanent loss, a lack of some good that should be there, a deformation rather than a fulfillment of human nature.

The source of bad or vicious actions is the human will. When the will makes a choice which is against the right order of things, it falls short of what a good choice should be and therefore is called vicious—that is, lacking something.

For Aristotle, virtue consists in the mean: it avoids the extremes of too much and too little. Since excess is possible in either direction, there are two vices corresponding to each of the virtues. In the case of prudence, for example, there may be an excess of prudence—overcaution, overdeliberation; or there may be a defect of prudence—too little deliberation, rash judgment.

Although we generally thus envisage virtue as the mean between extremes, from another point of view, as Aristotle again points out, the virtue is itself an extreme, since it is the best of a particular line of conduct, with the falling off from this peak of perfection being characterized as vice.[4]

The Supernatural Life of Virtue

1. The State of Man According to Christian Theology

Life according to the natural virtues represented the road to happiness for the Greeks, but it was not happiness itself. For they saw that final happiness consists not just in the search for truth, but in the contemplation and possession of truth. They knew that man had the deep thirst for truth and goodness that could be satisfied only by the full possession of truth and goodness, but they could see no natural satisfaction for that thirst.

From the standpoint of the Christian, the ethics of the Greek philosophers is not adequate. An ethics that is adequate will take into account the actual, existential condition of man, which is known, as far as the Christian is concerned, only through revelation. If the Christian stops at the philosophical answer, considering man just in his natural condition, he is talking about something that doesn't exist. From the standpoint of Christian revelation there is no such thing as a "natural" man. As soon as man was created he existed in a state of supernatural grace; that is, over and above the normal endowment of human nature, he was given certain gifts which enabled him to live the life that would lead to eternal life with God Himself.

Through the fall of our first parents, the gift of divine life was thrown away. Although man continued to be man, henceforth the conditions which allowed, him to achieve the highest fulfillment of human capacity were missing. Neither could existence in this state be called "natural," since man was not intended to live apart from God's grace.[5]

---

4 See Aristotle, *Nicomachean Ethics*, II, 8.

5 The word "nature" is used differently in the Augustinian and in the Thomistic traditions, and to confuse them leads to grave difficulties. Nature for St. Augustine means the actual, existential state in which man finds himself. Since the actual state of man after the fall is different because of the loss of the supernatural grace which belonged to

Once man had lost the gift of supernatural grace he was powerless to win it back—like the spendthrift who has thrown away his fortune. Only God Himself could repair the damage. Christ, the Man-God, reunited in His own person the human and divine natures, and through His death on the cross repaired the loss of the fall. Henceforth, through the rebirth of baptism, man is able to live again the life conferred by supernatural grace.

2. The Theological Virtues

Through the fruits of the Redemption, man can once more lead the divine life for which he was originally intended. But just as man needs the natural virtues to live well on the natural plane, so does he need virtues to live the life of grace—no longer the natural virtues, but the supernatural virtues, which God gives him to help him lead his new life.

The first, and indispensable, of the supernatural virtues, are the theological virtues of faith, hope, and charity. They are called theological virtues because they are given to us by God and unite us directly to His life. They are known to us, like all the supernatural virtues, only through revelation.

Faith, a divinely infused habit of the intellect, is the gift from God that initiates us into the divine life, making it possible for us to give our intellectual assent to things not in themselves evident to the intellect. The basis for this assent is the authority of God revealing.

Hope is a virtue of the will, which enables us to desire what would otherwise seem a goal inconceivably beyond our powers.

Charity, also a virtue of the will, is the great virtue which enables

---

his previous state, it is therefore possible for St. Augustine to speak of the nature of man being corrupted. For St. Thomas, on the other hand, using the terminology of Aristotle, to change the nature of man would be to change his kind of being, his essence; therefore St. Thomas stressed that the nature of man remained the same after the fall as before, the consequences of the fall consisting, not in the corruption of nature, but in the loss of the supernatural grace which nature needs for its perfect functioning. Regardless of the different and sometimes clashing terminology, both traditions stress the fact that man before the fall and man after the fall are the same being; in the one case, however, healthy, in the other sick and in need of curing.

us to love God as He should be loved.[6] The Christian sees charity
as the transforming virtue, the virtue that breathes life into all the
others. For just as a man may acquire technical skill as a painter or
musician and yet lack the inspiration of the true artist, so too a man
may perform all the outward actions of the virtuous man and yet
lack virtue. Charity is the great gift that pours the divine life into
the soul and makes all the virtues, natural as well as supernatural,
flourish and overflow the boundaries of selfish concern. "Morality
is not complete until the contrast of self and others ceases to be
relevant, and that belongs to the sphere of love, in which alone duty
and happiness are fully one."[7]

3. The Supernatural Cardinal Virtues and the Gifts

As further helps to the leading of the supernatural life man is
given the supernatural cardinal virtues of prudence, justice, temperance, and fortitude, which orient the natural cardinal virtues to
man's true end. (The special demands of the life of supernatural
virtue explain the contrast between the good man of Aristotle and
the Christian saint. Natural prudence or temperance, for example, is
often shocked by what looks like the imprudent or the intemperate
actions of some of the great saints of Christianity.)

A final set of supernatural helps, the seven Gifts of the Holy
Ghost, enable man to respond readily to the promptings of the Holy
Spirit. These Gifts are: Wisdom, Understanding, Counsel, Fortitude,
Knowledge, Piety, Fear of the Lord. Understanding, which helps us
to understand what is revealed, and Knowledge, which helps us to
discern the content of belief, are gifts associated with the virtue
of faith. The Fear of God, that is, the fear of the loss of God's
love, and Wisdom, the knowledge of things in their divine origin,
are Gifts especially associated with hope. All the Gifts, finally, are
founded in charity. (The Gift of Counsel refers to the strengthening
of man's practical reason, the Gift of Piety orders man in relation

---

6   See above, page 107.

7   D. J. B. Hawkins, *Nature as the Ethical Norm* (London: Blackfriars, 1951), p. 18,

to his fellow man, and the Gift of Fortitude strengthens us in the face of spiritual danger.)

Summary

Virtue is a kind of habit and has its seat either in the intellect or will, the specifically human powers, or in the sense appetites in so far as they are under the control of intellect and will. Virtues fall into two principal classes—intellectual and moral—according as they perfect the knowing or the desiring side of man's nature; the intellectual virtue of prudence is also termed a moral virtue because its matter is concerned with the moral life. The moral virtues are deeply interconnected, so that the health of one depends upon the stability of all. Vice is the contrary of virtue, and represents a permanent bad disposition opposed either to the attainment of truth or the performance of the good. The pattern of the virtuous life is completed only with the divinely infused supernatural virtues— theological and moral—if man is considered in his character as a being intended to work out a supernatural destiny.

CHAPTER 20

The Virtues of the Individual Person

It is not enough to know about virtue but we must try to have and use it.
ARISTOTLE, *NICOMACHEAN ETHICS*, X, 9.

Prudence, temperance, and fortitude are called the private or individual virtues because they are especially concerned with perfecting the individual person. Justice, as the virtue which perfects us in our relations with other human beings, is called by contrast the social virtue.

The distinction between individual and social virtues, though valid, is apt to be misleading. When we speak of perfecting the individual person we must remember that human fulfillment is not achieved in isolation. To seek happiness in indifference to the rest of mankind is to choose for a sterile selfishness rather than for the good.

There is no such thing as a strictly private act. We are so closely linked to all our fellow men by the bond of our common humanity that our individual failings or virtues are reflected in the whole of society. If I am a drunkard in private, even though I am careful not to harm any particular person, I am nevertheless sinning against society by dissipating energies and talents that could otherwise contribute to the common good. My private folly, my private extravagances, weaken the fabric of the whole. For the virtues, as we have already seen, are so tightly interwoven that an offense against any of the so-called private virtues is also a sin against justice, the social virtue.

The Virtue of Prudence

Prudence is a habit of the practical intellect which enables man to reason rightly about moral actions. St. Thomas defines it as "right reason about things that have to be done."[1] The only one of the moral virtues which is a habit of the intellect, it is sometimes called the master virtue, because as the virtue which perfects the intellect, the "seeing" power, it is its task to regulate the others. The various powers of desire, which are the seat of the other virtues, are blind powers. Left to themselves they know no limits. Even the virtues can run wild, as Chesterton says, and then they become vices. Hence the primacy of prudence as the virtue which furnishes the leaven of reasonableness and direction to our moral life.

There is both a knowing and a willing aspect to the virtue of prudence—as indeed to all virtues. The knowing aspect is apparent in the fact that planning and deliberation are necessary before we can choose in a way that will insure our reaching our good. This implies the capacity to learn and profit from past experience, for only in the light of experience can we develop the habit of making sound judgments about human conduct. For this reason Aristotle said that you cannot teach virtue to the young; they have not yet gained the breadth of experience required to form the virtue of prudence.[2]

We learn not only from our own experience but from that of others too: of friends, parents, teachers. This ability to learn from others—from the great teachers of the past as well as from living teachers—is called docility—not "tameness" or "meekness," but "teachability."

The second aspect of the virtue of prudence, the willing aspect, relates to the carrying out of what the prudent judgment prescribes. It is not enough to be able to judge well; we must be able to

---

1 *Summa Theologiae*, I-II, 57, 5.
2 *Nicomachean Ethics*, I, 3.

apply our judgments. Many people are capable of giving very good advice while they are themselves incapable of carrying it out, just as many people are good literary or musical critics without themselves being artists.

Prudence, then, must carry out the application of our moral judgments. In applying our decisions such things as the proper circumstances of time and place, the limitations of human nature, and so on, must be taken into account. Good advice, for example, if given at the wrong time can provoke a person to the contrary action. It is also a mark of prudence to anticipate the practical consequences of our actions, so that we will not prescribe a course of conduct that is foredoomed to failure. If, for instance, we make too many New Year's resolutions or take on an overambitious program of Lenten penance we usually end up by doing nothing. Inopportune social reform also violates this aspect of prudence. Prohibition is an example of an intended reform which was imprudent because it made impossible demands on human nature.

The Kinds of Prudence

Individual prudence is the virtue we all need to act rightly in view of our last end. But there are lesser ends to which man is also directed, way stations as it were on the road to our final destination. Such are the ends of family life and civic life. Prudence is needed here also for the right direction of our actions.

The wise guidance of family life is called domestic prudence —Aristotle called it economics. This is a virtue needed on the part of children as well as parents, for a prudent family life is not possible without the co-operation of all its members. Careless or extravagant children, for example, can undo the prudent financial planning of their parents.

Still another species of prudence is required for the wise governing of the political community. This is the virtue St. Thomas calls regnant prudence. Just as in the case of the family there is also a need in the state for a special prudence on the part of those who are subject to authority. Prudent cooperation on the part of the citizen in achieving the aims of the community is called political prudence, or as we would term it today, civic virtue.

A last species of prudence is military prudence, which has to do with the wise defense of the community by its armed defenders—primarily those in high command, but secondarily also by their subordinates.

In addition to these distinct species of prudence, there are what we might call specialized aspects of individual prudence: the problems calling for prudence in the field of law, of medicine, of commerce, of teaching, and all the other particular vocations.

Vices Related to Prudence

Imprudence in general may be by way of excess or by way of defect. Vices by way of excess have to do with an exaggerated concern for material goods, wealth, position, power, pleasure, and so on. Prudence may be wrongly applied, too, as when, for example, a thief lays careful plans for a robbery. (St. Thomas called this perversion of wise foresight "astuteness" rather than prudence, indicating that prudence wrongly applied is no longer prudence.)

Among the vices which result from a defect of prudence are rash judging—judging, that is, without sufficient reflection or care—and inconstancy, the habitual failure to carry out the judgments of prudence.

The Virtues of the Sense Appetites

Man's pursuit of goodness is complicated by the fact that he is a creature on the border line of two worlds, the world of spirit and the world of matter. Although we will the good in general as proposed to us by our intellect, our immediate choice is always of some thing or action in the order of concrete sensible things. But we react to sensible things in terms of pleasure and pain. The reasoned choice of the good cannot therefore be isolated from the feelings and passions that accompany the apprehension of our senses.

Although pleasure and pain are generally trustworthy indications of what is good or bad for us, they can mislead us in two ways:

we may overvalue pleasure and the avoidance of pain, so that they can draw us away from our right path; or, we may wrongly estimate what is good and bad for us—we know from experience that some pleasant things are harmful to us and that some painful things are really good for us. The blind drive of the senses toward pleasure and away from pain must therefore be controlled and guarded by reason. Since these drives are strong and unruly, special help in the form of virtue is needed in both the concupiscible and irascible appetites. The virtues which raise these drives to the properly human level, putting them under the control of reason, are temperance and fortitude.

The Virtue of Temperance

Temperance is the virtue which puts the concupiscible appetite in order. It is habitual right ordering of the desires for the sensible goods which we need for everyday living. It is defined as *the habit of the concupiscible appetite which subjects it to the rule of reason.*[3]

The main problems of temperance lie in two directions: problems relating to the desire for food and drink, and problems relating to sex. These drives, connected to the basic senses of touch and taste, are stronger than those connected with the other senses because they are so intimately linked up with the instinct for survival—of the individual on the one hand, of the race on the other. The principle by which the correct mean is determined in these desires is their right regulation according to the end in view.

In the case of food and drink, the end in view is bodily health, and thus the norm or standard would be that which best contributes to good health. Although this principle is constant, the circumstances in which it is applied will of course vary. Because of the great difference in the physical make-up of people, for example, a moderate meal for one person would be gluttonous for another. Or again, although right reason tells us that to use alcohol to the point of insensitivity is wrong, there are emergency situations when it may

---

3 See St. Thomas, *Summa Theologiae*, 141, 1.

be so used—as an anesthetic, for example.

The sex desire is implanted in us to insure the continuance and increase of the human race. This therefore will be the principle according to which right conduct in matters of sex will be judged. Sexual promiscuity has to be condemned on the score that it endangers the welfare of any offspring. Artificial birth control and abortion are clear perversions of the ends for which we have been given the sex instinct.

A final and important aspect of the virtue of temperance is that by placing the sense appetites under the control of reason, it links them to the higher side of man's nature, ennobling and spiritualizing them by raising them above the level of brute animal drives and giving them a share in the life of reason itself.

Vices Relating to Temperance

The vices of excess associated with the virtue of temperance relate to the immoderate love of goods in the sensible order: gluttony, drunkenness, sensuality, and so on.

The vice of defect associated with temperance is the general disregard or insensitivity to the goods needed for the reasonable wellbeing of the individual and of the race. A Jansenist or Puritanical distrust of sensible goods such as food and drink or of normal and necessary appetites such as the sexual desire, far from being a mark of virtue, is a vice, a falling off from the virtuous, the temperate, mean.

The Virtue of Temperance in the Light of Theology

The severe asceticism of some of the saints is occasionally assailed on the ground that it represents a vicious falling away from the true moderation which is the essence of temperance. The Christian, however, sees in the heroic self-denial of the saints the very peak of temperance, transformed by its supernatural motivation. Because of man's fall there is a disorder among his powers, and in order to discipline them and restore the lower powers to the control of reason, man may have to deny himself certain goods which are otherwise the objects of perfectly legitimate desires.

Temperance is not, however, a negative thing. On the contrary, it is an affirmation of the worth and dignity of material things as being creatures from the hand of God. Even inanimate things have been created for the honor and glory of God, and therefore they should be loved by us without greed or irreverence. Temperance is the virtue that insures that we will love God in His creatures with the love that is proper to them, not exploiting and perverting them with a disordered love.

The Virtue of Fortitude

The virtue of fortitude or courage is closely associated with the virtue of temperance because it also is concerned with our attitude toward pleasure and pain, this time however in relation to objects which represent great hardship or danger, especially the ultimate danger, the threat of death itself. Fortitude is the virtue which strengthens and moderates the irascible appetite, so that we can endure physical pains and face great danger reasonably. It especially illustrates the aspect of stability and constancy which is a mark of all virtue, and it may be defined as a habit of the irascible appetite which subjects it to the control of reason in the enduring or repelling of grave danger.[4]

The greatest danger which can confront man is the danger of death—the shattering of his very personality. Some sort of courage is always needed to face up to this inevitable prospect. Great self-control—and therefore the virtue—is needed to stand firm in those situations where it must be faced voluntarily: for the soldier under fire, for the doctor confronting contagious disease, for the martyr facing savage enemies. "Properly," says Aristotle, "he will be called brave who is fearless in the face of a noble death, and of all emergencies that involve death."[5]

The irascible passions, as we have seen (Chapter 12), are complex,

---

4   See St. Thomas, *Summa Theologiae*, II-II, 123, 2.
5   *Nicomachean Ethics*, III, 6; 1115 a 32.

involving both love and hate: love for the good perceived, hate for the obstacle which is a barrier to the good. The response of courage to a dangerous situation will also, therefore, be a complex one, including both fear and hope: fear because our lives are in danger, hope in the prospect of escape or of triumph.

Fear is always a condition of courage, for there are some things which all men should fear. "He would be a sort of madman or insensible person," says Aristotle, "if he feared nothing, neither earthquakes nor the waves, as they say the Celts do not."[6] Not lack of fear—for death is one of the things any normal man should fear —but the greater fear of doing something unworthy of man, is the mark of courage.

The other factor involved in courage is hope or daring—hope in the realization of the good which is at present beyond our power, or daring in the face of the evil we are trying to avoid.

Counterfeits of Courage

Not every bold action is courageous, and Aristotle scrutinizes five situations which produce a false appearance of courage:[7]

1. Actions which are performed for the sake of honor or to avoid disgrace do not meet the full requirements of courage. Although such actions may be virtuous, to win esteem or to avoid reproach are only accidentally associated with courage, whose essence consists in the facing of danger because the rule of reason calls for it.

2. The courage evinced by professional soldiers who assume that because of their superior skill or armament they have nothing to fear is only apparent. Once this superiority disappears such men are liable to be the first to run away.

3. The anger which is often a factor in courage is sometimes mistaken for the virtue. But the man who is spurred by uncontrolled anger acts rather as an animal than a human being. Such men are "pugnacious but not brave."

---

6 *Ibid.*, 7; 1115 b 26.
7 *Ibid.*, 8.

4. Overconfidence or wishful thinking can be a source of counterfeit courage. This is like the courage of the drunkard, for as soon as the intoxication of self-deception wears off rashness turns to cowardice.

5. The last example of false courage is the calmness which results from the complete misapprehension of danger—the courage of a man facing a lion thinking it is a rabbit. Aristotle instances the case of the Argives who boldly attacked the Spartans mistaking them for a much weaker enemy. When the truth became known, the Argives took to their heels.

Vices Relating to Fortitude

The vices relating to fortitude reflect the complexity of the virtue. Since courage calls for a proper fear in the face of death, there may be either excess or defect; the man who fears too much is called a coward and the one who fears too little is called rash.

In relation to the hope or daring which the virtue calls for, there may again be excess or defect. Once more the defect is termed cowardice, and the excess rashness or foolhardiness.

Summary

The virtues of prudence, fortitude, and temperance have to do especially with the perfecting of the person in his private activities and justice has to do with the perfecting of his actions in relation to the good of others. The first are called, therefore, individual virtues, while justice is called the social virtue.

Prudence, as the only moral virtue of the intellect, is called the regulatory or directing virtue. Besides the universally needed individual prudence, different states of life call for other species of prudence: domestic, regnant, political, military.

Temperance as a good habit of the concupiscible appetite, has to do especially with the moderation of sense desires in regard to pleasure and pain. Fortitude, the virtue of the irascible appetite, enables us to exercise rational control over fear and boldness in the face of great evil.

CHAPTER 21

Justice, The Social Virtue

Justice gives to each man his due, neither more nor less.
ST. THOMAS AQUINAS, *SUMMA THEOLOGIAE*, 64, 2.

The virtues of prudence, temperance, and fortitude are primarily concerned with our individual problems, problems that arise out of our response to the way things affect us. But besides being acted upon, we also act upon other things and other persons. The virtue that puts our public actions in order and relates them to our ultimate end is the virtue of justice. We may therefore define it as *a habit of the will which makes us render to each his due.*

Justice is a virtue of the will, of man's power to choose the good as rationally apprehended—the good in its general aspects, that is, as against the particular, individual goods with which the sense desires are concerned. It takes into account man's social nature and makes sure that in our choice of goods we will observe the reasonable good of other human beings.

The Kinds of Justice

In the *Republic* Plato equates justice with general human rightness. It is the harmonious fusion of all the other virtues. "Justice in this sense," comments Aristotle, "is not part of virtue but virtue entire."[1] Because of its universal application justice in this sense is called general justice.

---

1 *Nicomachean Ethics*, V, 1; 1130 a 9.

This meaning of justice emphasizes the inseparability of all the virtues—justice or general rightness is a part of any virtuous action, just as are prudence, temperance, and fortitude—but it does not give us the special virtue with which we are here concerned.[2] The general principle behind the special or cardinal virtue of justice is the insuring of what is due to others—both collectively in the community, and individually. There are accordingly two major divisions within the virtue according as it has to do with the common good or with the private good of other individuals. These divisions are termed respectively legal justice and particular justice.

1. Legal Justice

Legal justice defines the right relation of the individual to the common good, and is in turn divided into the two categories of equity and common legal justice.[3]

Justice from the standpoint of equity takes into account special circumstances which qualify the literal precepts of justice. Thus, for example, although justice says to render to each his due, it would be an act of folly to give back a loaded revolver to its drunken owner. Equity also deals with those situations which involve a mixture of rights. A builder may fail, for example, after he has completed nine tenths of his contract. Equity says he has some right to the value of his work even though he failed to complete it. Equity, in short, stresses rightness absolutely, the spirit or the intent as well as the letter of the law.

Common legal justice refers to the exact carrying out of the law for the sake of justice within the community. The strict letter of the law may have to be qualified, as we have seen, by the demands of equity.

---

2 St. Thomas, *Summa Theologiae*, 113, 1.

3 Legal justice is also sometimes called general legal justice—"general" as referring to the general or common good. "General legal justice" should not be confused with the wider term "general justice."

2. Particular or Individual Justice

Particular or individual justice—justice, that is, as it orders our actions in relation to the private good of our neighbor—is also divided into two categories: *distributive justice*, and *commutative justice*.

Distributive justice is concerned with the fair distribution of common goods (for example, a proportionate share in the natural resources of the community), of social benefits (education, civic honors, and so on), and of the common tasks and burdens (such things as taxes, civic offices, military duties). It is a proportionate justice, taking into account the individual circumstances of persons; a juvenile delinquent, for example, should not in fairness receive as drastic treatment as a mature criminal. A man who donates his time and energy to the service of the community deserves more honor from the community than the man who contributes nothing.

At the same time, distributive justice demands equality of treatment for persons of the same status. The teacher who shows favoritism to a student because of athletic prowess and the politician who gives public jobs only to his nephews are equally guilty of offending against distributive justice.

Commutative justice, or the justice of exchange, deals with equality in the exchange of goods, without any regard to the persons involved. This is the aspect of justice exhibited in the acts of buying and selling—the general exchange of goods and services on a roughly equal basis. In other words, where distributive justice stresses the proportional equality of persons, commutative justice stresses the numerical, the one for one equality of persons. The equality of what is exchanged is the principle behind this aspect of justice, which demands a fair return for another's goods or services. To drive a hard bargain by taking advantage of another's misfortune (to inflate food prices in time of famine, for example) or to take advantage of another person's weakness (for instance, to get a man drunk as a preliminary to doing business) or to cheat another person because of his ignorance of the true value of what he is exchanging, is to act unjustly, and in all such cases restitution is required if justice is to be re-established.

Although our own society tends to emphasize commutative as against distributive justice—we stress such slogans as "rugged individualism," "free enterprise," "every man for himself"—it should be recognized that distributive justice is prior in nature to commutative justice. Unless, for example, there is a fair distribution of the goods and opportunities of social life to start with, an insistence on commutative justice only aggravates the injustice within a community. It is no good to tell a man who has to sleep on park benches that such conduct is equally prohibited to rich and poor. Distributive justice must first insure the original good distribution of the necessities due to our nature, after which the freedom of exchange comes into play.

Justice in Relation to Other Individuals

Directly or indirectly all our moral actions affect the common good. Even a private act of intemperance, as we have seen, has its harmful reverberations within society. Nevertheless, consideration for or contempt of the good of others may refer more directly to individuals than to the common good. We shall therefore investigate first the problems of justice in relation to the good of other individuals, reserving for the next chapter the more complex problems of justice in relation to the common good.

Giving to others what is due them may take many forms. Our own society often tends to limit these problems to money affairs, but there are many intangible goods which in fairness we should share with our neighbors. The subordinate virtues which illustrate particular aspects of the cardinal virtue of justice highlight these special problems of justice. St. Thomas lists these subordinate virtues as religion, piety, respect for persons, gratitude, truthfulness, courteousness, liberality.

The natural virtue of religion stresses the fact that the worship of God is part of the natural law. Even without the benefit of divine revelation, there are clear enough evidences in nature of the existence of God and our dependence on Him to call for thanksgiving and worship. We therefore in justice owe certain duties to God as a person.

The natural virtue of piety has reference to the regard we owe to family and country. The respect for persons has to do with those placed in positions of authority. We owe them the respect due to their office and we owe obedience to those placed immediately over us.

Gratitude is the habit of rendering due appreciation to others for the good they do for us. We owe to others also the duty of truthfulness, and the return of love and courteousness.

Material possessions are given to man as a necessary instrument for the leading of a good life—to help him, in other words, develop the life of virtue and attain his final end. They have value and are truly desirable in so far as they are ordered to this end. It is possible to desire material possessions too much, however, and they become an end in themselves, instead of being used as means to an end. The virtue which moderates this desire is the virtue of liberality or generosity, which is related both to temperance and to justice—to temperance according as it regulates the desire for material goods, to justice according as it distributes their superfluity.

Vices Opposed to Justice

Opposed to the just mean of liberality are the extremes of avarice and prodigality. Both avarice and prodigality are offenses against justice because they deprive others of things they need in order to live well—the decent minimum necessary to a life of virtue.

The extremes of quarrelsomeness and adulation are the vices opposed to friendliness. The rules and techniques sometimes advocated as short cuts to the winning of friends and the influencing of people are a form of adulation to the extent that they are based on calculations of self-interest rather than a true esteem for others.

Lying, which is a deliberate false communication of our thoughts, can never be squared with justice, though circumstances may modify the seriousness of the untruth. The lie which is told as a joke, for example, is not as serious as the lie meant to harm another.

A humorous exaggeration not calculated really to mislead anyone would not be considered a lie. Similarly excluded would be the polite forms of everyday usage—"the boss is in conference"—which social convention has established as formulas for refusing to see someone. The prisoner's plea of "not guilty" is another such social convention. It means simply that the accused person contends that there is not enough evidence to convict him.

The careless use of these social conventions can easily lead, however, to the so-called "white lie," which no matter how mitigated by circumstances is still a violation of justice. The prudent person will take good care to avoid situations which might call for the use of the "white lie."

The failure to acknowledge the good done for us by other persons is the sin of ingratitude. There can also be vicious excess by way of too much gratitude. This vice is rare.

Neglect, physical or otherwise, of those closely related to us by family ties is a vice contrary to the virtue of natural piety. The love of country which this virtue calls for may also be vicious, both by way of excess and by way of deficiency.

The natural reverence for God, finally, may be vitiated by neglect, perjury, superstition, and idolatry.

The cruder forms of irreverence toward God, such as idolatry and superstition, have pretty well died out, but as Aldous Huxley points out they have been superseded by what he calls the "higher idolatry"—a much more insidious and pernicious form of idolatry. "The many varieties of higher idolatry," he says, "may be classed under three main heads: technological, political, and moral. Technological idolatry is the most ingenuous and primitive of the three; for its devotees, like those of the lower idolatry, believe that their redemption and liberation depend upon material objects—in this case gadgets. . . .

"Only a little less ingenuous are the political idolaters. For the worship of redemptive gadgets these have substituted social and economic organizations. Impose the right kind of organizations upon human beings, and all their problems, from sin and unhappiness to nationalism and war, will automatically disappear. . . .

"The moralists . . . commit idolatry inasmuch as they worship, not God, but their own ethical ideals, inasmuch as they treat virtue as an end in itself and not as the necessary condition of the knowledge and love of God—a knowledge and love, without which that virtue will never be made perfect or even socially effective."[4]

Summary

Justice is called the social virtue because it insures the rightness of our actions in relation to other human beings. Justice used in a wide sense to refer to human goodness in general is called "general justice." The strict usage of justice, where it refers to the cardinal virtue, has the following divisions:

I. Legal justice
  1. Equity
  2. Common legal justice
II. Particular justice
  1. Commutative justice
  2. Distributive justice

Subordinate virtues which illustrate special aspects of the virtue of justice, particularly in our relation to other persons (as distinct from the common good), are the virtue of religion, piety, respect for persons, gratitude, truthfulness, courteousness, and liberality. Excess or defect in any of these regards constitutes the vice of injustice.

---

4 Aldous Huxley, *The Perennial Philosophy* (New York: Harper & Brothers, 1945), Chapter 2.

CHAPTER 22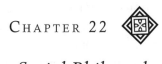

Social Philosophy

One man in misery can disrupt the peace of a city.
ANTOINE DE SAINT-EXUPERY, WIND, SAND, AND STARS, CH. 9.

Problems of justice arise not only in our private dealings with other individuals but also from our relationship to society as a whole. For the man who does not live in society, says Aristotle, is either a beast or a god.[1] Unless we live as an animal in the woods, we are dependent at least materially on the society within which we find ourselves, sharing in the physical heritage of the community: roads, buildings, cities, manners, and customs—all the accumulation of labor, skills, wealth, wisdom from past generations. Nor can we live as gods, in splendid isolation and independence, for mankind is one and we are "involved" in it. Even the sage or the saint who frees himself from the ordinary bonds of human weakness and dependence is impelled to share his illumination, to re-enter the cave, as Plato says.

The Nature of Society

Society in general refers to any union of persons which aims, under a constant authority, at a common end. The unity of a society is a moral unity, the common purpose of the group providing the bond of union. A mob of persons, though it may be united in a

---

1 See *Politics*, I, 2.

common purpose—in a street riot, for example—is not a society because it lacks the directing authority which insures the realization of its goal. Similarly, a group of animals can be called a "society" only metaphorically, since they lack the bond of some ideal goal rationally grasped.

Societies may be of many kinds, depending upon their origin and end. According to origin societies are natural, such as the family and the nation, or contractual, such as labor unions or veterans' organizations; according to their end, they are characterized as civil, religious, fraternal, and so on.

Social Philosophy and the Social Sciences

Social philosophy must be carefully distinguished from the social sciences. The social scientist—that is, the sociologist, political scientist, economist—establishes, connects, and explains matters of social fact. The social philosopher critically *evaluates* these facts, and tries to establish their purpose. The scientist gives the facts and says this is so. The philosopher evaluates the facts in the light of his own principles, metaphysical, psychological, and ethical, and says this *ought* to be so.

As soon as you have an idea of what man is—and we all have, either unconsciously absorbed, or consciously thought out for ourselves—you have an implicit social philosophy, for we cannot help but form further ideas about how men are related to each other. Whether you judge that men are intimately and naturally related to each other, or only accidentally and artificially related, a whole host of consequences follow which must be worked out and evaluated philosophically, unless we are content to drift and let others supply our social philosophy for us.

Is Man Social By Nature?

Is it the nature of man to be constantly at the throat of his fellow man, or is it his nature to live at peace with him? Is peace, as some men say, merely the interval between wars, something unnatural or, contrariwise, is it the state of warfare which is the disruption of the normal? Both points of view are upheld today, as they were at the time of the Greek sophists, and the first point for the social philosopher to establish is whether or not man is social or anarchic by nature.

Human society for Aristotle is something that flows from man's rational nature, since the fully rational life cannot be realized except in society. In the *Politics* he tells us that the gift of speech makes it evident that man is a more social animal than "bees or any other gregarious animals. Nature, as we say, makes nothing in vain, and man is the only animal whom she has endowed with the gift of speech. And whereas mere voice is but an indication of pleasure or pain, and is therefore found in other animals . . . the power of speech is intended to set forth the expedient and inexpedient, and therefore likewise the just and the unjust. And it is a characteristic of man that he alone has any sense of good and evil, of just and unjust, and the like, and the association of living beings who have this sense makes a family and a state."[2]

Of all human societies the family is the most basic, answering as it does to the most fundamental of human needs, both physical, as in the care of children, and moral, as in the need of human beings for love and companionship. (We know that an infant can die for lack of affection as well as for lack of physical care.) Beyond the family, Aristotle sees the more complex communities of man growing naturally out of the physical needs of man—the diversity of talents within mankind leading to the division of labor and the delegation of responsibility.

Is Man Anti-Social By Nature?

For the philosopher who holds that man is by nature anarchic, human society is an artificial and unnatural structure. The English philosopher Thomas Hobbes (1588-1679) envisaged man in the state of nature as living solely according to his passions and

---

2 *Politics*, I, 2; 1253 a 6. (All quotations from the *Politics* are taken from the translation of Benjamin Jowett [Oxford: The Clarendon Press, 1921].)

instincts. Man is a predatory animal, and the natural state of man is a state of war—*homo homini lupus*. "Hereby it is manifest," Hobbes says, "that during the time men live without a common Power to keep them all in awe, they are in that condition which is called Warre; and such a warre, as is of every man, against every man."[3] One of the deepest instincts in man, however, is the instinct for survival, and to keep from being exterminated primitive man chose to sacrifice his natural freedom in order to secure the benefits of peace. Accordingly he surrendered his liberty forever to a single strong man or group of men who guaranteed to keep order. This pact by which we voluntarily subject ourselves to an absolute ruler is called the social contract. Once this pact is established, all men must submit "their Wills, every one to his [the ruler's] Will, and their Judgments to his Judgment." And, "by this Authoritie, given him by every particular man in the Common Wealth, he hath the use of so much Power and Strength conferred on him that, by terror thereof, he is enabled to forme the wills of them all."[4]

The famous French philosopher Jean Jacques Rousseau (1712–1778) also rejected the view that reason and reciprocal help were the social bonds which united man in society. For him, too, the natural state of man is a state of total, unrestricted liberty. Unlike Hobbes, however, Rousseau made primitive man naturally good. The "noble savage" lives solely according to his feelings and is corrupted by society and by reason.

For Rousseau, too, the origin of the state is in a "social contract." Primitive man surrendered his private liberty to the collective will of the community, which Rousseau termed the general will. The general will can never be wrong, and as long as we obey it we are realizing our true freedom, whether we know it or not. The individual, in other words, can sometimes mistake our true will, and Rousseau would force us to be free by obeying the general will,

---

3 *Leviathan*, I, 13. Everyman edition (London and New York: J. M. Dent and E. P. Dutton, 1950) p. 103.
4 *Ibid.*, II, 17, 1; p. 143 of Everyman edition.

which is always right.[5]

Both Hobbes and Rousseau rest their doctrine on their view of the nature of man. Both stress the animal side of man, suppressing or denying his rational element. As against their doctrine are the facts of anthropology, which can unearth no evidence of the original "wild beast" state which preceded the imagined primitive contract, and the facts of human nature, which contradict both Hobbes' savage animal caricature of man and Rousseau's sentimental picture of innocent savagery. There is no need of the "contract" hypothesis to explain the existence of human societies. Man needs his fellow man for his reasonable development. Man is social because he is rational.

Rights and Duties in Relation to Society

Just as philosophers differ about the origin of society, so too they dispute the foundation of rights and duties. For those who hold that man is rational and free, and therefore social by nature, the foundation of right and duty is in the natural law. Our rational insight into the natural law tells us what we *ought* to do to realize our destiny, and our duties are precisely those things which the natural law prescribes for us as necessary. But as a correlative to this obligation, we have a claim on those goods which we need to carry out our duties. We have a right to them. Duties and rights are, then, something which flow out of the very nature of man. This is the reason why we describe certain rights, such as freedom of speech and conscience, as inalienable: they are rooted so deeply in human nature that to remove them is to destroy or mutilate the very personality of man.

Opposed to the doctrine that our rights and duties are linked to human nature itself is the view of those philosophers who, following Hobbes and Rousseau, root the rights of man in the state itself. In the original social contract by which, according to their opinion,

---

5 This is the philosophy from which springs the tyrannical principle that the majority will is always right. Rousseau's philosophy is truly the seed ground for future totalitarianisms.

the state is founded, the individual surrenders his basic liberty as the condition for a peaceful life in society. Henceforth the state itself becomes the fountainhead of rights and duties, specifying them and changing them at will.

The repercussions of these conflicting doctrines about the nature of rights and duties are apparent in the deep cleavages that divide modern society. The modern totalitarian state, in which there is no such thing as an unjust law, is the inheritor and exponent of the doctrines of Hobbes and Rousseau. Justice is what the state says it is, and if the citizen enjoys certain rights within the community, it is by the good leave of the state, which is free to withdraw those liberties again. Similarly the state tells the citizens what its duties are, and it may change them at will, so that what is a duty today may be a crime tomorrow.

Finally, to the illusions and distortions of the naturalist philosophers who helped prepare the way for the modern tyrannical state must be added the corrosive effect of moral skepticism. There are few greater enemies to man's freedom than the moral skeptic, for whom the words "right" and "duty" are empty sounds, since what does not exist or what is illusory is not worth struggling for. In the face of apathy and doubt the, ruthless and the strong take over and "right" becomes synonymous with "might."

The Common Good

Life in society is something which is called for by the very make-up of human nature, and man freely accepts it as required for his rational development. But a human society has a nature and a destiny which is distinct from that of the individual beings that go to make it up. A family group, for example, is something more than the mere collection of individuals that compose it. It has its own good to which the individual members of the family are called upon to contribute, sometimes at the cost of great sacrifice. Similarly the civil community has its own good, a collective good which is called the common good, and which is distinct from the private good of the individuals that go to make it up.

Two distortions have to be guarded against in the realization of the common good. First, the civil community is not a collection of anarchic atoms who are free to do what they want, while the state merely assumes the role of traffic policeman. In practice this means simply that the strong are free to dominate and exploit the weak within the community. Separate and special interests in the community must be subordinated to the demands of the common good, must be regulated, in other words, in terms of the natural law, which prescribes that one man's freedom cannot be exercised at the expense of another man's basic rights.

Some kind of authority, then, which will be vigilant in the protection of the common good is a requisite of the good society. This necessity can in turn, however, lead to the second basic error —the error which sees the civil community as more important than the human beings that make it up—the collective state, the totalitarian tyranny, which completely absorbs the individual into the community.

The good of the community is such a great good that the state can legitimately ask very great sacrifices of its citizens—their time, their wealth, their labor, and in time of great crisis even their lives. What it cannot ask is hate, falsehood, treachery, any evil doing on the part of its citizens; it cannot demand, in short, the sacrifice of the citizen's eternal life, for no temporal good—and if the state lasts a thousand years, it is still a passing good—no temporal good can outweigh the supreme worth of the immortal person. The just community, therefore, will strive to avoid the dangers of either anarchic individualism or monolithic totalitarianism, reconciling in a living and sensitive balance both the rights of the individual and the just claims of the common good.

Charity and the Common Good

The final fulfillment of man, as we have seen, is eternal friendship, personal union in the love of charity, with God. But we also know that man does not realize his destiny in isolation; he is bound up in a mysterious solidarity with the rest of the human race. God's call to love is therefore a call to mankind in common, and the love which binds us to God binds us equally to our fellow man. "There must be union in friendship between those who have the same end in common," says St. Thomas. "But all men share the same last end of happiness, to which they are divinely ordered. Therefore all men should be united with one another by a shared love."[6]

Summary

A society is a moral union of persons for a common end. Differing philosophies of man have given rise to opposing philosophies of society. Some hold that society is a natural organism, necessary for the proper fulfillment of human nature. Others hold that society is artificial, against nature, the result of a contract by which men exchange their natural, individualistic state of liberty for the advantages of community life.

Depending upon one's view of the state, rights and duties are seen either as rooted in the natural law, and therefore basically prior to the community, or they are seen as conventional and arbitrary privileges dispensed at the will of the community.

The purpose of society is the realization of a good which cannot be achieved in isolation by the individuals who make up the community. The true common good of a community cannot be opposed to the real good of any individual within the community. The extremes in the interpretation of the common good are its virtual denial in the laissez-faire state and its deification in the totalitarian state.

Beyond the bond of justice which holds the community together is the deeper tie of friendship, both natural and supernatural, which flows from a common nature and a shared destiny.

---

6 *Summa Contra Gentiles*, III, 117.

PART IV

THE UNIVERSE OF MAN

CHAPTER 23

The World of Bodies

The name body can be taken in many semses.
ST. THOMAS AQUINAS, ON BEING AND ESSENCE, CH. 2.

What Is a Body?

The first and most obvious things we know are bodies and their changes. This was the initial field of investigation for the early Greek philosophers, and for them the world of nature was simply the world of bodies. It soon became clear however that it was not easy to explain what a body is, and as various theories were developed the concept of nature itself underwent radical changes, though the identification of nature with the realm of bodies was to remain one of the most persistent meanings of the word down through the history of western philosophy. We will examine first the various meanings that have been attached to the word "body," and then we will be in a position to see how this has influenced the various interpretations of the word "nature."

The answers which have been given to the question, What is a body? can be grouped according to the different fields in which the intellect operates. The first answers seem to have been given in terms of quality—in terms, that is, of what is most obvious to us, the immediate sensible aspects of things.

Body As Quality

In their search for a key to the vast multiplicity and variety of bodies, the early Greek philosophers looked for some single principle behind all the different appearances of reality. For Thales, this single principle was water. For Heraclitus, fire. For others again, the basic reality was fourfold—earth, air, fire, and water. The differences between bodies could be explained by the principles of condensation and rarefaction—fire, for example, was simply earth in another and more rarefied state—and of attraction and repulsion (manifested in human beings as love and hate).

Anaxagoras of Clazomenae, in Asia Minor, a philosopher of the fifth century B.C., made the structure of bodies much more complex in his attempt to explain change. In each particle of body, he said, there is a little of every quality which falls under the senses. Thus a drop of water would contain minute quantities of every other thing in the universe—silver, copper, wood, cotton, flesh, blood, etc. It is called water because that is the element which predominates. Anaxagoras illustrated his doctrine from the mysterious change of food into the living body. I eat bread and it turns into flesh and blood, teeth, hair, sinews, bones. If bread produces these things, they must be in it to start with. A piece of bread therefore not only contains flour and water but also minute particles of teeth, hair, muscle, sinew, and so on. Digestion is the process which separates out the elements, redistributing them in the various parts of the human body.

The alchemists of the medieval and renaissance periods similarly stressed the importance of qualities. Every substance for them is composed of an identical primitive matter onto which is imposed a certain set of qualities. Substances vary according to the different sets of qualities. The secret of the transmutation of substances was to strip the primitive matter of one set of qualities in order to give it a new and different set. Whereas density was the quality most stressed by the ancient Greeks, color seems to have been the key quality for the alchemists. Color was the most important thing about gold, for example. If you could succeed in giving any other metal the same color as gold, you would have changed it into gold.

The alchemists were strongly influenced by the Platonic doctrine that the qualities of things are a reflection of eternal types or Ideas; this participation in the unchanging types is in fact what gives a body most of the reality it has, so that by changing the qualities of a thing you can change its basic character. This particular way of looking at things dominated the thought of physicists until the end of the seventeenth century, which saw the experiments that were to lead to a revival of the atomic theory of Democritus, with its emphasis on the quantitative rather than the qualitative aspects of things.

Body As Quantity

Democritus, another philosopher of the fifth century B.C., stressed quantity as the ultimate principle of things.[1] Qualities—colors, sounds, tastes, etc.—which earlier Greek philosophers had held to be part and parcel of bodies, do not belong to bodies at all, according to Democritus, but are rather the effect produced on our senses by solid bodies in motion. "According to convention," he says, "there is a sweet and a bitter, a hot and a cold, and according to convention there is color. In truth there are atoms and a void."[2] Atoms are the ultimate, indivisible particles of matter. Although they are made up of identically the same stuff, they differ in size and shape: some are large, some small; some are square, others round, and so on. According to their size and shape, they differ in their motions and in the way they are related to each other. The differences we see in things are accounted for by the varying combinations of these identically constituted atoms.

This primitive formula of Democritus is the prototype of one of the basic ways of looking at reality. For although the atomic theory

---

1 Democritus (fl. 400 B.C.) headed a school at Abdera, in Thrace. He was still alive when Plato founded his Academy. Only fragments of his writings have come down to us.

2 Diels, *Die Vorsokratiker*, Fragment 9.

of Democritus is a far cry from the modern atomic theory, "it was entirely in harmony with modern scientific thought in making the 'real' world of matter something entirely different from the vivid colored world perceived by the senses. The conception of the real world as a vast machine, colorless, odorless, soundless, had been introduced into human thought."[3]

Body As Number

Democritus represents a peak of what might be called the materialist or naturalist tradition in early Greek philosophy—the view that limits reality, including what we call mind or soul, to body and its manifestations. Another tradition makes mind prior to body, and puts all of reality under the control of law or design. Plato names Pythagoras as the originator of this tradition.

Pythagoras, as we have seen,[4] made important discoveries in the field of arithmetic, particularly about the properties of numbers. He discovered, too, that the notes in the harmonic scale varied according to fixed numerical proportions. Pythagoras was so impressed by the discovery that even the complex and apparently chaotic world of sound could be reduced to numerical law that he affirmed number to be the actual element out of which bodies are made. The number 1 is a point, 2 is a line, 3 a surface, 4 a solid. (These are the numbers necessary to define each of these figures.) With these four numbers as building blocks he constructed the entire universe. "The Pythagoreans supposed the elements of numbers to be the elements of all things, and the whole heaven to be a musical scale and a number," records Aristotle.[5]

The confusion of physical body with mathematical body was not limited to the Greek philosophers. We find the same doctrine in the seventeenth-century philosopher Descartes—another pioneer mathematician—who defined the essence of body as extension

---

3 J. W. N. Sullivan, *The Limitatioms of Science* (New York: The Viking Press, 1934), Chap. II, Section 1.

4 See Chapter 1.

5 *Metaphysics*, I, 5; 986 a.

in length, breadth, and depth. Descartes's philosophy of nature, or rather "mathematics of nature," was to influence profoundly modern concepts of the nature of bodies. We read in Sir Arthur Eddington, for example, that "if today you ask a physicist what he has finally made out the ether or the electron to be, the answer will not be a description in terms of billiard balls or flywheels, or anything concrete; he will point instead to a number of symbols and a set of mathematical equations which they satisfy. What do the symbols stand for? The mysterious reply is given that physics is indifferent to that; it has no means of probing beneath the symbolism."[6] Or again, in the words of Sir James Jeans, "Nature is more closely allied to the concepts of pure mathematics than to those of biology or of engineering."[7]

Body As Idea

George Berkeley, a bishop of the Church of Ireland, and contemporary with Oliver Goldsmith and Dean Swift, held that bodies are only sets of ideas. The only things I know, he says, are collections of sensations, which are present to me as conscious states. "Thus, for example," he says, "a certain color, taste, smell, figure and consistence, having been observed to go together, are accounted one distinct thing, signified by the name *apple*. Other collections of ideas constitute a stone, a tree, a book, and the like sensible things."[8] Ideas and sensation mean the same for Berkeley. Custom causes me to refer to certain bundles of ideas as though to something outside of me, which I call bodies. But actually I never know anything except ideas. I have never really experienced the existence of a body, and therefore I have no right to say that there are bodies.

When I say the table I write on exists, all I can mean by that is that if I am in the room I can perceive it; that is, I can see it, feel it, and so on. In the case of objects such as tables, trees, and other unthinking things, to be is to be perceived; "nor is it possible that

---

6 *Science and the Unseen World* (London: Allen and Unwin, 1929), p. 30.
7 *The Mysterious Universe* (New York: The Macmillan Company, 1932), p. 188.
8 *Principles of Human Knowledge*, I, 1.

they should have any existence, outside of the mind or thinking things that perceive them."[9]

This doctrine, which is called Idealism, is summed up in a well-known limerick by Monsignor Ronald Knox:

> There once was a man who said "God
> Must think it exceedingly odd
>   If he finds that this tree
>   Continues to be
> When there's no one about in the Quad."[10]

Where do our ideas come from if not from things? They are furnished directly to our minds by God. This explains also how things like tables and trees continue to exist when there is no one around to see them. Another limerick, an anonymous reply to that of Monsignor Knox, makes this clear:

> Dear Sir,
>   Your astonishment's odd:
> I am always about in the Quad.
>   And that's why the tree
>   Will continue to be,
> Since observed by
>   Yours faithfully,
>   God.

Body As Form

Plato follows in the footsteps of Pythagoras, stressing the greater reality of the spiritual as compared to the corporeal. In fact the Platonic doctrine so stresses the reality of the immaterial that at times it seems almost to argue away the existence of bodies. Plato does not say that bodies are nothing but they are so close to it that they cannot even be a source of certain knowledge. For him the 'really

---

9 *Ibid.*, I, 3.

10 Reprinted with the kind permission of Monsignor Knox.

real" is the world of perfect unchanging Ideas or Forms, and the world of bodies has reality only in so far as it reflects these eternal Forms.

In the *Timaeus* Plato speaks of a kind of receptacle for Forms, passive and indeterminate, which communicates something of its own indetermination and nullity to the Forms which it receives. Bodies, starting with the primary elements earth, air, fire, and water, are the offspring of the union of Forms with the Invisible and formless being which receives all things."

To the extent that bodies are a reflection of the eternal Forms, they participate in their being and intelligibility. But they also participate in the unsubstantiality and imperfection of the shifting surface on which the Forms are mirrored. The reflection of Form in bodies is therefore a distorted one, so mixed up with change and indetermination that the principal value of bodies is to serve as signs pointing our minds to the enduring and unchanging reality of the eternal types.

The extreme of this doctrine is found in the philosophy of Leibniz[11] who does away entirely with matter in his explanation of bodies, making them consist of pure forms which he calls monads. Each monad is a complete and self-contained reproduction of the whole universe. There is an infinite graduation of monads, starting with God, who by His omnipotent decree insures the harmonious interrelation of all the monads. Monads are graded according as they possess more or less self-consciousness. The higher ones are called souls or minds, although in fact each monad is spiritual in character. What we call bodies are like souls that have never become fully conscious. The apparent extension of bodies is only appearance. Modern developments of this doctrine substitute "points of force" or "energy" for Leibniz' pure forms.

---

11 Born 1648 in Leipzig, Leibniz was the first of the great German philosophers of modern times. He was an adherent of the philosophy of Descartes, which he modified considerably. He was one of the discoverers of differential calculus and a pioneer of modern symbolic logic. In addition to the fields of philosophy and mathematics he gained distinction as a lawyer, historian, and diplomat.

Body As Matter and Form

Aristotle discerned a twofold principle in bodies: form and matter.[12] In the things around us we see manifested different basic ways of being, so that we put things in different classes. There must be in things, then, some positive, determining principle which gives them the kind of being they have—tree as against lion, for example. This principle we call form.

But each individual corporeal being only partly realizes the possibilities of its way of being. A tree, for example, is not at one time everything a tree could be—maple and oak at the same time, let us say. Beings on this level, in other words, cannot exist except as limited; if you want that perfection of animal being we call lion, you cannot have simultaneously in the same being those perfections realized in giraffe or zebra. Along with the positive, formal principle which gives things their basic way of being, we are forced to recognize also the existence of a principle of limitation which circumscribes and confines beings. This principle we call matter. Dimension, consistency, color, taste, and all the other sensible properties which we associate with bodies, are the product of the limiting of form by matter.

This doctrine of the form and matter composition of bodies is called hylemorphism (from the Greek words for matter and form). It was taken over by St. Thomas Aquinas in the thirteenth century in opposition to the prevailing Augustinian position, which closely echoed Plato on this point. For St. Augustine, bodies were a reflection of varying degrees of order, form and number against the restless background of a previously created prime matter. In the Augustinian as well as in the Platonic position there was always the danger of the world of bodies slipping away from us as mere signs or symbols of a deeper reality. In the eyes of St. Thomas, the doctrine of Aristotle, while not effacing the symbolic dimension of corporeal creation, nevertheless endowed bodies with a separate reality and independence of their own, a position which he favored

---

12 See Chapter 7.

as better according with everyday experience.

Summary

The first inquiry into the nature of the world led to the investigation of the make-up of bodies. Many answers have been given to this question in the course of human thought, some of them reflecting partially valid aspects of bodies, others arguing away their very reality. For Aristotle and Aquinas, bodies are composite substances of formed matter, reflecting in their act of existence both the properties of quantity, such as figure and number, and the various qualities of color, sound, taste, and so on.

CHAPTER 24

The Realm of Nature

About nature consult nature herself.
FRANCIS BACON, INSTAURATIO MAGNA, PART 3, INT.

The Meaning of Nature

Out of the Aristotelian notion of form grew what was to become one of the basic meanings of the word *nature*. The form of a being is its principle of operation; the form, that is, gives a thing its fundamental pattern of activity which differs according as the basic ways of being differ. Form thus regarded as the principle of operation can be called nature.[1] From this point of view number and qualities as rooted in forms may also be considered as elements in the nature of a thing.

The sum total of individual natures can also be called nature. In this sense it corresponds to the word nature as used by the early Greek philosophers, standing for the ensemble of all bodies. Using nature in both the senses we have isolated, we can say that nature is made up of natures.

When we consider the nature of man our problem broadens. Man is corporeal and therefore belongs to nature considered as the sum total of bodily creatures. But on the side of his intellect and will man is open to another, noncorporeal order. What are we to call this other

---

1 From the Latin *nata*—the set of operations for which the thing has been born, we might say. The corresponding Greek word is *physis*, a word meaning growth. This is the source of our word "physics."

part of reality? It can also be called nature, though then it should be understood as nature on a different level. For some philosophers, anything above the corporeal order is called super-nature.

When the use of the word nature is broadened to cover that part of reality which is not corporeal, a further distinction again may be made. Nature may be limited in its application to the totality of creation, or it may refer to everything that exists, including God. ("God or Nature," says Spinoza.) In other words for some philosophers nature and the real are identified, though they may differ very widely about the meaning of reality; thus for the materialist philosopher, reality—and therefore nature—is body only, while for the idealist, reality—and therefore nature—is immaterial only.

For those who limit the word nature to the realm of the corporeal, any intrusion of man's intellect or will into the physical world demands a new set of distinctions: thus natural may mean the spontaneous, the elemental, the instinctive, as opposed to the artificial and acquired; for example, the state in which man is born is the state of nature as against the state of civilization, or the uncultivated and wild state of plants and animals as against the cultivated and the domesticated.

We may note, finally, that in a theological context the state of nature may be opposed to the state of grace.

Nature As Caused

One of the marks of Aristotle's philosophy is its stress on purpose in nature. Nature is not an aimless thing. If we have digestive organs it is because there is food to be digested. If we have eyes it is because there is something to see. And similarly if we have intellects it is because reality is intelligible. If I ask the "why" of things I can hope for an answer. The whole endeavor of science and philosophy presupposes this over-all reasonableness of reality. Everything must have its adequate reason, though our intellects may not always be able to discover it.[2]

---

2 Our intellects, as we have already seen, are geared to a particular, limited range of

From the very fact that things have being, then, they are intelligible. Things may have the full reason of their being in themselves, in which case they are said to be self-sufficient and their own nature is their explanation; or they may have part of their explanation in things outside themselves—some other being is needed to explain them. Beings that are not self-sufficient, not self explaining, are the only ones of which we have direct experience, for everything that falls under our senses bears the mark of having come into existence, of depending therefore on something prior to itself for its existence and for its explanation.

If a thing's reason for being must be sought outside itself, then instead of using the word "reason" we can use the word "cause." The word "cause" indicates that we are dealing with beings that are not self-sufficient, that have a beginning of some kind. The term "cause," in other words, is more restricted than the term reason." It answers the question "Why" about things that come into being. We may define a cause as *any positive factor*—as against a negative factor, such as a necessary condition—*on which something depends for its existence*. The product of the causal action is called an *effect*.

The Fourfold Division of Cause

Greek philosophy at first contented itself with assigning a single cause in attempting to explain the reason for a thing. The philosophers of nature looked for some single kind of matter, such as water or fire, as the source out of which all things came. Other philosophers, as we have seen, designated numbers or forms as the single explaining principle of things. Assimilating the partial truths in all these positions, Aristotle asserted that four different kinds of cause contributed to the production of any bodily substance. Two of these causes are intrinsic to the thing, the others extrinsic.

The union of matter and form in the thing are the intrinsic causes of its being. The form, as we have seen, is the positive, determining

---

reality. Being may offer too much or too little intelligibility for us, just as the sun may offer too much or too little light for our eyes.

principle which gives a thing its basic way of being. The matter is the passive, determinable principle, the principle of limitation without which the form could not be realized.

The extrinsic factors in the production of a new substance are again twofold. The first is the activity from without which is required to bring about the actuality of a hitherto unrealized possibility—this outside factor is necessary because if the possibility could realize itself it would never remain a possibility. The second extrinsic factor is the goal or purpose for which the new being comes into existence. These last two factors are called efficient and final causes.

The Origin of the Fourfold Division of Cause

The discrimination of the four kinds of causality, the four different ways in which we can answer the question "why," probably came about originally from the analysis of works of art, of human production. In the making of a statue for example, there is a real dependence of the final result on the kind of material we use—wood, stone, plastics, etc. Hence our first kind of cause, the material cause, is *that out of which* the thing is made. Again we may observe that the kind of statue we make depends on the form we impress on the matter—the Venus de Milo, for instance, as against "The Thinker" of Rodin. Thus the formal cause is the likeness or form which tells us *what the thing is.*

The efficient cause is *that by which* the effect is produced—in this case the sculptor. (The sculptor's chisel would be called an instrumental cause.) The final cause is *that for the sake of which* the activity is performed, and it may refer either to the work itself or to the agent who produces the work. Thus we may say that the end or aim of the work of art is to show forth the likeness of Venus or, referring to the artist, we may say the whole chain of activity was motivated by the artist's desire to produce a work of beauty or to earn money. Whichever motive dominates is called the principal end; other motives are called secondary ends.

By analogy from works of art, Aristotle extended the notion of a fourfold causality to the works of nature. Each thing in nature is a formed matter, brought into being by a cause external to itself, and ordered to some goal. To understand a thing is to discover the causes that have made it. To trace these lines of causation was to be from henceforth the goal of scientific exploration.

Summary

Nature may refer (1) to the individual bodily thing considered in its active, substantial character; (2) to the sum total of individual bodily natures, with anything outside the world of bodies being called supernature or supernatural; (3) to the totality of creatures, as distinct from the Creator; (4) to all reality, including God; (5) in a theological context, nature is used in opposition (or contrast) to supernatural, which refers in a wide sense to anything relating to the order of grace, in a narrow sense to the union in charity with God.

A cause is any positive factor on which something depends for its existence. There are four basic kinds of cause: intrinsic—formal and material; and extrinsic—efficient and final.

PART V

THE UNIVERSE OF BEING

CHAPTER 25

In Quest of Being

The formal object of the intellect is being, just as color is the formal object of vision.
ST. THOMAS AQUINAS, *SUMMA CONTRA GENTILES*, II, 83.

Beyond the question of what it means for a thing to be a body, or to be a living being, or to be a human being, there is the even deeper question of what it means to be at all, or of what it means to be in one way and not in another. If the philosopher is to push his exploration of reality to the deepest point, he must investigate the mysterious universe of being.

The Philosophy of Being

Any approach to reality which seeks to discover exactly what it means for a thing "to be" can be called a philosophical approach. The investigation of being itself, however, in its simple, intelligible purity—as it applies to God, angel, man, atom, to any being whatsoever—is philosophical investigation in the strictest sense. Aristotle called this science the First Philosophy, because it studies first principles and first causes. He also called it Theology, the science of God, since if we trace the lines of being far enough they will take us back to God as the ultimate source of all being.[1] The name metaphysics was eventually given to Aristotle's "first philosophy," partly because of a historical accident, partly because it is an apt name. An

---

1 See *Metaphysics*, VI, 1.

early editor of the works of Aristotle, Andronicus of Rhodes (cir. 50 B.C.) placed the treatises on being after the books dealing with physical things. Because it had no title of its own he simply labeled it "After the Physics." (The "meta" in "metaphysics" is the Greek preposition meaning "after.") Since for man the natural path of understanding is from the visible things of nature to those higher realities which do not fall under the senses, the name metaphysics— coming after physical things —is a fitting name, and it has persisted as the most general name for this body of knowledge.

Ontology, the science of being, is another name given to the philosophy of being. The name was first coined by the French philosopher Duhamel (1682) from the Greek words 'on, 'ontis (being) and *logos* (science), and later was given wide currency by the German philosopher Wolff (1730).

The Awareness of Being

Our primary contact with being is through the medium of our senses, which make us aware of the various things existing around us—flowers, trees, mountains, butterflies, birds, human beings. Behind the manifold sensible appearances of these things we are aware in a vague, confused way of one common trait—all exist or are capable of existing—which enables us to give to all of them the name "being." This is the common-sense awareness of being. This ordinary everyday awareness of being is, however, unscientific —confused, unreflexive, common to child and adult alike. The awareness of being is there, but it is implicit, taken for granted. This intuition of the being embedded in the sensible reality, this common-sense certitude that things exist, is not yet the metaphysical awareness of being; if it were, even the child would be a metaphysician.

A special effort, a trained sensitivity of the intellect, is required to penetrate through the partial, particularized manifestations of being—the manifestations of color, movement, quantity, so many veils, as it were, which must be pushed to one side so that being, just being in all its intelligible purity and richness, is brought into focus for the intellect's contemplation. Not until then is the being which is the special concern of the metaphysician laid bare.

In other words, there is more than one way for the intellect to take hold of reality. It may stop at the rough, superficial aspects of things, the surface likeness with which reality is engrained, or it may penetrate to the inmost structural likenesses which radiate out of the very core of reality. The name *total abstraction* is given to the first way of seizing reality, *formal abstraction* to the second. The nature of our concept of being will vary according as we take either of these approaches to reality.

Total and Formal Abstraction

Common sense can get immediately at the actual existence of material things, and it can use a vague recognition that the different things which it lumps together have something in common. It stops however at the widest and most obvious strata of universality. It sees, for example, in dog, cat, horse, elephant, the universal "animal." It sees in gold, silver, platinum, the universal "metal." In all of these together it sees the universal "bodily substance," and it sees that the latter class is larger, more universal than the former ones. This kind of abstraction, where there is relatively little content, is called *total abstraction*.

But the intellect can grasp individual realities in a different way. It can contemplate reality through one or other of the specific features, the formal structures, which make this reality to be what it is. The philosopher, for example, sees in dog, cat, horse, elephant, the intelligible content "sentient being." The biologist sees the intelligible content "vertebrate mammal," and so on. This kind of abstraction, where the movement of the intellect is intensive and penetrating rather than extensive and discursive is called *formal abstraction*.

Total abstraction, the simple taking of the whole out of the parts, is the abstraction characteristic of common sense. Formal abstraction, the penetration to the intelligible articulation within the whole, is the abstraction characteristic of scientific knowledge.

The Degrees of Formal Abstraction

Formal abstraction itself may take place on different levels, as the intellect penetrates further and further into the heart of reality. On the first level of formal abstraction, the intellect concentrates on the material qualities of things, such as colors, sounds, hot and cold, rough and smooth, seeing them apart from the individual in which they are found. Thus redness, for example, is the same whether the intellect is first aware of it as given to it in a red rose or in a red flag. This is the level of the natural sciences and of the philosophy of nature, which studies the moving, changing qualities of material being.[2]

The intellect may, however, move to a still deeper plane, discovering a new universe of forms and their relations to each other. This time not only are the individual and changing characteristics of things transcended, but also their qualitative characteristics, so that the intellect focuses its gaze solely on those universal aspects of material bodies which have their roots in quantity. Here are exposed the secrets of extension and numerical structure, and on this level we find the mathematical sciences and the philosophy of mathematics.

The most profound and ultimate layer of reality to which the intellect can penetrate is the level of being itself, which is common to all reality, since the least that can be said of a thing is that it is not nothing. On this level the intellect sees what it means for a thing to be, and the concept being, which for common sense was the widest and emptiest of all, suddenly becomes for the philosopher the richest and most meaningful. No longer imprisoned in those sensible realities which are first presented to us by the senses, the concept of being is abstracted by the intellect from all conditions of individuality, of quality, of quantity, and we consider solely what it means for a thing to be. This is the level of metaphysics, and the exploration of this new world of meaning is the work of philosophy at its highest pitch.

---

2 For a fuller treatment of the degrees of abstraction, see the last chapter, "The Perennial Philosophy."

The Analogy of Being

The word "being" applies to everything that is or can be, even to possibilities, for whatever is not nothing is being. (If we can't say "being," we can only say "nothing.") Being, then, is something that belongs to all things. Yet one being is not another being, nor one way of being another way of being. Things, in other words, not only agree in that they are all beings, but they also differ by their very being.

Any being whatsoever may evoke the whole universe of intelligibility which is implicit in the word "being," and yet every being is unique, isolated, separate from every other being; in a certain sense every being is final, ultimate. We are confronted in short with one more instance of the mystery of sameness and difference. And in trying to penetrate this mystery we must not forget the primary data revealed by our intellectual intuition of being —namely, that being is common to everything that is, but that at the same time things differ by their very being.

We say that God is a being and that a stone is a being. Man is a being and a possibility is a being. But the being of God is infinite, and the being of a stone finite. My being is actual, but the being of my grandchildren is potential. They can all be called being in that they are all "not nothing." But they differ in the way they are "not nothing": all the distance between potential and actual, between finite and infinite. The likeness we assert for such beings when we apply the same word, being, to them cannot be found, then, in terms of what they are, for the gap between a finite being and God is infinite. The likeness must be sought elsewhere.

Besides direct likenesses, such as those between members of the same class, there are indirect likenesses "founded solely on the similitude of two relations, as when we say of a ship's captain that he is king on board, to express that the captain is to his ship what the king is to his realm."[3] It is this second kind of likeness, an indirect

---

3   A. D. Sertillanges, *Foundations of Thomistic Philosophy* (St. Louis: B. Herder Book Company, 1931), p. 79. Cf. St. Thomas, *Summa Theologiae*, I, 13, 1-5; *Truth*, 2, 11.

likeness, which is found between otherwise dissimilar beings. The likeness affirmed by the word being is the likeness of a certain proportion which is found within any being whatsoever. For the being each thing has is proportionate to its kind of existence. A stone, for example, exists in the way proper to mineral being and it differs from the way in which an animal or an angel exists. All are beings, but they differ in their very way of being, for an animal may be said to have in some way more being than a stone, just as an angel would express more being in its existence than would a tree or a flower.

To express this likeness of proportionality, we say that the term being is used analogically. Analogical is from the Greek word meaning proportion. There is a likeness of proportion between beings and at the same time a dissimilarity of being. Being is proportionate to the essence in which it is found, but essences themselves are of different kinds. Thus we can say that beings have something in common because they are beings, yet differ by their very being.

Two extremes of error are possible if we ignore the analogical character of being; if we forget, in other words, what we started out with—the awareness of the simultaneous sameness and difference of being. The one extreme cancels out the "difference" aspect of things and says that when you call things being you mean exactly the same thing in each case. Then all being becomes one. God, man, stone: all are one because all are being. This doctrine, that all things are one, is called *Monism*: a special form of Monism is *Pantheism* which does not distinguish between the being of God and the being of anything else.[4]

The other extreme of error is to emphasize the difference of beings to the point where their "sameness" aspect is denied. This doctrine, which is given the name *Radical Pluralism*, says that strictly speaking no two things should ever be given a same name, not even the name being, since they are completely different. The American philosopher William James[5] went so far as to suggest that the word

---

4 We have already met this doctrine in Parmenides. See Chapter 3.

5 William James (1842-1910), a brother of Henry James, the novelist, taught at Harvard where he held professorships first in philosophy and later in psychology. A gifted

Universe, which means combined into one, should be changed to the word "Pluriverse" as better expressing the true nature of reality. Reality, from this point of view, is broken up into a number of disconnected chunks which have nothing whatever in common, not even being.

Only the awareness of the essentially analogical character of being enables us to steer a path between the extremes of these two errors. The principle of analogy is the sole means which enables us to explore the mysteries of reality without doing violence to its nature.

Summary

The ultimate question we can ask of anything is about its very being. The science which explores the mystery of being is philosophy in the strictest sense, and is called metaphysics or ontology. Being as we first know it is the vague, general being of common sense. To disengage being from its sensible matrix is the goal of formal abstraction at its highest level. The intuition of being on this level of abstraction reveals it as analogous, realized proportionately in its different subjects. The recognition of being as analogous enables us to avoid the extremes of Monism, which lumps together all beings as one, and Pluralism, which fragmentizes reality into an infinity of totally unrelated parts.

---

writer, his espousal of the pragmatic philosophy and his brilliant studies in experimental psychology exercised a profound influence on intellectual life in America.

CHAPTER 26

Transcendentals of Being

And just as it is with being, so too with the one and the good, which are convertible with being.

ST. THOMAS AQUINAS, *SUMMA THEOLOGIAE*, I, 6, 4.

The concept of being is a magic key which unlocks the door to a whole new universe of meaning, for the reality which it brings before the mind is so luminous with intelligibility that it overflows the limits of its idea—it is so rich in import that we have to use new concepts to express these new flashes of meaning. These new concepts do not add anything to being for whatever they express is also being; they simply make explicit for us what is already implicit in the idea of being.

The Ways of Adding to Being

St. Thomas points out in a classic text[1] that there are two ways in which we can unfold these latent meanings of being. The first is to express the basic ways of being itself; that is, whether or not the being is, at least relatively, "a being in itself," equipped for separate existence, so to speak, such as a tree, a bird, a man, or whether its way of being is such as to require existence in something else, as in the case of being red, or round, or smiling. In this case we have to

---

1 *Truth*, 1, 1. The quotations which follow are taken from this text. Translated by Robert W. Mulligan, S.J. (Chicago: Henry Regnery, 1952).

do with the division of being into substance and accident.

The second way is to make explicit the manners of being that are common (analogously) to all beings whatsoever. In this second case we have to do with what are called the transcendentals of being. Being itself is transcendental in the sense that it rises above all divisions and categories. The other transcendentals are simply other ways of saying being, of describing characteristics of being that are coextensive with being but which the concept being itself does not make explicit. They are so many ways, in other words, of saying what all beings whatsoever—infinite or finite, actual or possible— manifest in common.

Within this second way of making explicit the modes of being there are again two points of view possible. We can first consider the mode of being expressed by each being absolutely, taken just by itself. In this way the mode of being "expresses something in the being either affirmatively or negatively. We can, however, find nothing that can be predicated of every being affirmatively and, at the same time, absolutely, with the exception of its essence by which the being is said to be. To express this the term *thing* is used ... there is, however, a negation consequent upon every being considered absolutely: its undividedness, and this is expressed by *one*. For the *one* is simply undivided being."

Instead of considering every being absolutely, we can also consider the mode of being expressed by every being relatively, according, that is, as it is considered in relation to something else. Here again there is a twofold distinction.

"The first is based on the distinction of one being from another, and this distinction is expressed by the word *something*, which implies, as it were, *some other thing*. For just as being is said to be *one* in so far as it is without division in itself, so it is said to be *something* in so far as it is divided from others.

"The second division is based on the correspondence one being has with another. This is possible only if there is something which is such that it agrees with every being. Such a being is the soul, which, as is said in [Aristotle's] *The Soul*, is 'in some way all things.'

The soul, however, has both knowing and appetitive powers. *Good* expresses the correspondence of being to the appetitive power, for, and so we note in the *Ethics*, the good is 'that which all desire.' *True* expresses the correspondence of being to the knowing power, for 'all knowing is produced by an assimilation of the knower to the thing known.' "

Some philosophers would put in a further addition to being at this point, namely, beauty, as "the splendor of all the transcendentals together." Beauty implies according to St. Thomas a simultaneous relation to both intellect and will. It relates to the will according as it gives pleasure. It relates to the intellect according as it implies a kind of knowledge. Beauty, in short, is good considered under a special relation—according, that is, as it is known.[2]

We will endeavor to explore these various facets of being, starting with being in its transcendental aspects. Since "thing" says little more than "being," and "something" resolves into the same property as "one," we will limit our study to unity, truth, goodness, and beauty.

Ways of Adding to Being

I. Special Manners of Being:
    1. Absolutely . . . . Substance
    2. Dependently . . . . .Accident:

                                             quantity
                                             quality
                                             relation
                                             action
                                             passion
                                             time
                                             place
                                             posture
                                             habitus

---

2 Cf. St. Thomas Aquinas, *Summa Theologiae*, I, 5, 4 ad I.

II. Manners of Being which belong to all Being in general:

1. Absolutely
   - Affirmatively ..... { being / thing
   - Negatively .... one

2. In relation to some other being
   - Negatively .... something
   - Affirmatively ..
     - as related to intellect. . true
     - as related to will .... good
     - as related to intellect and will ...... beautiful

Unity

St. Thomas characterizes unity as "the absence of division within a being."[3] What this implies is that every being has its distinctive nature, is constituted essentially in a uniquely determined fashion, so that if its basic structure is changed it becomes another kind of being. There is something, in other words, that makes a tree, for example, to be what it is. As long as those elements essential to being a tree are there, the being remains the same—one and the same thing. Although its accidental properties can change, it remains substantially one. Potentially it can be basically changed, of course, turned into wood pulp, or ashes, for example, but then its way of being is changed. If a thing loses its basic unity, in other words, its being has been changed.

Unity, like being itself, is analogical. The undividedness of a being is proportionate to its metaphysical richness. In bodies you will find the undividedness of substance and accident, form and matter. In a mineral, the undividedness of physical and chemical properties. In a plant, the undividedness of physical and chemical properties, but something more also—the undividedness of life. There is more unity, in other words, in a plant than in a stone. Similarly an animal holds together in its unity more elements than the plant, adding the

3 See *Summa Theologiae*, I, 11, 1.

distinctive forces of animal life to those of vegetable life. Unity, in short, is proportioned to the degree of being realized in a given subject, to the point where in God, the supremely undivided Being, the highest unity of all is realized and even the distinction between essence and existence disappears.

Truth

Besides considering each being taken just by itself, we can consider it, as we have seen, in a relational way—as related, that is, to a knowing and willing subject. All being, as being, is capable of being known. This relationship of being known is at the base of the various meanings we can assign to the term "truth."

We have already met one meaning of the word truth—the truth of knowing.[4] We say a judgment is true if what I affirm (or deny) in my intellect squares with the corresponding reality outside my mind. The truth of the intellect, in other words, is dependent on things—it does not make the things it knows, it discovers them.

There is, however, another kind of relationship between our minds and things—the relationship that exists in the making of something artificial. Here there is a real dependence of the thing made on our intellects, because it will be made according to the idea we have in mind to start with. The kind of house we build, for example, will depend on the plans we draw up. If what we plan comes up to our expectations, we say it is true to our intentions.

The dependence of an artifact on our intellects is of course a kind of secondary dependence, since we do not give the new thing its being but only its new arrangement. Also, there is no guarantee that the thing I make will come up to my preconceived plan. The cake I actually make or the portrait I paint may not correspond at all to my original plan. In other words a kind of falsity is possible in artificial things, a falsity which follows from the lack of agreement of the thing made and the idea of its maker.

Just as we see a dependence of artificial things upon the plans we

---

4 See Chapter 11.

think up, so too we can see the marks of a certain dependence of natural things on the mind of their maker. The universe, in other words, shows signs of having been made according to some plan, and a plan implies an intellect.

But because the being itself of natural things, and not only their extrinsic arrangement, is given to them, they must be dependent on God, the first cause of all beings, who alone can give things their very being. Since God is all-powerful, things can not fail to come up to His intention or design—they agree necessarily with their idea in the mind of their Creator. This correspondence of things with their idea in the mind of God is called their truth—their metaphysical or ontological truth. All being squares with its pattern in the mind of the Creator, and therefore all being is true. "The true is what is," says St. Augustine.

A thing is said to be true to the extent that it is. Truth—which is simply being viewed from a certain aspect—is realized proportionately, and the higher we go in the state of being the more truth we find, until at the very summit of being we find Truth itself, the Absolute Truth because the Absolute Being.

Since error is not possible for the Supreme Being, things must measure up to their rule; ontological error—falsity of being, in other words—is in the strict sense impossible. In a qualified sense we may say that a thing is false to the extent that it fails to realize what is ideally possible for it. A fig tree that does not bear fruit, for example, is not all that a tree of this species could be. A human being is said to be false to his nature to the extent that he fails to live up to the standard proper to a human being.

Besides the truth of knowing, logical truth, and the truth of being, ontological truth, we might also note that there is still a third relationship between our intellects and things to which we give the name truth: the agreement or otherwise between what is in our minds and the words we speak. If my spoken words correspond to my thoughts, I say I am speaking the truth. If not, I say I am speaking falsely. This kind of truth is called moral truth.

Since beings in their very origin depend on the mind of the Creator who first thinks them before bringing them into being, it is a mark of all being that it can be known—not by our minds necessarily, but at least by the mind of God. Thus all the various meanings of the word truth derive ultimately from their being known first by the mind of the Creator.

The Good

Just as all beings are capable of being known, so too all beings are capable of being loved, if not by us, at least by their Creator, who would not have brought them into being if He had not loved them. All things, then, are worthy of being loved or desired—on the metaphysical, if not the moral, plane—for their own sake. This aspect of desirability is designated by the term good. And the more a thing is what it should be, the more it is desirable. A being is fully good of its kind when it is perfect; that is, finished, completed. "Something is desirable," says St. Thomas,, "according as it is perfect."[5] But all beings, to the extent that they exist at all are to that extent perfect, and to that extent, therefore, desirable or good. Hence we can say that all beings are good: whenever we can say "being," in other words, we can also say "good."

But beings are desirable not only in themselves, but to others, and this is a further mark of all being, that it tends to overflow, to communicate itself to others.

The simplest level on which the superabundance of being manifests itself is the level on which one thing may serve as a means to the accomplishment of the good of another; for example, food is used by the animal for energy. Under this aspect the good is called *useful*.

The highest aspect of good is the good which is loved for its own sake, simply as worthy of being loved. Good under this aspect is called *worthy* or *virtuous*.

The joy or pleasure which accompanies the realization of the good

---

5 *Summa Theologiae*, I, 5, 1.

which is loved for its own sake is called the *pleasurable* good.[6]

We have already met these distinctions in moral philosophy, where we saw that strictly speaking there is only one being, the supreme being, worthy of being loved for its own sake. Hence neither the useful good, which is a pure means, nor the pleasurable good, which is a dependent good, should be loved for their own sake. The right order of goods, then, from the lower to the higher, will be the useful, the pleasant, and the worthy.[7]

The Problem of Evil

"Whence do we evil?" asks Evodius, a friend of St. Augustine, in the beginning of St. Augustine's book *De libero arbitrio*.

"You start a question," St. Augustine answers, "which, when rather young, greatly harassed me, and drove and cast me headlong and worn among the heretics."

The dramatic story of St. Augustine's nine-year long espousal of the Manichaean heresy and his gradual liberation from its errors is told in his *Confessions*. The solution St. Augustine there offers to the problem of evil has become integral to the perennial philosophy.

St. Augustine was first attracted to the religion of the Manichees[8] by his difficulty in understanding how a world created by a God who is good could have evil in it. In order to overcome this difficulty, he affirmed that reality was made up of two eternal beings, one evil and the other good, each constantly warring against the

---

6 See St. Thomas, *Ibid.*, 6.

7 See H. Renard, *The Philosophy of Being* (Milwaukee: The Bruce Publishing Company, 1946), p. 184.

8 The roots of the Manichee sect have been traced back to the Persian priest Zoroaster (sixth century B.C.) who taught that the universe is made up of the commingling of two principles, one the element of darkness (Ahriman)) and the other the element of light (Mazda), which are constantly at war with one another. Mani (third century A.D.), the founder of the sect called Manichee, combined this doctrine with elements he took from Christianity and other sources. The religion he founded enjoyed wide popularity throughout the Mediterranean basin and persisted in spite of persecution into the early Middle Ages. The term "Manichaean" has come to stand for any doctrine which makes evil a positive thing—which says, for example, that material beings as against spiritual are evil.

other: "And because piety constrained me to believe that the good God never created any evil, I conceived two masses, contrary to one another, both unbounded."[9] The clash of these two beings explains the mixture of good and evil in the universe. It also explains the contradiction in human nature: when I do something evil, it is the principle of darkness working through me; my good actions are the working of the principle of light.

St. Augustine decided finally that an explanation of this kind raises more difficulties than it solves, for while it safeguards the goodness of God it makes Him limited in power and circumscribed in being—God is no longer God, in short. Augustine found the key to his problem in the Neoplatonic doctrine of the hierarchy of being—the great universal ladder of being from the lowest to the highest.[10]

God, the highest Being, exhausts the fullness of being. If there is to be any being other than the Infinite Being of God, then such beings must necessarily be merely partial realizations of being. But only an Infinite Being is unchangeable by nature. Any other being therefore will have a principle of change within it. And wherever there is the possibility of change, there is the possibility of less being or no being.[11]

In this intrinsic mutability of all things other than God, St. Augustine finds the explanation of physical evil. Evil is the privation of good, a lessening of a being from what it should be. So far is evil from being something positive or real in itself that if a thing were to become purely evil it would cease to exist at all: "For corruption injures, but unless it diminished goodness, it could not injure. Either then corruption injures not, which cannot be; or which is most certain, all which is corrupted is deprived of good. But if they

9 *Confessions*, V, x, 20.

10 On the hierarchy of being, see below, page 228.

11 "And I beheld the other things below Thee, and I perceived, that they neither altogether are, nor altogether are not, for they are, since they are from Thee, but are not because they are not what Thou art. For that truly is which remains unchangeably" (Confessions, VII, xi, 17).

be deprived of all good, they shall cease to be . . . so long therefore as they are, they are good: therefore whatsoever is, is good. That evil then which I sought, whence it is, is not any substance."[12]

Everything that comes from the hand of God is, then, good, but some things are better than others, "being unequal to this end, that they all might *be*." Evil is therefore a relative term, indicating some lack in a being otherwise good. But the very imperfection and cor-ruptibility which makes us call some beings evil is the condition of the greater good and harmony of the whole, just as the fading of the individual notes or syllables as they succeed one another is the indispensable condition of music or poetry: "Behold, these things pass away, that others may replace them, and so this lower universe be completed by all his parts."[13] Even the presence of sinners in the universe does not deface its perfection, for God foresees the disordered will of the sinner and out of that defective will brings good: "Nor by their wickedness do they effect that under the rule, power, and wisdom of the All-ruling God, the beauty and order of the universe should in any way be deformed, since to their wills of whatever sort, though evil, certain fitting bounds are assigned to their power, and the due measure to their deservings, so that even with them, thus placed under the fitting and due order, the universe is fair."[14]

Moral evil, the evil brought into the world through the free choice of creatures, represents a much more difficult problem than physi-cal evil, and ultimately an impenetrable mystery. We know, however, that if God creates beings with free will when He knows that some of them will use their freedom wrongly, it must be because the gift of freedom is worth this terrible risk. And it remains true that evil

---

12 *Confessions*, VII, xii, 18. Cf. St. Thomas: "Evil in a substance consists in its lack of something which it is naturally apt to have and ought to have. It is no evil to a man not to have wings because he is not by nature apt to have them . . . but it is an evil to him not to have hands, because he is by nature apt to have them, and ought to have them, if he is to be perfect." *Summa Contra Gentiles*, III, 4.

13 Confessions, IV, xi, 16.

14 *On the Literal Interpretation of Genesis*, XI, 21.

in this case too is a privation, the absence of a good that should be there. An evil choice is always a choice of some good; its evil lies in its not being good enough. "There is no efficient cause of evil," St. Augustine says, "but rather a deficient one."[15]

Beauty

Still another universal aspect of being is beauty. Beauty is the radiance of being in all its transcendental aspects together—unity, goodness, and truth as reflected in the three components of beauty: integrity, proportion, clarity.[16] The *integrity* or wholeness of a thing refers to its completeness, its perfection (and by implication its unity). In other words, a thing is not fully beautiful until it is all its nature calls for—until it fully realizes its kind of being. *Proportion* refers to the harmonious arrangement of parts within a being in relation to its end. This due order of parts within a being dispos-ing it toward its end is its ontological good. The brilliance of form radiating from a being is its *clarity*; this is the splendor of its form as knowable, its inner "intelligible radiance," its ontological truth.

Although ultimately, St. Thomas says, the beautiful can be reduced to the good, nevertheless it differs from it in concept. It is a special kind of good—that which pleases on being apprehended. It is not the good simply, but rather the good of the intellect—a good which satisfies on being known. Similarly it differs from the true taken simply (which is being in its illuminating aspect) in that it arouses love for the object known.[17]

---

15 *The City of God*, XII, 7.

16 "Three things are required for beauty: first, integrity or perfection . . . ; also due proportion or harmony; and again, clarity." St. Thomas Aquinas, *Summa Theologiae*, I, 39, 8. On beauty as the combination of all the transcendentals, see Maritain, *Art and Scholasticism*, note 63b (New York: Sheed and Ward, 1930). See also E. Chapman, "The Perennial Theme of Beauty and Art," in *Essays in Thomism*, edited by Robert E. Brennan, O.P. (New York: Sheed and Ward, 1942).

17 See St. Thomas Aquinas, *Summa Theologiae*, I; 5, 4, *ad* 1; I—II, 27, 1, *ad* 3. See also Maritain's comment on these texts, *op. cit.*, n. 56.

Ugliness

To the degree that things realize themselves in being, they are beautiful, for wherever there is being there is some degree at least of unity, goodness, and truth.[18] But to the degree that multiplicity, evil, falsity, vitiate a thing's nature, there is a relative ugliness. Just as in the case of evil, ugliness represents a deficiency in a being otherwise beautiful. And again, as in the case of evil, a relative ugliness of one of the parts may be the condition of the greater beauty of the whole. Finally, to complete the analogy, we can say that if a thing were to become totally ugly it would dissolve into nothingness.

Summary

The transcendentals are so many ways of making explicit the modes of being that are coextensive with being itself. They do not add anything new to being but they express special aspects of being. Unity refers to the undividedness of a being. Like all the transcendentals, it is an analogous concept and is realized proportionately in the different orders of being. The transcendental truth is ontological truth, the truth of being. There is no ontological falsity, except in the derived sense in which it refers to artificial things. The transcendental good is the good of being itself seen as desirable. Evil is the privation of being, the lack of a good which should be present. Beauty is being as it manifests the qualities of integrity, proportion, and clarity. Ugliness is the deficiency or lack of any of these qualities.

---

18 "There is nothing which does not participate in the beautiful and the good, since every being is beautiful and good according to its own form." St. Thomas Aquinas, *Summa Theologiae*, I, 39, 8.

CHAPTER 27

The Divisions of Being

Existence does not exist.
CAJETAN, QUOTED BY MARITAIN, PREFACE TO METAPHYSICS, P. 20.

Besides those most general aspects of being which are found in common in all beings and which we studied as the transcendental aspects of being, there are special aspects of being which reveal certain lines of division running through creation. The divisions within being unfold for us according as we adopt the standpoint of intelligibility, of existence, or of action.

Essence and Existence

In any being we consider there is a twofold aspect: every being has some kind of existence (actual or possible), and it is a some-thing, it has an intelligible consistency that makes it what it is and differentiates it from all other beings. Of any being whatsoever, in other words, we can ask the two questions, "Does it exist?" and "What is it?"

The first aspect, the existence aspect, is the product of the direct touch of the intellect with reality, with the intelligible treasure of existence which is blindly conveyed by our senses. This intuition of existence is basic, primary, in the sense that you cannot get behind existence; existence is the absolute starting point; the alternative to existence is nothing. This is the aspect of being implied in the famous phrase, "To be or not to be, that is the question." Before a thing can be this or that it has first of all to be.

The second aspect of being gives us the "whatness" of the thing—tells us that it has a definite, intelligible structure, even though we may not always know exactly what it is, or know it clearly. The name for this second aspect of being is *essence* or *quiddity*; quiddity—the "whatness" of a thing—is the essence as presented in a definition, while essence in itself is what the thing is—i.e., what the definition defines. Still a third name, *nature*, is used to designate what we mean by essence; nature is essence considered as the principle, the source, of the operations or activities which the thing is made (*nata*, born) to produce.

Any confrontation of being must present this twofold aspect —the intellect oscillates as it were between the two poles, essence and existence. For whatever comes into the intellect has both intelligible consistency and some kind of existence, actual or possible, and neither aspect can be totally separated from the other. It is a fact, however, that the philosopher is often tempted to close his eyes to the existence of things, since it cannot be frozen, so to speak, within a concept. The act of existence overflows with intelligibility; it is so rich in intelligible values that no concept can capture it.[1] It is caught only in the direct and immediate touch of the intellect, which has to keep itself keyed to its highest pitch in order not to lose the subtle and infinitely varied values of this supremely intelligible object.

One of the most serious errors a philosopher can make is to stop at the realm of essence to the forgetfulness of the more elusive values of existence. The rich constellation of mathematical essences may beguile the philosopher—Descartes turned physics into geometry, for example. The realm of logic, the inner, stable universe of beings of reason, may also offer itself as a better and neater world than the untidy realm of change and contingence. But a truly realist

---

1 This is what Cajetan means when he says, "Existence does not exist." In other words, "existence" considered as a concept in our minds is not the "actual existence" which is attained in our immediate judgments of reality. See J. Maritain, *A Preface to Metaphysics* (New York: Sheed and Ward, 1939), Lecture II.

philosophy will always guard against this temptation to spin reality out of its own substance; it will always refer its abstractions back to their existential source, constantly renewing and refreshing itself at the inexhaustible fount of existence itself.

The Meaning of Essence

Essence may be used in a wide or a narrow sense. In its broadest use, it refers to any aspect whatever of intelligibility, man, tree, stone, sweetness, greenness, health, etc. In this sense it means the "whatness" of anything whatsoever, from the standpoint of its being able to be understood.

But of the many things that are apparent to us in knowing some are obviously more basic than others. Thus where I see a tree, I see besides the aspect of living being such other things as green, tall, waving, and so on. But the tree may change in color, or it may stop waving in the wind, and it still remains a tree. It cannot stop living, however, and remain a tree. Living, therefore, is something more basic to being a tree than these other aspects. Or in a human being, such things as color, posture, age, may vary, but other things such as rationality and animality cannot be absent without the disappearance of the human being. In brief, of all the intelligible aspects of things that come into our understanding, some are basic to the thing, some are not. A man must be rational, but he need not be old, or playing baseball, or brown-haired. When I say what a man is, then, I have to say such things as rational and animal, while those other things are not implied in being a man. I may use the word essence, therefore, in a narrower sense, to refer just to those elements which make a thing what it is basically.

Essence considered in this strict sense limits or ties down existence to this or that *kind* of existence. It gives the thing its fundamental pattern, its intelligible structure. It is what a thing necessarily is if it is at all. It is that element in the thing which cannot be altered without resulting in a *different kind* of being.

The Distinction Between Essence and Existence

Looking at the things around us, trees, human beings, and so on, we realize that they are not all they could be—they do not exhaust the possibilities of their kind of being. Indeed it is possible for an essence—a new species of animal, for example—never to be realized at all in actual existence, or for a species once come into existence to be destroyed utterly, like some of the classes of pre-historic animals.

This is a mark of the real distinction between essence and existence in the things of our world. For the creature feels a double pull: toward the nothingness from which it is drawn, and toward God, for whom it was created, and whose love alone keeps it from slipping back into the void.

This drama is played out on a conscious level in human beings, but we can see its echo even in nonhuman creatures, for it is the law of their being too that their essence seeks to realize itself more and more fully in existence. Reflecting both the source from which they come and the end for which they were destined, they seek to be more and more like God, whose essence fully exhausts existence. "The very physical world, created as it is for God's glory, tends with a kind of blind love towards its author."[2]

The Knowledge of Essence

There are obvious and important differences in the kind of knowledge we have of different things. We know some things well, others obscurely. I know myself, for example, better than I know a dog or a cat because I know myself from the inside, so to speak, whereas my knowledge of the dog or the cat is from the outside. My knowledge of essence, in other words, varies. Sometimes it is clear, as in the case of triangles, and circles and numbers, sometimes it is so dark that we can hardly say anything beyond the fact that a thing is something.

---

2 E. Gilson, Spirit of Mediaeval Philosophy (New York: Sheed and Ward, Inc., 1936), p. 364.

Although we can know essences, our knowledge is never exhaustive. There are always depths of intelligibility inviting the further penetration of our intellect, so that if we were truly to exhaust the meaning of anything we would need an intellect capable of comprehending being absolutely. It seems apparent, furthermore, that our intellects are geared to a definite and limited order of reality, and that both the things below and the things above this order are dark to us—the former in the direction of matter, because there is not enough for our intellects to lay hold of, too little intelligibility, too little being; the latter because there is too much being, too much intelligibility, so that our intellects are overwhelmed, dazzled, just as our eyes may be blinded by too much light.

It is possible to make too great demands on the intellect, insisting as did Descartes on a degree and absoluteness of clarity of which it is not capable. Such philosophers make no provision for those partial insights into reality which, though not exhaustive, really tell us something, even if in an incomplete manner, about the way things are. To recognize that we do not have complete and exhaustive knowledge is not, as Descartes suggested, to throw suspicion on the value of the intellect. It is simply to accept the fact that we are finite beings, and that our intellect is limited. There are colors and sounds which some instruments—and some animals—can detect beyond the range of our eyes or ears. Yet none of us would say that what our eyes and ears report to us is false or useless. Similarly we can recognize the limitations on our intellect without depreciating its dignity or its value.

Substance and Accident

Instead of considering beings from the standpoint of their intelligibility, we may consider them in their mode of existence outside our intellects. From this point of view all being is either being which exists on its own, in at least a relatively independent fashion, or else exists in another, in such a way that it has no existence apart from the other. The first way of being is found in such things as a maple tree, a robin, a race horse, a human being—independent centers of existence and activity, beings that go on being what they are behind the restless face of everyday change. These beings are called substances. We may define a substance as *a being whose nature it is to exist in itself.*

The second way of being is called accidental, and it refers to the partial, secondary, surface changes and manifestations of the basic way of being—the green garb of the maple tree, the song of the robin, the speed or the sleekness of the race horse, the health or the wisdom or the cheerfulness of our next-door neighbor. These ways of being could not exist on their own, any more than the grin on the face of the cat can be found apart from the cat. The basic characteristic of these ways of being, then, is that they depend on some prior being for their existence. We may define an accident therefore as *a being whose nature it is to exist in another.*

The depth to which an accident is rooted in the being of a substance may vary. Thus we could not conceive of a body without dimensions, though other accidents, like the green of a leaf, the quick movements of a bird in flight, the melancholy disposition of a Monday morning, may come and go. Some accidents therefore are called *necessary* and others *contingent.*

The True and False View of Substance

Besides the capacity to exist on its own, substance in finite beings manifests a second aspect—it is the ground or support for those dependent ways of being we call accidents. This aspect of substance is not essential, however, since it is not found in God, who is supremely substance.[3]

The erroneous consideration of substance solely as the support for accidents has led to what we might call the flowerpot view of substance—as though substance were a receptacle into which so many accidents are inserted, like flowers in a pot. Substance on the

---

3 For the sense in which substance can be properly predicated of God, see H. Renard, *The Philosophy of Being* (Milwaukee: The Bruce Publishing Company, 1946), p. 200 ff.; and Henry J. Koren, *Introduction to the Science of Metaphysics* (St. Louis: B. Herder Book Co., 1955), p. 186.

contrary is the primary being of the thing, and accidents are the secondary ways of being by which substance is manifested to us. Beings as we know them are more or less perfectly realized and change according as their perfection increases or diminishes. Thus they are both being and becoming. The fluctuating, accidental surface manifestations of the being presuppose the underlying consistency, the enduring substance, the being behind the change. Accidents are none other than partial manifestations of substance itself. They are not "secondary beings pasted on like so many parasites,"[4] but they are the attenuated and diffused being of the substance itself, radiated and refracted in so many partial reflections.

The Knowledge of Substance

Substance as such cannot be perceived by our senses: we cannot see it, touch it, imagine it. Our senses do indeed perceive beings which are substances, but it is the color, the taste, the shape of the thing which is known by our senses, not its being or its substance. The existence of substance is known only by an insight of the intellect, which sees that behind the becoming of sense phenomena there exists the being which is the subject of the change. Putting it another way, if all beings are accidents—which alone are directly disclosed to us by our senses—then all beings exist in others, which contradicts the very notion of being. It contradicts too, the evidence of our everyday experience which tells us that there are many independent beings of many kinds. We say therefore that there are as many substances as there are individual beings.

The Classification of Accidents

There are nine classes of accident according to Aristotle, and they can be grouped as follows:

I. Those characterized by the substance itself in which the accident has its being:

---

4 A. D. Sertillanges, *Thomas d'Aquin*, I, 78. Quoted by H. Renard, *The Philosophy of Being* (Milwaukee: The Bruce Publishing Company, 1948), p. 204.

1. *Quantity* (resulting from the matter of the substance).
2. *Quality* (issuing from the form of the substance).
3. *Relation* (ordering the substance to something).

II. Those characterized by some extrinsic reality which is referred to the subject:

4. *Time* (the measure of the subject's duration).
5. *Place* (the measure of extension).
6. *Posture* (site). (The measure of the disposition of parts.)

III. As concerned in production, causality, change:

7. *Action* (characterizing the principle).
8. *Passion* (characterizing the term).

IV. As descriptive of exterior appearance:

9. *Habit* (vesture, ornament).

Act and Potency

The concepts of act and potency give us a third general way of dividing the term being. These are concepts which arise out of a consideration of the fact of change, and we have already met them in their historical origin in Aristotle. (See Chapter 7.)

In what way are we to understand change? If we were to forget that our judgments must be anchored in objective reality it is easy to see how the intellect by itself might be led to the denial of an obvious fact, declaring that change is unreal. For, as Parmenides observed, a thing is or it is not. A thing is what it is, and thus bluntly considered seems to be incapable of becoming.

If change cannot be explained in terms of the being which is to be changed—since the existing thing is already all that it can be— possibly we should look for the explanation at the opposite pole, in terms of what the thing is going to become. But what the thing is going to become is not yet in existence, and what does not yet exist cannot be the source of change. What does not yet exist cannot account for the existence of anything real.

Our apparent dilemma forces us to a further exploration of the notion of being. The analysis of the earlier Greek philosophers left out of consideration a kind of intermediary stage of being, midway, as it were, between being and nonbeing. The possibility of change is found not in what the thing actually is, nor in what it is going to be, but rather is determined by what the thing is able to be. The full being of a thing is not only what it actually is at this moment but also what it is able to be. Let us compare two different realities to see how this can be.

A block of marble has a certain set of possibilities belonging to it which are different from the possibilities which belong to a pail of water. The block of marble can be turned into dust or carved into a statue. It can be used as a cornerstone, or a tombstone, and so on. The pail of water can be used to wash in, or to water plants. The water can be turned into steam or ice. We can do many things with our pail of water which we cannot do with the block of marble.

Now let us isolate these two sets of possibilities, the possibilities of marble and the possibilities of water. We have seen that they are different. Since they are still only possibilities, are they nothing? If we say they are nothing, then can two nothings be different from one another?

If we are to say the two clusters of possibilities are different then we have to grant they are something. They are certainly not beings in the full sense of the word, in the sense that the pail of water and the block of marble are real. But neither can we say that they are nothing. Somewhere in our notion of being we have to find room for them. Our concept of reality has to be expanded to make room for possibilities, for whatever is not nothing is real.

The full reality of our block of marble, then, is not only what it actually is at this given moment, but also what it can be; and the full reality of our pail of water is both what it actually is and what it is able to be. The fact that a being can become something else is part of its very make-up, and it is with respect to this possibility of becoming something else that we find the explanation of change. It is, for example, with respect to the ability to be heated, which is a real constituent of water, that the source of actual heat makes water hot.

The Definition of Change

Commenting on Aristotle's definition of change as "the act of a being in potency in so far as it is in potency," St. Thomas explains the definition of change as follows:[5] A thing may be in any one of three situations—in act only, in potency only, or somewhere between act and potency. An entirely potential thing is not in a state of change; neither is a thing finished and in perfect act in a state of change. Change therefore is the state of being in between being-in-act and being-in-potency. We can illustrate this with an example:

Water that is only potentially hot is not yet in a state of change. Water that has become hot is no longer changing to hot; it is hot. But if our water is only partly heated, lukewarm, let us say, then it is being changed to hot. Change in our body of water, in other words, refers to the progressive stages from being cold through increasing stages of warmth until we can say it is actually hot. At this point there is no longer any process of change. The change is finished with the realization of the new way of being which was the goal of change.

The imperfect stage of being lukewarm is called the state of change with reference to the future state of being hot to which it is ordered. If the relationship to the future state of being hot were ended—if we stopped heating the water, for example—then the change would be at an end. Our water then would be lukewarm simply, lukewarm in act, we would say, and not changing into hot. In other words, the imperfect act of being hot—which is the state of being lukewarm—is imperfect only with respect to being hot. If we no longer consider that relationship, then the state of being lukewarm is being in act only. In short, our lukewarm water from one point of view is changing, from another it is not changing. It is changing as it is referred to a further, more perfect act of being; in this respect, it is "being in potency." As it is referred to an anterior, less perfect state, it is called "act"; it is an "imperfect act," however,

---

5 From the *Commentary on the Physics*, Bk. III, lect. 2. This text is quoted at length in Renard, op. cit., p. 24.

because it is in potency to further perfection. To illustrate again:

Lukewarm water, as referred to the cold water which was the starting point of change, is in act—but "imperfect act" as compared to the "perfect act," the hot water which is the goal of change; it is also in potency as referred to the further perfection of which it is capable, the act of being hot. In other words, the same water, viewed in relation to the starting point of change may be said to be in act (imperfect) or, viewed in relation to the goal of change, may be said to be in potency.

We now have the elements necessary to explain our definition of change. Change implies a prior composition of act and potency. The act of a thing is what it already is. Its potency is what it can be. It is not with reference to a thing's act that it changes, because a thing in act is already all that it can be at a given moment and in a certain respect. The change that takes place must be, then, with reference to the thing's potency. Hence the phrase in our definition, "in so far as it is in potency." But the various stages of relatively imperfect being along the path to the realization of the new way of being can also be called "act" in so far as they are new realizations of being in relation to the potency with which we started out. These stages are, however, "imperfect act" in relation to the final goal of change because they fall short of that ultimate perfection. Change, therefore, is the imperfect act of being in potency to the new way of being toward which it is ordered. Or, in the definition of Aristotle, "Change is the act of a being in potency in so far as it is in potency."

The Extrinsic Principles of Change

The principles we have just examined are the intrinsic principles of change. But a thing cannot realize its own potencies, for then there would be no reason why it should ever be in potency. Therefore we have to look outside the thing for the further explanations of change. This is found in the efficient and final causes, which are called the extrinsic principles of change.

The efficient cause is the action from a being outside—the first cause in the order of existence—which communicates to the thing acted on the perfection which was there in potency only. The final cause is the reason why an action is initiated—the first cause in the order of intention.

The Relation of Potency and Act to Matter and Form

In bodily creatures as well as purely spiritual beings there is a realization of being which we can call act. But it is an incomplete, partial realization as compared with the exhaustive realization of being within each order of spiritual being. To express the fact of this new kind of limitation when we enter the realm of bodies we may use the terms "form" and "matter" instead of "act" and "potency." Form and matter therefore indicate a deeper mark of limitation: limitation not only according to essence, according to the basic way of being, but also limitation within that kind of being, so that only part of the type is realized.[6]

The Knowledge of Act and Potency

We have already seen that form and matter do not mean anything like our everyday words "shape" or "stuff." They are conceptions arrived at as the result of a rational analysis, and any attempt to picture them in the imagination or to reduce them to something visible or tangible destroys their meaning. The same is true of the concepts of act and potency. Act, for example, does not mean action or activity in the popular usage of these terms. It refers rather to the basic "to be," the primary existence of a thing, which philosophy terms "first act." "Second act" is used to refer to the operations of a being, the sense which the everyday term "activity" usually carries. The word potency, finally, in its philosophical sense refers to possibilities of being, and only secondarily to the everyday usage of "power." Much of the difficulty attaching to the philosophical uses of these

---

6   Thus whereas in angels the only way they can be differentiated is according as they realize different essences, in the case of corporeal beings there

terms disappears if we remember that "what is imperceptible to sense is not necessarily nothing."[7]

The Hierarchy of Being

Only an infinite being could exhaust the possibilities of existence. We have to say therefore that only in God is there no shadow of possibility. Only God, in other words, is unlimited Act. All other beings are composed of act and potency, for no matter how much perfection they possess they are at least in potency to existence, since they had to be brought into being.

Highest in the scale of created beings are the angels who are pure spirits, beings perfectly in act, for each exhausts the possibilities of its finite way of being.[8] Each angel is a complete species or class of being all by itself, realized in a single act of being, as though, for example, every possible manifestation of humanity were realized in a single, enduring flash of existence.

When we come to the order of bodily creatures we find the same combination of act and potency. But in contrast to the order of pure spirits, we find in bodies a relative poverty of being, so that the possibilities of each class can be realized only partially and in piecemeal fashion. Thus the kind of being represented by the class *animal* is realized in each of the different kinds of animal, and the individual being of each animal in turn is realized only in successive stages. And there will always remain vast potentialities in this order which will never be realized.

The dynamic progression within reality is epitomized thus by Dr. Chapman: "The philosophical awareness of existence opens

---

7 W. D. Ross, Aristotle, quoted by M. J. D'Arcy, *The Mind and Heart of Love* (New York: Henry Holt and Co., 1947), p. 179. For a fuller treatment of the notions of first act and second act, see G. Klubertanz, *Introduction to the Philosophy of Being* (New York: Appleton-Century-Croft, 1955), p. 113.

8 Although philosophy cannot prove the existence of angels, the type of being they represent, that of a pure spirit of a limited nature, is perfectly conceivable and therefore can be discussed as one of the possible ways of being.

the intellect to the metaphysical drama of how beings composed of essence and existence, potentiality and actuality, and, if they are material, form and matter, struggle to realize themselves more fully in existence by achieving more unity, truth, goodness, beauty, substantiality, and accidence, while at the same time resisting the pull towards non-being, multiplicity, falsity, evil, and ugliness. Even at the successful conclusion of this drama, the gap between essence and existence branding all contingent beings will not be completely overcome, and will point to the Being whose essence is existence, self-subsisting act, absolute unity, truth, goodness, beauty, and all else that He is infinitely."[9]

Summary

Being discloses certain basic divisions within itself according as we adopt variously the standpoints of intelligibility, existence, or action. Being as an object for the understanding is disclosed in its essence-existence aspect. Existence, as referring to the act by which a thing is placed outside of nothingness, is the ultimate datum for the intellect. But existence is always the existence of *something*, of an essence. Essence itself may be understood in a wide sense, as referring to any intelligible "whatness," or in a narrow, more precise sense, as referring to just those elements which must be present in a being in order to make it the kind of being it is. "Substance" is used of beings that exist "on their own," independently of other beings. The term "accident" is used of those secondary and dependent aspects of being which could not exist save as manifestations of a more primary being. Being is further divided into the concepts "act" and "potency." Act refers to the full actualization of being, potency to unrealized possibilities of being. Act and potency are the intrinsic causes of change, as against the extrinsic efficient and final causes.

---

9 Emmanuel Chapman, "To Be—That Is the Answer," in the Maritain Volume of *The Thomist* (Jan., 1943), p. 146.

CHAPTER 28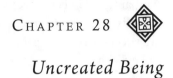

Uncreated Being

Dost thou hope to sound the depths of God, To reach the limits of the Almighty?
THE BOOK OF JOB, 11:7.

The Knowledge of God

Before the intellect rises to the formation of scientific or philosophic judgments it has certain natural, spontaneous insights into the nature of man and the structure of reality, a kind of reflection, if it is not clouded by prejudice or false teaching, of the native evidence of things in the mirror of the intellect. Among these insights is the knowledge of the existence of a superior being upon whom the world is dependent.

In the words of St. Thomas, "There is a certain general and confused knowledge of God in all men . . . because by his natural reason man is able at once to arrive at some knowledge of God."[1] The findings of modern anthropology confirm this observation. No matter how remote in time or how primitive in culture, it is impossible to find a tribe or a nation which has not believed in the existence of some kind of a god, however vague or twisted their idea might be. "There is," says Otto Karrer in *Religions of Mankind,* "a *'consensus generis humani,'* an agreement of mankind so far as our present knowledge extends, in the belief that there exists an absolute

---

1 *Summa Contra Gentiles,* III, 38; see also *Summa Theologiae,* I, 2, 1, ad 2.

and supreme Being above ourselves which has ordered the universe and human life in particular. . . . History knows of no people godless and devoid of religion, though here and there particular groups, schools of thought or governments may combat religion."[2]

The fact remains however that this primitive knowledge of God is likely to be extremely hazy and indefinite, for although, as St. Thomas says, men for the most part know that there must be some cause of the order they see around them, "Who or of what kind this cause of order may be, or whether there be but one, cannot be gathered from this general consideration."[3] It is important, therefore, to explore these primordial insights of common sense systematically, delineating the evidence in the stronger light of philosophical reflection.

The philosophical formulation of the arguments for the existence of God goes back to the time of Plato and Aristotle. A number of the arguments, such as those from order and causality, are found in common in nearly all philosophers. These arguments do not depend upon any particular philosophical system precisely because the evidence for them is accessible even to common sense. In other words, the evidence on which they rest is so basic that any philosopher who refused it would automatically block himself off from a great part of reality.

Whether The Existence of God Is Self-Evident

Some philosophers have maintained that the existence of God is so evident that it forces itself on our minds as soon as we are aware of what the name God means. Probably the most famous exponent of this view is St. Anselm, a philosopher and theologian who almost a thousand years ago set free an idea which has fascinated and tantalized the minds of men ever since.[4]

---

2 *Religions of Mankind* (New York: Sheed and Ward, 1936), pp. 80-81.

3 *Summa Contra Gentiles*, III, 38.

4 St. Anselm, born in 1033, in the north of Italy, entered the Benedictine Order at an early age. He helped found a new monastery at Bec, in Normandy, where he taught and wrote for many years. Eventually he became Abbot. Still later he was appointed

Anselm thought that we could know that God exists merely by considering all that is implied in the definition of God. We can all, even the atheist, he says, have at least the idea of God in our minds; this is the idea of the most perfect being we can think of, "a being than whom nothing greater can be conceived." If we analyze what is implied in such a notion, we are forced to recognize that the most perfect being we can think of must be an actually existing being. For if we think of the most perfect being as nonexisting then it would not be the most perfect being of which we were thinking. To illustrate, let us list side by side the characteristics of the most perfect being, the one existing, the other not existing:

BEING A	BEING B
all-powerful	all-powerful
all-just	all-just
all-knowing	all-knowing
all-wise	all-wise
all-loving	all-loving
everlasting	everlasting
unlimited, etc.	unlimited, etc.
existing in my thought only	existing both in my thought and in reality.

Which of these, Being A or Being B, is the more perfect? Clearly we have to answer Being B, since a being that exists both in thought and in reality is more perfect than one that exists in thought alone. In fact we cannot even call Being A a perfect being, since it does not possess actual being. It is literally impossible, then, even to think of God, the infinitely perfect being, except as actually existing. Therefore, Anselm concludes, God exists.

Anselm's argument is not as strange as it looks at first sight. Its

---

the Archbishop of Canterbury, and suffered exile from England twice following on quarrels with the Crown over the question of Investitures. He died in exile in Holland in the year 1109. For the statement of his argument see the translation of the *Proslogium* in Sidney N. Deane's *Anselm* (La Salle, Ill.: Open Court Publishers, 1944). This edition contains also the reply of Gaunilon to Anselm.

validity depends on his explanation of knowing. Working in the tradition of Plato and St. Augustine, Ansehn holds that our knowledge is intuitive in character, derived from flashes of the eternal, unchanging types which are reflected in our souls. To know means to scan with the eye of the mind this inner sky of intelligible reality. In this inner world of ideas St. Anselm sees the idea of the perfect being, and as part of the make-up of this idea the note of actual and necessary existence. All he has to do to show the existence of God is to point out the content of this idea for others to look at. Just turn your gaze, he says in effect, and take a good look at what is there for everybody to see. Thus for St. Anselm the argument might be more properly called a pointing out than a proof.

The History of the Argument

Anselm's argument was held as a matter of course by a majority of the philosophers of the Middle Ages after his time. It was held as a reproach against the philosophy of St. Thomas in the thirteenth century that there was no room in it for this argument. Descartes made the argument a keystone in his philosophical system, and he was followed in this by such famed philosophers as Spinoza, Malebranche, and Leibniz. Even today the argument is not without its supporters. Descartes expressed the argument thus: "When the mind . . . reviews the different ideas that are in it, it discovers what is by far the chief among them—that of a Being omniscient, all-powerful, and absolutely perfect; and it observes that in this idea there is contained not only possible and contingent existence, as in the ideas of all other things which it clearly perceives, but existence absolutely necessary and eternal. And just as because, for example, the equality of its angles to two right angles is necessarily comprised in the idea of a triangle, the mind is firmly persuaded that the three angles of a triangle are equal to two right angles; so, from its perceiving necessary and eternal existence to be comprised in the idea which it has of an all-perfect Being, it ought manifestly to conclude that this all-perfect Being exists."[5]

Criticism of the Argument

The first objector to Anselm's argument was a contemporary, a monk called Gaunilon. Gaunilon said that he could think of a perfect island, an island with "an inestimable wealth of all manner of riches and delicacies in greater abundance than is told of the islands of the Blest." Now an island that exists is more perfect than an island that does not exist. It does not follow, however, that this imagined perfect island actually exists.

Anselm countered Gaunilon's argument by pointing out that the idea of God is unique among the ideas we find in our mind. The concept of God is the *only* idea which includes existence as part of its make-up, as part of its very definition. The idea of island, however, does not include the note of necessary existence. If I were to break down the idea into its essential elements I would find that I do not have to think of "actual existence" in order to think of "island." The same is true of any other idea I think of except one— the idea of God. For the note of existence, actual and necessary existence, enters into the very definition of God. He is existence, this is His very Being, and this is what I cannot help but see when I think of Him.

St. Thomas also denied the validity of Anselm's argument. Maintaining that all knowledge comes by way of the senses, he disagreed with St. Anselm about what an idea means. Whereas for St. Anselm ideas are independent realities, more real than sensible realities and directly affecting us, for St. Thomas the inner world of ideas is an abstraction from sense experience. The only actual existences we experience immediately are those of the sensible world around us. Since God cannot be an object of sense experience we cannot have direct knowledge of His existence but have to argue from the sensible world as an effect of God's power. It is true that if we want

---

5 The Principles of Philosophy, I, 14, edited by Elizabeth S. Haldane and G. R. T. Ross, Everyman edition (London and New York: J. M. Dent and E. P. Dutton, 1931), p. 170.

to think of God we cannot think of Him except as actually existing. But the necessity of which we are aware is simply the necessity within the thought-structure which we call the definition of God. It is not an intuition of an actual existence apart from our minds.

The validity of St. Thomas' criticism depends upon the explanation of man's knowing. Anselm's argument can be accepted only at the price of adopting an Augustinian or Cartesian philosophy of man, with all the difficulties and drawbacks which the history of thought shows are inherent in these positions. If on the other hand we hold to the Aristotelian-Thomistic interpretation of the nature and knowledge of man, the argument of St. Anselm has to be rejected.

The Five Ways of St. Thomas

For St. Thomas the proofs for the existence of God take as their starting point some fact common to all the beings in the world around us: that they are changing, caused, contingent, imperfect, ordered. These facts are evaluated in the light of one of the laws of being; for example, that every effect has a cause. From this, they proceed to the conclusion of a Supreme Being who is the explanation of the beings with which our examination started. The philosophical proofs for the existence of God are, in short, metaphysical in character: "The point of departure is being, the point of arrival is being, by way of the laws of being."[6]

St. Thomas reduces the philosophical arguments for the existence of God to five in number, which he calls the five "ways" to God.[7] He uses the word "way" rather than "proof" or "argument" because although the arguments lead us to the *fact* of God's existence, the very Being Itself of God is so infinitely beyond the power of our expression that our knowledge of Him is at best incomplete and

---

6 Olgiati, Key to the Study of St. Thomas (St. Louis: B. Herder Book Company, 1929), p. 79.

7 *Summa Theologiae*, I, 2, 3.

analogical: "The supreme knowledge we can have of Him is to know that He is above all our thoughts."[8]

The Proof from Motion or Change

St. Thomas' first argument is based on the implications of the fact of motion or change. (Motion for St. Thomas means all the kinds of change that are possible.) The things around us have a limited way of being. They are not at any given moment all they could be. Their being is so poor that it has to be realized in stages, piecemeal so to speak, on condition that they change; thus, different possibilities of a single human being are realized in all the changes from infancy to old age, but they cannot be realized simultaneously. And the same is true, of course, for all the other sensible things we know.

What needs explaining here, according to St. Thomas, is the bringing about of the new ways of being which are implied by the fact of change, for a thing cannot give itself what it previously lacked. (Otherwise we would have to say that something comes from nothing, as though water were poured from an empty jug.) The only thing that could bring a new way of being into existence would be some previously existing being.

That previously existing being itself is either changed or unchanged. If it is unchanged, then we have what we are looking for, a "first mover unmoved"; that is, a being that changes without itself being changed.

If, however, the being that brings about the change is itself a changing being, its changes in turn must be brought about by something else. But there cannot be an indefinite series of such movers since if there were no first being to initiate the series of changes there would be no series at all. Nor does it make any difference if we make the series endless; this would be like saying that a watch does not need a mainspring to make it function provided it has an endless number of wheels. Even supposing an infinite series of

---

8 Truth, 2, 1, ad 2; quoted by Sertillanges, *Foundations of Thomistic Philosophy* (St. Louis: B. Herder Book Company, 1931), p. 57.

changed beings, the infinite series itself would need explaining. "It is contrary to reason to say that an actually existing motion can have *its sufficient reason, its actualizing raison d'être, in a series of movers, each one of which is moved by some external cause.* If all the movers receive that impulse which they transmit, if there is not a prime mover which imparts movement without receiving it, then motion is out of the question, for it has no cause."[9]

It is not a question, then, of going back forever and ever in a series of dependent movers, but rather of rising above the whole series to a new level, of recognizing that the subordinate series itself is dependent at each moment of its existence on a mover of a superior order.[10] The first mover unmoved is not merely the initiator of a chain of movements, like the man who winds up a clock, but "by its action here and now has an influx upon any actual motion."[11]

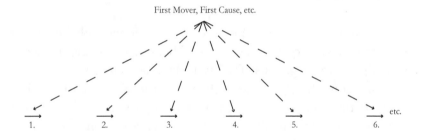

Fig. 1. Each successive change or cause depends not only on the preceding members of the series, but at the same time depends on the continuing influence of the First Mover and First Cause for its preservation in being.

---

9   R. Garrigou-Lagrange, God, *His Existence and Nature* (St. Louis: B. Herder Book Co., 1939), Vol. I, p. 265.

10 See diagram, p. 238.

11 H. Renard, The Philosophy of God (Milwaukee: The Bruce Publishing Co., 1950), p. 35.

First Mover, First Cause, etc.

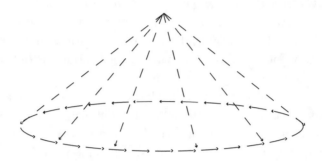

Fig. 2. Even in an infinite series, not only must the existence of each of the elements in the series of changes or causes be accounted for, but the very series itself is dependent as a whole upon the First Mover and First Cause.

To summarize: we see the things around us constantly becoming something else, acquiring new ways of being. But a being that lacks something cannot give itself what it lacks. Therefore when a thing becomes something else it must be under the influence of another being. If this other being also changes, then the source of its change must be sought in something else. But we cannot go on forever with a series of dependent agents, since then there would be no first mover and therefore no subsequent movers. To account therefore for the actual fact of change there must be a first mover which is itself unmoved. "And this everyone understands to be God."[12]

The Argument from Efficient Causality

The first way of St. Thomas considers things from the standpoint of their becoming. The second way looks at them from the standpoint of their being. As in the first way, we start with an observed fact of everyday experience: there is an order of efficient cause and

---

12 *Summa Theologiae,* I, 2, 3.

effect; some beings, that is, bring other beings into existence. What about the being that brings the effect into existence? Is it itself caused or uncaused? If it is caused, it cannot be its own cause, for then it would be "prior to itself," it would exist before it existed. We are forced therefore to look for a cause for our cause, which cause in turn is either caused or uncaused.

But just as a series of changes, the one depending on the other, has to be explained no matter how long the series, so too for a series of dependent causes. If there is no first cause—that is, no efficient cause which is itself uncaused—there will be no secondary or intermediary efficient causes. Even if we supposed an infinite series of such subordinated causes, we would still need, just as in the case of an infinite series of moved movers, a first independent cause of the whole series. To account, therefore, for the sequences of caused causes which we do find in the world around us, we must admit the existence of a first cause, itself uncaused, "which all men call God."

If the influx of the first efficient cause were for a single moment withdrawn, all the secondary causes dependent on it would instantly cease to exist. We must recognize accordingly that dependent or secondary causes depend on the first cause not only for their beginning but also for their continuing in existence. "If the question `Why did it begin?' needs answering, so does the question `Why does it go on?', and just as it must be maintained that unless something had produced it it could not have begun to be, so also it must be maintained that unless something was preserving it it would collapse into nonexistence."[13]

The remaining arguments for the existence of God all stress likewise the insufficiency of the world around us to explain itself: things are contingent—they could have not been, do not possess their existence necessarily; things manifest varying degrees of perfection—of goodness, beauty, and so on; there is an endowed order—both in the heart of individual natures and in reality as a whole. To explain

---

13   E. I. Mascall, *He Who Is* (New York: Longman's, Green, and Company, 1943), p. 46.

the fact of contingent, imperfect, and regulated being we must conclude to the existence of a being who is necessary, perfect, and the
giver of order. And in all these aspects of reality, just as in the case
of the facts of change and efficient causality, we are led to recognize the necessity of the *present* effect of God's power in sustaining
the universe in being:

> "He lives and reigns, throned above Space and Time.
> New every morning the creative Word
> Moves upon chaos. Yea, our God grows young.
> Here, now, the eternal miracle is renewed.
> Now, and for ever, God makes heaven and earth."[14]

The Knowledge of God from the Five Ways

Each of the five ways tells us something about the perfections of
God. From the first way we know God as a being who is the cause
of change without Himself being changed; as a being, that is, in
whom there is no shadow of potency. Since there is no possibility
of change in God He must be pure Act—otherwise there would be
the possibility of change through the addition of what He lacked.
Since He exhausts every possibility of being, God must be said to
be infinite.

From the second way we know God as uncaused, which is to say
that He does not receive existence but *is* existence; to exist is His
very being. The third way shows us that God is the absolutely necessary being. The fourth way tells us that God as the exemplar of
all perfection is the supreme Good and infinite Love. The fifth way
tells us that God is the First Intelligence who orders all being.

All of these marks together give us the knowledge of God as a
Person—a being that is one, self-subsistent, intelligent, and free.

We must recognize, of course, that no idea we can form about the
nature of God will ever be adequate because we can never in this
life know God directly. We are saved from agnosticism, however, by

---

14 Alfred Noyes, *The Unknown God* (New York: Sheed and Ward, 1934), p. 367.

recognizing that since no effect can be greater than its cause, we can therefore affirm of God at least as much perfection as is evident in the world of which He is the cause. "Thus we are led to know," says St. Thomas, "the existence of God and those things which necessarily pertain to Him according as He is the first cause of all things, exceeding all things caused by Him."[15]

Because the perfections of creatures are limited and partial, when we assert them of God we must think of them as having all limitation and imperfection removed. (This is called "the way of remotion.") And because God is infinite, we must also think of them as realized to an infinite degree. (This is called "the way of excellence.")

Finally, to avoid the pitfall of anthropomorphism, the error, that is, of casting God in the likeness of man, we must remember that any concept we apply to God is used analogously. This means that God and man are proportionally, not essentially, related. We can say equally of man and God that the way they exist is proportionate to what they are—thus:

$$\frac{\text{The existence of man}}{\text{The essence of man}} \quad . . \quad \frac{\text{The existence of God}}{\text{The essence of God}}$$

No matter how great the difference between what man is and what God is, the proportion between the way in which existence is realized in relation to their kind of being remains constant.

Other Ways to the Existence of God

A recent book bearing the title *The God That Failed,*[16] recounts the disillusionment which led a number of Communist writers to reject the god of Communism. As against this god that fails, others, like St. Augustine in his *Confessions,* tell of how they discovered the God that never fails—of how from the very living out of a human life we can come to know of the existence of the true God. For besides

---

15 *Summa Theologiae,* I, 12, 12.
16 Richard Crossman, *The God That Failed* (New York: Harper & Brothers, 1950).

the "ways" of the speculative intellect, the practical intellect has its "ways" too to the knowledge of the existence of God.[17]

These ways are sometimes called the moral arguments because they rest on facts of man's moral life—the facts of conscience, for example—which become meaningless or delusive if God does not exist. Such arguments in their popular expression are not philosophical, though they are a valid reflection of those intelligible necessities within being upon which the intellect consciously or otherwise bases itself. We have to do, in short, with a special case of what St. Thomas called connatural knowledge.[18] There can be, that is, a kind of lived knowledge of the truth, a knowledge which receives its test and confirmation in our daily lives, in this case the knowledge of the radical insufficiency of certain facts of man's moral life to explain themselves apart from God.

The Argument from Man's Higher Aspirations

The most significant fact of our moral lives is the basic choice between good and evil which sooner or later confronts every person who reaches the use of reason: that decision which puts either self at the center of reality or which recognizes something higher than self. This is the decision that determines the whole cast of a man's life: either God exists, and our aspirations to truth, to justice, to something higher than ourselves really reflect what is deepest in our nature; or God does not exist, and we should logically deny our ideals and aspirations and, denying all interests but our own, become "beaked and taloned graspers of the world." Paul Claudel puts the contrast thus:

"Here is a man of sound judgment, right mind, and feeling heart. How then can he imagine that what is strongest, best, most life-giving in his nature, is what deceives him, and is to him a source of illusion and error? Whereas the coarsest parts, passion, egoism, material instinct—those whose field is narrowest and can never

---

17   See J. Maritain, *Approaches to God* (New York: Harper & Brothers, 1954).
18   See Chapter 10.

go beyond their instrumental value without knocking straightway against death—that these are the sole certitude and the sole legitimate groundwork of our nature?"[19]

Sometimes the choice is wrongly made and it is only after the bitter testing that the knowledge is gained of a life lived wrongly, of misspent years: "Too late have I loved Thee, O Thou Beauty of ancient days," was the anguished cry of St. Augustine.

The Path of Created Beauty

Another of the "paths" of the practical intellect is, for Jacques Maritain, by way of artistic making and "creation in beauty," for beauty is but one more of the many mirrors of God. The artist engaged in the manifestation of beauty in his works cannot but be led, consciously or unconsciously, to God as the principle of all beauty. And he quotes in illustration the famous passage from Baudelaire: ". . . it is this immortal instinct for the beautiful which makes us consider the earth and its various spectacles as a sketch of, as a *correspondence* with, heaven. The insatiable thirst for all that is beyond, and which life reveals, is the most living proof of our immortality. It is at once through poetry and *across* poetry, through and *across* music, that the soul glimpses the splendors situated beyond the grave; and when an exquisite poem brings tears to the eyes, these tears are not proof of an excess of joy, they are rather the testimony of an irritated melancholy, a demand of the nerves, of a nature exiled in the imperfect and desiring to take possession immediately, even on this earth, of a revealed paradise."[20]

The Testimony of the Mystics

The testimony of the mystics, the "friends of God," those rare and favored souls who know of God because of the closeness

---

19 Paul Claudel, *Ways and Crossways* (New York: Sheed and Ward, 1933), p. 112. Cf. Dostoevski, in *Notes from Underground*: "Can I have been constructed simply in order to come to the conclusion that all my construction is a cheat? Can this be my whole purpose? I do not believe it."

20 Quoted in J. Maritain, *Approaches to God*, pp. 85, 88.

of their union with Him, was in the eyes of Henri Bergson[21] the strongest confirmation of the arguments for the existence of God. When these great souls testify in unison of their knowledge of the existence of God as a lived experience, the only adequate explanation is, in the words of Bergson, "the real existence of the Being with whom they believed themselves in communication."[22]

We may add that such heroic sanctity, so much goodness, such treasures of wisdom poured out so prodigally, could not be the fruit of illusion. The only adequate explanation of the grace, the freedom, the nobility which they show forth in their lives is the inspiration and influence of the God whom they proclaim.

Summary

The invisible God, through His effects in the visible universe, can be known even to common sense. The history of the universal belief of man in the existence of God testifies to the strength of this evidence. From its earliest days philosophy has sought to formulate scientifically adequate proofs for the existence of God. Although some philosophers have thought that the existence of God can be known intuitively, philosophers in the Aristotelian-Thomistic tradition reject this position as implying an erroneous theory of human knowing. The traditional arguments as summarized by St. Thomas in the Five Ways start from some fact in the sensible universe and proceed by way of the laws of being to the existence of the Being who is God. Although we can know the fact of God's existence, our knowledge of His nature is incomplete and analogous.

---

21 Henri Bergson (1859-1941) is the exponent of the doctrine called "creative evolution." A dynamic philosophy recalling the ancient Heraclitean doctrine of universal change, it challenged the static, mechanistic philosophy of materialism which prevailed at the time.

22 Quoted in Jolivet, *Cours de Philosophie*, p. 303.

CONCLUSION

CHAPTER 29

The Perennial Philosophy

We are like dwarfs seated on the shoulders of giants. We see moe things than the amcients and things more distant, but it is due neither to the sharpness of our sight nor the greatness of our stature, it is simply because they have lent us their own.
BERNARD OF CHARTRES, IN JOHN OF SALISBURY, METAL., III, 4.
(TRANSLATION THAT OF E. GILSON.)

In our philosophizing in previous chapters we have had occasion from time to time to explore the various fields of knowledge and the way in which they differ from one another. It is now time for us to co-ordinate all these separate insights and consider the problem we left unanswered in our opening chapter: the definition of philosophy in the strict sense. To get our definition into sharper relief we shall first distinguish philosophy from other ways of knowing to which it is closely related and with which it is sometimes confused.

Philosophy and Common Sense

As we found to be the case with the term "philosophy" itself we can assign both a broad general meaning and a strict technical meaning to the expression "common sense."

In its wide, popular meaning common sense is simply the conglomeration of generally held opinions and beliefs, more or less well founded, more or less mixed up with error and prejudice, which make up the voice of the community—"what everybody knows." It may also refer in this broad usage to good practical sense in everyday affairs—to "good horse sense."

In a philosophical context the expression has had a number of meanings. For the Romans, common sense meant the vulgar opinions of mankind.[1] For St. Thomas it was a technical expression for the unifying sense.[2] For certain modern philosophers it has meant a kind of instinct or special feeling for the truth.[3]

None of these usages square with the strict interpretation we have given to the expression "common sense" above. (See Chapter 11.) It is important therefore to recall the exact sense in which we have used it. Common sense refers to the spontaneous activity of the intellect, the way in which it operates of its own native vigor before it has been given any special training. It implies man's native capacity to know the most fundamental aspects of reality, in particular, the existence of things (including my own existence), the first principles of being (the principles of identity, noncontradiction, and excluded middle), and secondary principles which flow immediately from the self-evident principles (the principles of sufficient reason, causality, etc.).

One of the points that links philosophy and common sense is that they both use these principles. They differ however in the way they use them. Common sense uses them unconsciously, unreflectively, uncritically. They can be obscured or deformed for common sense by faulty education, by cultural prejudices, by deceptive sense imagery. Philosophy on the contrary uses these principles critically, consciously, scientifically. It can get at things demonstratively, through their causes. It can therefore defend and communicate its knowledge.

The certainties of common sense, the insights of a reasoning which is implicit rather than explicit, are just as well founded as the certainties of philosophy, for the light of common sense is fundamentally the same as that of philosophy: the natural light of

---

1 See Cicero, *De Orat.*, I, 3; Seneca, *3rd letter to Quintillion*, Sect. 3.

2 See above, p. 71.

3 This doctrine was first held by Thomas Reid (1710-1796), the originator of the school of thought which is known as the Scottish Common Sense School.

the intellect. But in common sense this light does not return upon itself by critical reflection, is not perfected by scientific reasoning. *Philosophy, therefore, as contrasted with common sense is scientific knowledge; knowledge, that is, through causes.*

A second point which links philosophy and common sense is that they take all reality for their province—common sense blindly, in a kind of instinctive response of the individual to the totality of experience; philosophy consciously, in the endeavor to give every aspect of reality its due. This claim of philosophy to know the whole of reality does not mean that the philosopher makes pretense of knowing everything—the human intellect cannot exhaust the mystery of the smallest being in the universe, let alone everything. It remains true, nevertheless, that all things are the subject matter of philosophy, in the sense that the philosopher takes as his angle of vision or point of view the highest principles, the ultimate causes, of all reality. Along with common sense, then, *philosophy seeks the comprehensive, all-inclusive view of reality; it is the knowledge of all things.*

Philosophy is thus close to common sense and at the same time different from it. It differs from common sense because it holds its conclusions scientifically, with a clarity and depth inaccessible to common sense. It is close to common sense because it shares the universality of common sense and a common insight into the fundamental structure of reality. We might even say that philosophy grows out of common sense, and that common sense taken in its strict meaning is a kind of foreshadowing, a dim silhouette, of philosophy proper. Any philosophy, therefore, that strays very far from common sense is suspect. If it goes so far as to contradict the basic certitudes of common sense, then it is guilty of denying reality itself, and on this point common sense can pass judgment on it.

Philosophy and the Different Orders of Scientific Knowledge

We have said that philosophic knowledge differs from common-sense knowledge because it is knowledge through causes. This is the characteristic of all knowledge which can be called scientific, as Aristotle pointed out long ago. You have scientific knowledge when you can give the causes of a thing, its necessary reasons. You can explain the reason why. You can tell what will happen whenever those causes are found under the same conditions. Common-sense knowledge can tell you that water expanding into steam will exert pressure; scientific knowledge tells you why and can predict with certainty the degree of pressure that a given amount of steam will exert on a measured surface.

But, as we have seen, there are different kinds and different fields of scientific explanation. Some branches of investigation get at the immediate or proximate causes of things, others get at the remote or ultimate causes. It is, therefore, one of the tasks of philosophy to find the hierarchy and order of the different sciences.[4]

The Principle of Order of the Branches of Knowledge

Using the word "science" in the older sense to cover all kinds of certain knowledge through causes, our present task is to find some principle by which we can differentiate between the various fields of scientific inquiry. One possible approach to this problem is through a consideration of the kinds of causes stressed by the different kinds of knowing; thus, for example, the concern of the physical sciences is seen to be with material causes, the special interest of mathematics with formal causes, while philosophy especially stresses formal and final causes.[5] Another approach is in terms of method; philosophy and mathematics, for example, are deductive in a way not possible for the natural sciences, whose method is mainly inductive. But the ideal principle of differentiation is found, according to the philosophy of Aristotle, in the various degrees of formal abstraction.[6]

---

4 "It is the function of the wise man to put things in order, because wisdom is primarily the perfection of reason and it is the charactcristic of reason to know order." St. Thomas, On the Ethics of Aristotle, lect. 1.

5 See W. R. Thompson, *Science amd Common Sense* (New York: Longmans, Green and Co., 1937), Chapter 7.

6 For the kinds and levels of abstraction, see above, Chapter 25.

Science and Philosophy on the First Level of Abstraction

The first level of abstraction is the level on which the intellect abstracts from the concrete individuality of material things and studies the qualitative characteristics they possess in common. This sphere of knowledge is coextensive with that part of reality which falls directly under our senses—the universe of changing bodies. This is the domain the Greek philosophers called "physics," and it presents, as they saw, a double aspect: an aspect of change and an aspect of permanence. Beneath the restless tides of change which make up the horizon of the senses, there is a stabilizing reality to which the intellect can reach, a permanence of structure which guarantees the constancy of things and their operations, and thus renders possible a *science* of changing bodies.

In investigating this realm of nature the intellect can oscillate between two poles. It can try on the one hand to penetrate to the inner intelligible structure of things, to find out their essential constitution, their unchanging inner nature or being. Or it can on the other hand turn to the peripheral aspect of things, to the qualities they display and the operations they perform, things which are immediately verifiable by the senses and capable of measurement.

To illustrate: my curiosity may be aroused by a certain plant I run across. I can ask this kind of question about it: How does it fit into the general classification of plants? What is its cellular structure? What kind of food sustains it? To answer this kind of question I have to turn to the report of my senses. Or I can ask another kind of question: What is the difference between a live plant and a dead plant? What are the characteristics of living being? What is a soul? I can answer this kind of question only in the light of the intelligible values of being itself.

Because this plane of abstraction offers two ways of understanding the real, we say that there are two distinct kinds of knowledge, which we may term the ontological and the empiriological according as the intellect penetrates the inner nature of things or as it moves toward their sensible appearances.[7] The first kind of knowledge is called the philosophy of nature: *philosophy* because it stresses the being aspect of things; *of nature*, because it is limited to the being of changing, material things.

The second kind of knowledge is called today physical science, natural science, empirical science. It is called *science* because it reaches stable knowledge through causes. It is called *physical*, *natural*, or *empirical* because it deals with the area of sensible, material reality (*physics* is from the Greek word for nature; *nature* and *empirical* both indicate the realm of the sensible).

Thus the natural sciences and the philosophy of nature share the same subject matter—the world of changing bodies—but study it from different points of view.[8] Even on this plane, we see verified, though in a relative way, the statement that science deals with proximate causes, philosophy with ultimate causes, for the questions which the philosophy of nature asks—what is change, what is a body, etc.—are about things that are taken for granted, taken on faith, so to speak, by the physical sciences. They are the questions that are ultimate for this order of reality.[9]

Philosophy and Mathematics

A second genus of knowledge is constituted by those sciences which have developed out of man's penetration into that deeper layer of reality where being is disclosed in its quantitative aspects.

---

7 We are using here the terminology proposed by Maritain in his *Philosophy of Nature* (New York: Philosophical Library, 1951).

8 In the technical language of philosophy the subject matter of a science is called the *material object* of that science. The point of view from which it is studied is called its *fomal object*. Man, for example, is the material object of the sciences of anthropology, anatomy, political economy, sociology. The formal aspect or point of view from which man is studied varies of course with each of these sciences, and is the principle by which they are differentiated from each other; thus, anthropology studies man as an animal, anatomy, according to his skeletal structure, etc.

9 Because they are not the absolutely ultimate questions—for the philosophy of nature leans on the principles of metaphysics—we say that the philosophy of a nature is an imperfect or dependent wisdom; cf. Aristotle: Physics is also a wisdom, but it is not the first kind" (*Metaphysics*, IV, 3; 1005 b 1).

Analogously to the division we found on the first level of abstraction we are obliged again to separate the mathematical sciences from the philosophy of mathematics. Thus, where arithmetic studies the properties of numbers, or geometry the nature of plane surfaces, the philosophy of mathematics studies the being itself of number, quantity, and so on.

We might note here the special character of mathematical physics which is a kind of mathematics of nature. In this science the intellect moves from one plane of abstraction to another; though formally mathematical, since its method of analysis is mathematical, it is materially physical: *what* is analyzed is physical reality —(this is the "physics" part of mathematical physics).

Metaphysics or the First Philosophy

The third level of abstraction brings us finally to the domain of philosophy in the strict sense—the plane on which the intellect grasps being as being, *being* isolated in all its intelligible purity as against its partial revelation in *this* or *that* being. Here the intellect penetrates through the veils of matter to the very nerve of reality, to being in its full transcendental value, as it is realized analogically, from the least of existing things to the greatest. This is the heart of philosophy, metaphysics, the philosophy of being, the *First Philosophy* of Aristotle.

Philosophy and the Higher Wisdoms

Aristotle offered the name theology as an alternative to first philosophy because the tracing of causes to their origin brings us back to that part of reality which is permanent, unchanging, eternal—to God Himself, "for God is thought to be among the causes of all things and to be a first principle." Hence for Aristotle, metaphysics is "the divine science."[10]

The religions of Judaism and Christianity, however, brought to

---

10 *Metaphysics*, I, 2; 983 a 8; cf. Cicero: "Wisdom is the knowledge of things divine and human" (*De Finibus* II, 12, 37).

the world the knowledge of a wisdom higher than the wisdom of philosophy: the knowledge of things divine which is given to us by God Himself through revelation. It became necessary therefore to distinguish more explicitly than did the Greeks between the purely rational, philosophical knowledge of God—which is called natural theology—and the knowledge of God we receive through revelation—which is called, in its systematic formulation, revealed or sacred theology.

There is, in other words, more than one path to the knowledge of God and therefore more than one wisdom. The wisdom of sacred theology is called a higher wisdom than philosophy because its subject matter, the knowledge of God in His inmost nature, His inmost life, is higher than the subject matter of philosophy.

But some of the truths given to us through revelation are also known to us by reason. The fields of philosophy and theology, in other words, overlap. It is important, therefore, to define their boundaries and determine their relation to each other. To secure this final element in our definition we must turn aside temporarily and examine more closely the relations between revelation and reason.

Reason and Revelation

Historically the efforts to reconcile the valid claims of both reason and revelation have run all the way from the denial of reason in favor of revelation to the deification of reason and the denial of the very possibility of revelation. Along the lines of the first extreme, some theologians have held that God's revelation has disclosed all the things that are really important for man to know, and that the search for further knowledge is dangerous and illusory. Tertullian, a second century writer, sets the type. St. Bernard and St. Peter Damian in the twelfth century, and the Franciscan Spirituals at the end of the Middle Ages to some extent reflect the type.[11] St. Paul is their favorite authority: "See to it that no one deceives you by

---

11 See E. Gilson, *Reason and Revelation im the Middle Ages* (New York: Sneed and Ward, 1938), Chap. 1.

philosophy and vain deceit, according to human traditions, according to the elements of the world and not according to Christ" (Col. 2:8).[12] Misguided zealots like Tertullian who defend revelation by destroying reason are fortunately rare and we need not spend time on them.

1. "Faith Seeking Understanding"

A considerable distance from this uncompromising fideism, but still frequently blurring the lines between faith and reason is that strong tradition which, basing itself on St. Augustine, holds that faith is the indispensable condition of understanding. For St. Augustine—his own intellectual and moral history so taught him —natural reason by itself is hopelessly inadequate to the pursuit of ultimate truth. Faith paves the way for reason by disciplining the soul and spiritualizing the intellect. Since the intellect is led by love, the role of the will in knowing is primary. Christian wisdom, in short, implies right desire as well as true insight.

The prolific family of St. Augustine—it extends from St. Anselm and St. Bonaventure through Malebranche and Pascal right down to Kierkegaard and Newman—stresses, thus, the importance of docility, with reason drawing its sustenance from faith: "Whence shall I begin? With authority, or with reason? The natural order is that authority should precede reason when we wish to learn anything," St. Augustine says.[13] And again, "If you cannot understand, believe in order that you may understand."[14]

The Christian wisdom of St. Augustine showed in time an unfortunate tendency among some of his lesser disciples to degenerate into a kind of Christian theologism, and "faith seeking understanding"

---

12 Needless to say, this is a one-sided interpretation of St. Paul who also tells us that "the invisible things [of God] are clearly seen . . . being understood through the things that are made" (Rom. 1:20); a text that has been rightly interpreted as the divine charter for natural theology (and therefore for philosophy).

13 *De moribus Ecclesiae*, I, 2, 3.

14 *Sermon* 118. This and the preceding text are quoted in Father D'Arcy's article on "The Philosophy of St. Augustine," in *A Monument to St. Augustine* (New York: Sheed and Ward, 1930), p. 159.

only too often meant the reduction of theology to philosophy, with a proliferation by mediocre philosophers of bad reasons for what they believed.

2. The Sundering of Faith and Reason

At the opposite pole to the fideist is the extreme rationalist, who holds that human reason is ultimate and rejects the very possibility of revelation. (The term "naturalism" is sometimes given to this position.) The rationalist in effect deifies reason, since he refuses to admit the possibility of anything higher—of God, for example. Instead of submitting his intellect to truth, he declares that he is the arbiter and measure of truth.

A less extreme version of rationalism is that of philosophers like Descartes who believe in the fact of revelation but hold that nothing revealed can be understood; the gap between reason and faith is so great that they cannot be related to one another. Thus, for philosophers like Descartes and his followers, the mind gives a blind assent to the data of revelation and the intellect goes about its business of philosophizing in complete indifference to theology.

These positions must be further distinguished from the position of those who, lacking the gift of faith in a divine revelation, concede nevertheless that such a revelation is possible and not inconsistent with reason. For such persons, though, reason is in fact the last court of appeal, the only wisdom open to man.

3. The Harmony of Faith and Reason

The concord of faith and reason, with the careful safeguarding of the nature and rights of each, was not achieved until the time of St. Thomas, who opposed equally those who introduced philosophy into theology and those who tried to reduce theology to philosophy.[15] St. Thomas first carefully distinguished between theology and

---

15 The essential elements of the solution worked out by St. Thomas had been laid down long before him, and especially by the twelfth-century Jewish philosopher, Moses Maimonides. It remains true, however, that St. Thomas was the first to bring together and synthesize those elements into an orderly solution.

philosophy so that the nature of one could not be confused with the other.

It is the nature of philosophy to proceed solely by way of rational evidence and demonstration based on such evidence; therefore we should never appeal to revelation in support of a philosophical thesis. It is the nature of theology to base itself on the word of God, drawing out the implications of revealed truth in the light of faith; although it may use philosophy as an instrument, it cannot be reduced to philosophy.

Within theology itself St. Thomas distinguished between truths which, though revealed, can also be known by the unaided intellect, such as the existence and unity of God, and revealed truths which are beyond reason, such as the Trinity and the Incarnation.[16] Even though reason can discover truths of the first kind, they are nevertheless revealed because they are essential for man to know and unaided reason can attain them only with difficulty and at the constant risk of error. Once understood, however, they are known and not believed; that is, they are held as philosophy, and not on faith. The second class of truth, secrets of God's inner being which are of their very nature forever inaccessible to reason, will never be held other than as faith, for "what belongs to faith cannot be proved demonstratively."[17]

Having thus distinguished between believing and knowing, between faith and reason, St. Thomas is careful to make the point that although they are distinct they are not separate: "The gifts of grace are added to nature in such a manner that they do not remove but perfect it. So it is with the light of faith that is infused in us gratuitously: it does not destroy the light of natural knowledge with which we are by nature endowed."

A truth in one order cannot contradict a truth in another order.

---

16 See *Summa Contra Gentiles*, I, 3.

17 This and the following texts in this section are taken from In Boeth. de Trin., III, 1, ad 3. Quoted by A. C. Pegis, in the Introduction to On the Truth of the Catholic Faith (Summa Contra Gentiles) (New York: Doubleday and Company, 1955), Vol. 1, pp. 24-26.

A truth in philosophy cannot contradict a truth of faith: "Now although the natural light of the human mind does not suffice for the manifestation of the things that are made manifest by faith, yet it is impossible that what is divinely taught to us by faith be contrary to the things with which we are endowed by nature. For one or the other would then have to be false, and since both come to us from God, God would be to us an author of falsehood, which is impossible."

Because a truth of the natural order cannot possibly contradict a truth of the revealed order, the philosopher or scientist is free to investigate nature as far as his researches can carry him, in the full confidence that he cannot discover any truth that will contradict revelation.[18]

On the other hand, theology exercises a kind of negative jurisdiction over philosophy and the empirical sciences, in the sense that where there is an apparent contradiction between reason and faith, the theologian claims the right, in view of the infinitely more sure source of his truth, to tell the philosopher or the scientist that he has erred somewhere and must go over his reasons again. "For if in what the philosophers have said we come upon something that is contrary to faith, this does not belong to philosophy but is rather an abuse of philosophy arising from a defect in reason."

To sum up: Wisdom is knowledge about the ultimate reality, the unchanging being of God Himself, but is realized according to different lights: philosophical wisdom according to the natural light of reason; theological wisdom according to the light of faith. The two wisdoms, though related, are distinct, and to confuse one with the other is to destroy it. *Philosophy therefore seeks its goal by the natural light*

---

18 See the following on this point: "The position of Aquinas may be considered a healthy one in that it assures the rational investigator, the philosopher or the scientist, that he need not fear to pursue his independent studies. Nothing he can firmly establish can possibly be counter to true religion. Some historians have thought that this attitude of Aquinas has helped to free European thought from the fear of undermining religion and so has helped to make possible the independent pursuit of natural science." Stallknecht and Brumbaugh, *Spirit of Western Philosophy* (New York: Longmans, Green and Co., 1950), p. 206.

of reason alone.

The Definition of Philosophy

We now have all the elements necessary for us to define philosophy in its strict sense. First, we have seen that it differs from the everyday knowledge of common sense in that it is scientific knowledge of things through their causes. Second, since philosophy studies being itself it shares with common sense an interest in the whole of reality as against the parceling out of reality which is characteristic of the natural sciences. Our third point is that philosophy differs from the physical sciences not only in terms of the greater universality of its subject matter, but also in terms of its approach to its subject matter: whereas the physical sciences concern themselves with proximate or secondary causes, philosophy deals with first or ultimate causes. Finally, philosophy differs from revealed theology in that it uses reason alone to reach its answers, whereas the light of theology is the light of faith.

Our definition of philosophy epitomizes all these elements: *Philosophy is the knowledge of all things in their first principles or causes as seen by the natural light of reason.*

This definition of philosophy has grown out of the gradual differentiation in time of the various orders of knowledge. This differentiation unfortunately was not achieved without violence and difficulty, each order of knowledge—theology, philosophy, mathematics, the empirical sciences—all tyrannically claiming at one time or another to be the sole interpreter of reality.

The truth is that the full knowledge of anything comprises all that can be discovered about it on all the levels of investigation —scientific, mathematical, and philosophic; and the man of religious faith will further integrate this knowledge with what revelation tells him in those areas where philosophy opens onto theology. We separate out the various aspects of a thing for detailed study, but only in order to make a final integration which will restore all those separate facets of the thing into a unified whole. In brief, we "distinguish in order to unite."[19]

Christian Philosophy

Considered in its essence according as we have just defined it, philosophy to the extent that its nature is fully realized must be the same for all men at all times and all places. In this strict sense there cannot be a Christian philosophy any more than there can be a Christian mathematics or a Christian grammar, for philosophy as such, in its pure nature, is the work of reason alone—"the perfect work of reason," St. Thomas calls it.[20]

But the definition of philosophy is an abstract essence, and abstractions are not found except in a mind. Philosophy is in fact formulated by living men who are part of an age and environment which they cannot help but reflect—if only in their choice of problems—in their philosophizing. It is in this context, the state of philosophy, the concrete conditions under which it is realized, as contrasted with the bare essence or nature of philosophy, such as we have expressed it in our definition, that it becomes possible to speak of Christian philosophy (or of Indian philosophy, or of Marxist philosophy). Thus with reference to the Middle Ages we can quite properly speak of a Christian philosophy as contrasted with Arabian or Jewish philosophy; or, in the case of modern philosophy we can speak of English philosophy as against the philosophy of the Continent.

In a period such as the European Middle Ages when the Christian religion predominated, it was inevitable that the dominant theological preoccupations of the time should be reflected in philosophy. This relationship could be a harmful one, as when, for example, theology attempted to swallow up philosophy, but in general the interchange between philosophy and theology which gives Christian philosophy its distinctive character has been a fruitful one for philosophy. Under the stimulus of theology, philosophy has investigated areas of reality which might otherwise have lain fallow

---

19 For the interrelationship of the different levels of knowledge and the divisions of philosophy, see Charts on p. 260.

20 *Summa Theologiae*, 45, 2.

forever. In the endeavor to explain the data of revelation, philosophers have explored and deepened such key concepts as those of nature, personality, freedom. There has even been a more positive contribution in the actual disclosure to philosophy of truths hitherto ignored or but dimly perceived; the definition of God as being, for example, comes from the Scriptures; the distinction between nature and person is another such gift of theology to philosophy.[21] Negatively, the external control of theology over philosophy has helped to keep it from error.

Besides the work of enlightening and fertilizing the human reason, the Christian sees in theology the further effect of healing and elevating. For although philosophy by essence is solely dependent on the natural reason, and is therefore autonomous in its own order, as realized existentially by actual, living, human beings, "it benefits by being exercised in a subject enjoying the radically changed conditions of existence effected gratuitously by the life of grace and the infused intellectual and moral virtues and gifts, in whom they mutually strengthen each other and are integrated into a vital synergy."[22]

In the light of this relationship between philosophy and theology, Jacques Maritain defines Christian philosophy as "philosophy itself in so far as it is situated in those utterly distinctive conditions of existence and exercise into which Christianity has ushered the thinking subject, and as a result of which philosophy *perceives* certain objects and *validly demonstrates* certain propositions, which in any other circumstances would to a greater or lesser extent elude it."[23] Professor Gilson points out that Christian philosophy is a family of philosophies, including in its extent "all those philosophical systems which were in fact what they were only because a Christian religion existed and because they were ready to submit to its influence."

---

21 On this point see the masterly study of Professor Gilson, *The Spirit of Mediaeval Philosophy*, translated by A. H. C. Downes (New York: Charles Scribner's Sons, 1936).

22 Emmanuel Chapman, 'Living Thomism," in *The Thomist*, Vol. IV, No. 3 (July, 1942), p. 385.

23 *An Essay on Christian Philosophy* (New York: Philosophical Library, 1955), p. 30.

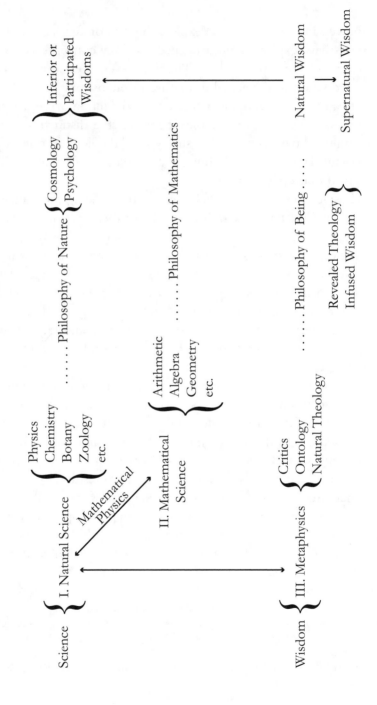

The Levels of Knowledge

Science
I. Natural Science
{ Physics
Chemistry
Botany
Zoology
etc. } ...... Philosophy of Nature { Cosmology
Psychology } Inferior or Participated Wisdoms

Mathematical Physics

II. Mathematical Science
{ Arithmetic
Algebra
Geometry
etc. } ...... Philosophy of Mathematics

Wisdom
III. Metaphysics
{ Critics
Ontology
Natural Theology } ...... Philosophy of Being ......
{ Revealed Theology
Infused Wisdom }

Natural Wisdom → Supernatural Wisdom

The Divisions of Philosophy

1. *Aristotelian Division:*

Propaedeutic of Introductory...	Logic
Speculative Philosophy.........	{ Physics Mathematics Metaphysics
Practical Philosophy..........	{ Ethics Politics
Poetical Philosophy	Art

2. *The Thomistic Division*

Propaedeutic.................	Logic	
Speculative Philosophy.........	Philosophy of Nature	{ Cosmology Psychology
	Philosophy of Mathematics	
	Philosophy of Being	{ Ontology Natural Theology
Practical Philosophy..........	Philosophy of Art	
	Philosophy of Morals	{ Ethics Political Philosophy

3. *The Wolffian Divison:*

Metaphysics	{ General Special	{ Ontology Psychology Cosmology Theodicy (Natural Theology)
Normative Sciences	{ Logic Ethics Aesthetics	{ General Special

NOTE: The divisions given for Aristotle and St. Thomas are implicit in their writings. Wolff (1679-1754), a disciple of Leibniz, stressing the ontological aspects of the philosophy of nature, made it a division of metaphysics. Some philosophers in the Aristotelian-Thomistic tradition today prefer to follow him on this point.

Against this background he defines Christian philosophy as "every philosophy which, although keeping the two orders formally distinct, nevertheless considers the Christian revelation as an indispensable auxiliary to reason."[24]

It remains true, nevertheless, that no matter what its conditions of formation or exercise within the individual philosopher, the worth of any philosophy depends when all is said and done upon its truth, the firmness with which it is based on rational evidence and the rigor with which it demonstrates its conclusions, so that if a philosophy that calls itself Christian falls short of what the essence of philosophy demands, to that extent it is a decadent philosophy.

The Perennial Philosophy

What should we call the philosophy we have been trying to develop in the course of this work? Many names are possible. For instance, since it is a philosophy developed in accordance with the principles of Aristotle, it can be called the Aristotelian philosophy. This is not to say that it is a mere re-working of Aristotle's philosophy. It implies rather that we have built upon certain basic insights into the nature of reality which were first disclosed by Aristotle. And what was first seen by Aristotle to be the way things are, is still the way things are, for the structure of reality does not change from generation to generation. But while the philosophy of Aristotle is in this sense ageless, it is also true that by the very nature of its constitution as a science always open to the mystery of being it is susceptible to endless growth and enrichment. The treasures of intelligibility enfolded in the least act of existence are inexhaustible, so that while the basis of philosophy does not change, its horizon is boundless; philosophy will be finished only when the last metaphysician on earth for the last time closes his eyes on being.

If you wish to emphasize the rock solid foundation of our philosophy in the nature of things as they are, you can call it the Realist philosophy. Stressing the collective labor which has gone into its

---

24 *The Spirit of Mediaeval Philosophy* (New York: Sheed and Ward, Inc., 1938), p. 37.

elaboration over the centuries, it may be termed the Common philosophy. Or, since metaphysics is the archstone of our philosophy, we can call it the philosophy of being.

Among those who have expressed the philosophy of being in a Christian context, St. Thomas Aquinas is outstanding. Much in the way that Aristotle gathered up and synthesized all that had been done before him in philosophy, so did St. Thomas in his day epitomize in a new and daring synthesis all that was worth rescuing in the name of truth. He did more. He deepened his Aristotelian inheritance so profoundly as in effect to transform it, for in virtue of his unique metaphysical intuition of existence, philosophy with St. Thomas "for the first time in its long history was able to reach deeper than the level of inextinguishable essences to the fathomless undercurrents of existence irradiated by them."[25] Those for whom St. Thomas has thus transposed the philosophy of being from an essentialist to an existentialist key will frequently signify this profound transformation by calling the philosophy of being Thomist rather than Aristotelian.

Stressing the great teachers who have elaborated and transmitted the philosophy of being in the schools of Europe, the name Scholastic is sometimes used as synonymous with the Thomistic philosophy. The term is open to serious objection, however, in that it is equally used to designate the philosophy taught in general in the medieval universities—which was in fact a good deal more likely to be Augustinian than Aristotelian in its inspiration.

The ultimate appeal of any philosophy, however, will be not in terms of its originators or its teachers, but in terms of its truth. In the language of St. Thomas himself, "the study of philosophy is that we may know not what men have taught but what the truth of things is."[26] In the sense that it is the expression of truth, and therefore everlasting, the philosophy of being is called the perennial philosophy, the enduring philosophy. Given this emphasis, the

---

25 Emmanuel Chapman, "To Be—That Is the Answer," in the Maritain volume of *The Thomist* (Jan., 1943), p. 144.

26 *In De Coelo et Mundo*, I, X, led. 22.

perennial philosophy is not the particular philosophy of any person or school, but simply the philosophy collectively worked out through the centuries by innumerable anonymous toilers in the vineyard of truth. The perennial philosophy, in short, is philosophy itself, which because it is true is therefore perdurable.

Philosophy is perennial in another sense, in its need for constant renewal. For although the principles of philosophy are timeless, they are nevertheless worked out in time, and it is the task of the philosopher to incarnate the bloodless abstractions of philosophy afresh for each new generation, and confronting the ever new and ever more complex problems of society, to bring "new treasures out of old." In the words of Emmanuel Chapman, "The perennial philosophy by its very nature must be always freshly present. Not ancient or neo, but current and living, it should be ready to answer the most crucial questions of today. The philosophy in touch with existence has the challenge within itself to deepen and perfect itself, and keep itself in a constant state of renewal."[27]

---

27 *Loc. cit.*, p. 152.

READING LIST

The bibliography which follows is confined to works in the classical realist tradition. The student who is thoroughly grounded in this philosophy will find little difficulty in extending his investigations to new fields.

A useful complement to the student's first studies in philosophy is the reading of some history of philosophy. The following are recommended:

Copleston, F. C., *History of Philosophy* (Westminster, Md.: The Newman Press). Volume I: Ancient Philosophy—Greece and Rome (1946). Volume II: Mediaeval Philosophy—Augustine to Scotus (1950). Volume III: Mediaeval Philosophy—Ockham to Suarez (1953).

Martin, Clark, Clarke and Ruddick, *A History of Philosophy* (New York: Appleton-Century-Crofts, 1941).

Stallknecht, N. P., and Brumbaugh, R. S., *The Spirit of Western Philosophy* (New York: Longmans, Green and Co., 1950).

Thilly, F., and Woods, L., *A History of Philosophy* (New York: Henry Holt and Co., 1951).

Thonnard, F. J., *A Short History of Philosophy* (New York: Descleé & Cie, 1955).

Other "Introductions to Philosophy" which can be consulted usefully:

Bremond, A., *Philosophy in the Making* (New York: Benziger Brothers, 1930).

De Raeymaeker, L., *Introduction to Philosophy* (New York: Joseph A.

Wagner, Inc., 1947).

Hocking, W. E., *Types of Philosophy* (New York: Charles Scribner's Sons, 1929).

Maritain, J., *Introduction to Philosophy* (New York: Sheed and Ward, Inc., 1930).

Perry, R., *A Defense of Philosophy* (Cambridge, Mass.: Harvard University Press, 1931).

Stallknecht, N. P., and Brumbaugh, R. S., *The Compass of Philosophy* (New York: Longmans, Green and Co., 1954).

Wild, J., *Introduction to Realistic Philosophy* (New York: Harper & Brothers, 1948).

General Studies in the Philosophy of St. Thomas Aquinas:

Chesterton, G. K., *St. Thomas Aquinas* (New York: Sheed and Ward, Inc., 1933). This has been reissued in a paperback edition by the Image Book Division of Doubleday Co., 1955.

D'Arcy, M. C., *Thomas Aquinas*, rev. ed. (Westminster, Md.: The Newman Press, 1954).

Gilson, E., *The Christian Philosophy of St. Thomas Aquinas* (New York: Random House, 1956).

Maritain, J., *St. Thomas Aquinas* (New York: Sheed and Ward, Inc., 1936).

Sertillanges, A. D., *Foundations of Thomistic Philosophy* (St. Louis: B. Herder Book Company, 1931).

Vann, G., *St. Thomas Aquinas* (London: Hague and Gill, 1940).

For the Explanation of Philosophic Terminology:

Runes, D., *Dictionary of Philosophy* (New York: Philosophical Library, 1942).

Wuellner, B., *Dictionary of Scholastic Philosophy* (Milwaukee: The Bruce Publishing Company, 1956).

Recommended Readings for Part 1

Plato, *Euthyphro*, *Apology*, and *Crito*; conveniently collected along with the death scene from the Phaedo (New York: Liberal Arts

Press, 1948).

—— *Republic*, translated with commentary by Francis Cornford (New York: Oxford University Press, 1945). Read Books I—IV and VIII—IX.

Aristotle, *Metaphysics*, Bk. I. This is conveniently found in the edition of R. McKeon, The Basic Works of Aristotle (New York: Random House, 1941).

Burnet, J., *Greek Philosophy from Thales to Plato* (London: Black, 1948).

Guardini, Romano, *The Death of Socrates* (New York: Sheed and Ward, Inc., 1949).

Jaeger, W., *Aristotle* (Oxford: Oxford University Press, 1949), Chapters I—IV.

Weaver, R. M., *Ideas Have Consequences* (Chicago: University of Chicago Press, 1948), Chapter I.

Wild, J., *Introduction to Realistic Philosophy* (New York: Harper & Brothers, 1948), Chapter I.

Advanced Readings

Cornford, F., *Before and After Socrates* (Cambridge: Cambridge University Press, 1932).

—— *Plato's Theory of Knowledge* (translation of and commentary on the Theaetetus and Sophist) (London: Kegan Paul, 1935).

—— *Plato's Cosmology* (translation of and commentary on the Timaeus) (London: Kegan Paul, 1937).

—— *Plato and Parmenides* (translation of and commentary on the Parmenides) (London: Kegan Paul, 1939).

Hamilton, Edith, *The Greek Way* (New York: W. W. Norton, 1930).

Jaeger, W., *Paideia, The Ideals of Greek Culture* (New York: Oxford University Press, 1939-1944).

Livingstone, R. W., *Portrait of Socrates* (London: Oxford University Press, 1928).

More, P. E., *Platonism* (Princeton: Princeton University Press, 1931).

Nettleship, R. L., *Lectures on the Republic of Plato* (London: The

Macmillan Company, 1898).

Stace, W. T., *Critical History of Greek Philosophy* (London: The Macmillan Company, 1920).

Taylor, A. E., *Plato, the Man and His Work* (New York: The Dial Press, 1929).

Wild, J., *Plato's Theory of Man* (Cambridge, Mass.: Harvard University Press, 1948).

Recommended Readings for Part 2

Lewis, C. S., *The Abolition of Man* (New York: The Macmillan Company, 1947).

Maritain, J., *Three Reformers* (New York: Charles Scribner's Sons, 1929).

Mouroux, J., *The Meaning of Man* (New York: Sheed and Ward, Inc., 1948).

Neill, Thomas P., *Makers of the Modern Mind* (Milwaukee: The Bruce Publishing Company, 1949).

Ramuz, C., *What Is Man?* (New York: Pantheon, 1948).

Advanced Readings

Adler, M. J., *What Man Has Made of Man* (New York: Longmans, Green and Co., 1937).

St. Augustine, *Confessions*, translated by E. B. Pusey, Everyman Edition (New York: E. P. Dutton, 1947).

Gilson, E., *The Christian Philosophy of St. Thomas* (New York: Random House, 1956).

Maritain, J., *Existence and the Existent* (New York: Pantheon, 1948).

——*The Range of Reason* (New York: Charles Scribner's Sons, 1952).

——*Scholasticism and Politics* (New York: The Macmillan Company, 1940).

Sheed, F. J., Communism and Man (New York: Sheed and Ward, Inc., 1938).

Textbooks

Brennan, R., *The Image of His Maker* (Milwaukee: The Bruce Publishing Company, 1948).

——*Thomistic Psychology* (New York: The Macmillan Company, 1941).

Renard, H., and Vaske, M., *The Philosophy of Man*, rev. ed. (Milwaukee: The Bruce Publishing Company, 1956).

Vann, G., *The Heart of Man* (London: Longmans, Green and Co., 1945).

Woodworth, R. S., *General Psychology* (New York: Henry Holt, 1938).

For the writings of St. Thomas, the most convenient edition is *Basic Writings of St. Thomas*, edited by A. C. Pegis (New York: Random House, 1945), 2 vols. *Introduction to St. Thomas*, edited by A. C. Pegis (New York: Modern Library, 1948). Valuable also are *St. Thomas Aquinas: On The Truth of the Catholic Faith: Summa Contra Gentiles: Book One: God*, newly translated with an introduction and notes by Anton C. Pegis (New York: Doubleday Image, 1955); *Book Two: Creation*, newly translated with an introduction and notes by James F. Anderson (New York: Doubleday Image, 1956); *Book Three: Providence*, newly translated with an introduction and notes by Vernon J. Bourke (New York: Doubleday Image, 1956); *Book Four: Providence* (cont.), newly translated with an introduction and notes by Charles O'Neil (New York: Doubleday Image, 1956).

Recommended Reading for Part 3

Aristotle, *Nicomachean Ethics*, Bks. VIII and IX (on friendship).

Plato, Republic, Bk. I; also the Laches (on courage) and the Charmides (on temperance).

St. Thomas Aquinas, *Summa Theologiae*, I-II, 90-97 (on the natural law).

D'Arcy, M. C., Christian Morals (London: Longmans, Green and Co., 1937).

Maritain, J., *The Person and the Common Good* (New York: Charles Scribner's Sons, 1947).

——*The Rights of Man and the Natural Law* (New York: Charles Scribner's Sons, 1943).

Sheedy, J., *The Christian Virtues* (Notre Dame: University of Notre Dame Press, 1949).

Advanced Readings

Adler, M., *A Dialectic of Morals* (Notre Dame: University of Notre Dame Press, 1941).

D'Arcy, M. C., *The Mind and Heart of Love* (New York: Henry Holt and Company, 1947).

Maritain, J., *Man and the State* (Chicago: University of Chicago Press, 1951).

——*True Humanism* (New York: Charles Scribner's Sons, 1938).

Rommen, H., *The Natural Law* (St. Louis: B. Herder Book Company, 1948).

Von Hildebrand, D., *Christian Ethics* (New York: D. J. McKay, 1952).

Textbooks

Bourke, V. J., *Ethics* (New York: The Macmillan Company, 1951). Gilson, E., Moral Values and the Moral Life (St. Louis: B. Herder Book Company, 1931).

Renard, H., *The Philosophy of Morality* (Milwaukee: The Bruce Publishing Company, 1953).

Recommended Readings for Part 4

Maritain, J., *The Philosophy of Nature* (New York: Philosophical Library, 1951).

——*Science and Wisdom* (New York: Charles Scribner's Sons, 1940).

Sullivan, J. W. N., *The Limitations of Science* (New York: The Viking Press, 1934).

Thompson, W. R., *Science and Common Sense* (New York: Long-mans, Green and Co., 1937).

Whittaker, S. T., *From Euclid to Eddington* (Cambridge: Cambridge University Press, 1949).

Advanced Readings

Conant, J. B., *On Understanding Science* (New Haven: Yale University Press, 1947).

Joad, C. E. M., *Philosophical Aspects of Modern Science* (London: Allen and Unwin, 1948).

Sheen, F. J., *Philosophy of Science* (Milwaukee: The Bruce Publishing Company, 1934).

Whitehead, A., *The Concept of Nature* (Cambridge: Cambridge University Press, 1920).

Textbooks

McWilliams, J., *Cosmology* (New York: The Macmillan Company, 1928).

Nys, D., *Cosmology* (Milwaukee: The Bruce Publishing Company, 1942).

Smith, V., *Philosophical Physics* (New York: Harper & Brothers, 1950).

A translation of the *Principles of Nature* of St. Thomas, and his *Commentary on Books I and II of the Physics of Aristotle* will be found in: Kocourek, *An Introduction to the Philosophy of Nature* (St. Paul: North Central Publishing Co., 1948).

Recommended Readings for Part 5

Gilson, E., *The Unity of Philosophical Experience* (New York: Charles Scribner's Sons, 1937).

Lecomte du Nouy, P., *Human Destiny* (New York: Longmans, Green and Co., 1947).

Lewis, C. S., *The Problem of Pain* (New York: The Macmillan Company, 1948).

Maritain, J., *A Preface to Metaphysics* (New York: Sheed and Ward, Inc., 1939).

Noyes, A., *The Unknown God* (New York: Sheed and Ward, Inc., 1934).

Advanced Readings

Garrigou-Lagrange, R., *God, His Existence and Nature* (St. Louis: B. Herder Book Company, 1946).

Gilson, E., *Being and Some Philosophers* (Toronto: Pontifical Institute, 1949).

Maritain, J., *The Degrees of Knowledge* (New York: Charles Scribner's Sons, 1937).

——*Existence and the Existent* (New York: Pantheon, 1948).

Mascall, E., *He Who Is* (London: Longmans, Green and Co., 1943).

Phelan, G., *St. Thomas and Analogy* (Milwaukee: Marquette University Press, 1941).

Textbooks

Benignus, Bro., *Nature, Knowledge, and God* (Milwaukee: The Bruce Publishing Company, 1947).

Joyce, G., *Principles of Natural Theology* (New York: Longmans, Green and Co., 1924).

Renard, H., *Philosophy of Being* (Milwaukee: The Bruce Publishing Company, 1946).

——*Philosophy of God* (Milwaukee: The Bruce Publishing Company, 1951).

Smith, G., *Natural Theology* (New York: The Macmillan Company, 1951).

SUGGESTED TOPICS

Topics for Essays, Part I

Before and After Socrates.

The Place of Philosophy in Education. (Compare Plato, *Republic*, Bks. VI and VII, and Newman, *Idea of a University*, Discourse VI.)

The Problem of the One and the Many.

Plato and Aristotle Compared.

Topics for Discussion

Chapter 1

What are some of the marks which distinguish philosophy from other kinds of knowing?

How would you explain the following sentence: "The teaching of English, of history, of economics, of science is at the same time a teaching of philosophy"?

Does philosophy have any practical value?

Chapter 2

Make a list of things that are real even though our senses cannot perceive them.

Can you find any grounds for the comparison of man as a microcosm to the world viewed as the macrocosm?

Are numbers real things?

Where do numbers exist when you are thinking about them? When you are not thinking about them? If there were no human beings would there be any numbers?

Chapter 3

Is there anything in the world of bodies which does not undergo change?

How are the paradoxes of Zeno answered? If you cannot answer Zeno should you agree with him?

Chapter 4

How does the Sophist view the nature of man? What are the basic causes of Sophistry?

What is the counterpart in our society of the Sophist? What is the effect of the Sophist on society?

Chapter 5

Is there any truth to Socrates' contention that knowledge is virtue; ignorance, vice?

Is there any evidence for Socrates' view that the one who inflicts injustice is harmed more than the one who receives it?

Did Socrates' accusers have any kind of reasonable case against him?

Chapter 6

What is an Idea for Plato as against a sense experience? What is the meaning of meaning for Plato?

How far did Plato succeed in reconciling Heraclitus and Parmenides?

What is Plato's view of the nature of man?

Chapter 7

What does knowing mean for Aristotle?

What is the meaning of meaning for Aristotle?

What is Aristotle's view of the nature of man? How does it differ from Plato's? Which doctrine agrees better with everyday experience?

How far does Aristotle agree with Plato? How does he differ?

Topics for Essays, Part II

The Problem of Skepticism.
The Mystery of Knowing.
The Levels of Freedom.
Friendship in Aristotle.
The Unity of Man.

Topics for Discussion

Chapter 8

Which is more important, the knowledge of man or knowledge of the material universe?

What philosophy of man is implied in the dictum that "man is what he eats"?

What are the distinctive signs by which man is differentiated from the brute animal?

Chapter 9

What are the different levels on which assimilation is possible? Can I really know the President of the United States just through news pictures or other such representations?

If there were no human beings would there be any physical objects? How do you know?

Does the problem of the universals have any practical meaning or is it just an academic exercise?

Chapter 10

How do we know we have internal senses?

What is the difference between a sense image and a concept? What does Pascal mean when he says, "We know the truth not only by the reason but also by the heart"?

Chapter 11

What are some of the common causes of error?

How would you proceed in a discussion with a skeptic about whether we can know anything?

Is there any truth in the saying that "the search for truth is more important than the finding"?

Chapter 12

What is meant by saying that love is at the root of all the emotions?

Can love and hate of the same thing exist together?

How do we know we have free choice?

Chapter 13

What are the different meanings of the term "freedom"? Can you illustrate with examples from everyday life?

What are the philosophical and social implications behind the saying, "Man is born free, and everywhere he is in irons"?

How can a person be subject to a code of laws and still be called free?

Chapter 14

What are the different kinds of love according to St. Thomas?

What did St. Augustine mean when he said, "Love and do what you will"?

How does the love of friendship contrast with the love of charity?

Chapter 15

How would you go about proving to the materialist that the soul exists?

Would the soul of man separated from his body still know things?

What is implied in the saying, "When I sit down so do my thoughts"?

Chapter 16

Comment on the quotation at the head of the Chapter.

Pascal speaks of "the grandeur and the misery of man." What does he mean?

Topics for Essays, Part III

The Virtues and How They Are Related.
The Purpose of Human Life.
The Natural Law.
The Bill of Rights and the Natural Law.
The Common Good.
Friendship and Charity.

Topics for Discussion

Chapter 17

Some philosophers contend that the desire to be happy is selfish. What is your opinion on this point?

What did John Stuart Mill mean when he said, "Better Socrates dissatisfied than a pig satisfied"?

Can you find instances from your everyday life of the confusion of ends and means: in the home? in school? in business? Should ethics be separated from religion?

Chapter 18

How do we know the first principles of morality? How well can we know them?

Do animals have rights?

Why do people differ in their ideas of right and wrong? Is conscience a matter of feeling?

Chapter 19

Do all the virtues have to do with morality?

How are the cardinal virtues interrelated?

Are the intellectual and moral virtues interrelated?

Can the moral life of man be adequate without the supernatural virtues? Without the intellectual virtues?

Why are there four cardinal virtues?

Chapter 20

Is it possible to be overprudent?

Does the practice of temperance indicate a contempt for material creatures?

Does the virtue of courage imply the absence of fear?

How are the virtues of temperance and fortitude related to the sense appetites? to prudence?

Can you think of examples of counterfeit courage?

Chapter 21

How does commutative justice differ from distributive justice? Is the "white lie" always immoral?

What does Huxley mean by "the higher idolatry"?

Chapter 22

How does social philosophy differ from the social sciences? What is the evidence for the contention that man is by nature anti-social? that he is by nature social?

What are the rights of the state in the education of children? in the waging of war? in the infliction of capital punishment?

How do you reconcile the rights of the person with the claims of the common good?

Topics for Essays, Part IV

The Philosophy of Science.

How Bodies Are Constituted.

The Meaning of Nature.

The Doctrine of Final Causes.

Topics for Discussion

Chapter 23

What are some of the ways in which the term body has been interpreted?

Did Berkeley really mean that a mountain is only a set of ideas?

Chapter 24

What are the various meanings of the word "nature"? How was the doctrine of the four causes developed?

What are the causes that go into the production of an automobile? of an oak tree?

How is causality related to change?

Suggest common terms from everyday speech which imply the notion of final causes.

Topics for Essays, Part V

The Ways of Adding to Being.

The Problem of Evil.

The Principles of Change.

The Principles of Act and Potency and the Argument from Motion.

Anselm's Argument for the Existence of God.

The Five Ways of St. Thomas.

Topics for Discussion

Chapter 25

What is the difference between total abstraction and formal abstraction?

Can you find instances of analogy in the everyday use of language?

Can you name anything that is not being?

Chapter 28

What different kinds of unity can you think of?

How does the truth of knowing differ from the truth of being? Is evil anything positive? Are poisons evil? Is the devil evil?

Chapter 27

How does existence differ from essence?

Is the difference really in things or does it exist only in thought? Is potential being nothing?

What are the principles of change?

Is the doctrine of matter and form reflected in everyday speech?

Chapter 28

Is there any sense in which the existence of God is self-evident?

How would St. Anselm answer the objection that you cannot jump from the ideal to the real?

Can natural theology substitute for religion?

How can a finite mind have a natural knowledge of an infinite God?

Do you have to be a philosopher to know from reason that God exists?

What are some of the ways to God besides the five ways of St. Thomas?

The atheist says you do not need God to explain the universe. How would you answer him?

Topics for Essays, Conclusion

The Definition of Philosophy.

Philosophy and Common Sense.

Reason and Revelation.

Christian Philosophy.

The Perennial Philosophy.

Topics for Discussion

Chapter 29

How is philosophy related to common sense?

How is philosophy related to the physical sciences?

If a scientist and a philosopher give contradictory answers about the same thing how are we to decide who is right?

Is it proper to speak of a "Catholic" philosophy?

Can reason and revelation contradict one another?

Should philosophy change with every generation?

INDEX

Abstraction, degrees of, 201 f; levels of formal, 250 ff; total and formal, 201

Accident, classes of, 223; defined, 222

Act and potency, as explanation of change, 224 f

Act, first and second, 228; in Aristotle, 48; in St. Thomas, 48 n; knowledge of, 228; meaning of, 226 Agent or active intellect, 73 Alcibiades, description of Socrates, 26 Allegory of the cave, 42

Altruistic love, 106

Analogy, 202 ff

Anaxagoras, on the constitution of bodies, 184

Anaximenes, doctrine of, 9; quoted, 10w

Anger, passion of irascible appetite, 93

Appetite, concupiscible, defined, 90; concupiscible, passions of, 91; irascible, defined, 90; irascible, passions of, 92 f; meaning of term, 89 n; rational, 94 ff; sense, 89 ff; sense, virtues of, 159 ff

Aristophanes, description of Socrates, 26

Aristotle, and the constitution of bodies, 189 f; and the science of metaphysics, 199; compared with Socrates and Plato, 51 f; critique of Plato's view of justice, 165; critique of Socrates' moral teaching, 32; definition of change, 225; doctrine of act and potency, 48; doctrine of form and matter, 47; explanation of change, 49; explanation of knowing, 50; his relation to Plato, 46; life and works, 45 f; on the agent intellect, 73 n; on courage, 162 f; on the degrees of knowledge, 50 f; on false kinds of courage, 163; on friendships, 106; on friendship as moral bond of society, 108; on the happy life, 133 f; on knowledge by connaturality, 77; on man as social by nature, 174f; on purpose in nature, 192; on social nature of man, 172; on virtue, 147, 152; teaching on man's nature, 51

Art, as habit of the practical intellect, 150

Athens, rise of, 21 f

Aversion, passion of concupiscible appetite, 91

Baudelaire, on the existence of God, 243

Beauty, as a transcendental, 215 Being, analogy of, 202 ff; hierarchy of, 213, 228; its common-sense meaning, 200; transcendentals of, 206 ff

Bergson, H., on the existence of God, 243